Political Parties and the State in Post-Communist Europe

It is not possible to understand the nature and functioning of post-communist political parties without understanding their relationship with the state. On the one hand, few parties in the region would be able to survive and perform without state resources as they lack strong roots within the wider society. On the other hand, the relatively weak states inherited from the communist period offer parties and elites opportunities for various forms of rent-seeking within state institutions. But how can we understand the relationship between parties and the state? How do the party-state links work in practice and do they exhibit any cross-national or cross-party variation? Are there any discernible patterns of party-state linkages among the post-communist democracies?

Political Parties and the State in Post-Communist Europe addresses these questions. The party–state linkages are analyzed alongside three analytical dimensions: state financing of parties, their legal regulation, and party patronage within the state institutions. The book brings together case studies of post-communist countries, as well as cross-country comparative analysis, each addressing at least one of these analytical dimensions. Besides providing a framework within which studies of party–state relationship can be undertaken, the book thus brings comparative evidence on the extent and the manner in which parties in the region use the state for their own purposes.

This book was previously published as a special issue of *The Journal of Communist Studies and Transition Politics*.

Petr Kopecký is a Research Fellow of the Netherlands Organization for Scientific Research based in the Department of Political Science at Leiden University.

Political Parties and the State in Post-Communist Europe

PETR KOPECKÝ

Routledge
Taylor & Francis Group

LONDON AND NEW YORK

First published 2008 by Routledge
2 Park Square, Milton Park, Abingdon, Oxon, OX14 4RN

Simultaneously published in the USA and Canada
by Routledge
711 Third Avenue, New York, NY 10017

Routledge is an imprint of the Taylor & Francis Group, an informa business

First issued in paperback 2016

© 2008 Petr Kopecký

Typeset in Times Roman by Techset Composition, Salisbury, UK
Printed and bound in Great Britain by MPG book Ltd, Bodmin, Cornwall

British Library Cataloguing in Publication Data
A catalogue record for this book is available from the British Library

Library of Congress Cataloging in Publication Data
A catalog record for this book has been requested

ISBN 13: 978-0-415-43959-6 (hbk)
ISBN 13: 978-1-138-97881-2 (pbk)

Contents

The online edition of this journal is hosted by Metapress: *taylorandfrancis.metapress.com*

For details of past and future contents of this and our other journals as well as guidance
on gaining access to this journal online please visit our website at *www.tandf.co.uk/journals*

Preface

This collection of essays examines the relationship between political parties and the state in post-communist Europe. Observers of post-communist politics generally agree that this relationship is very important for understanding the performance of the new East European democracies in general and of their political parties in particular.[1] There are at least three interrelated reasons why the state–party linkage is highly significant. First, parties in the post-communist region generally lack strong roots within the wider society. As a result, very few of them would be able to survive and perform without state resources. Second, the principal task of post-communist parties and elites has been to rebuild the institutions of the state. As a consequence, parties in the post-communist countries have been in a unique and strong position to define the rules of the game so as to cement their position within the state institutions. Third, the state structures inherited from the communist period are relatively weak in resisting intervention by political elites. As a result, post-communist states offer parties and elites opportunities for various forms of rent-seeking within state institutions.

While there is little doubt about the importance of the party–state relationship, there is less agreement about – and indeed knowledge of – how these links work in practice, and whether they exhibit any cross-national, cross-party or cross-temporal variation. The present collection aims to fill this void. The studies assembled here are not guided by a tight theoretical or conceptual framework of party–state linkage. The contributors were encouraged to adopt their own analytical approach in the study of a specific country. However, my intention from the outset was to widen the focus of most existing research, and move beyond the study of state financing of political parties as the main or even the sole indicator of the party–state link. Therefore, in addition to (or even instead of) state party finance, all contributions also consider party patronage within state institutions, and the legal framework within which political parties operate, as two other key dimensions of the party–state relationship. It is particularly the matter of party rent-seeking within the state that gives this collection a relatively novel focus at both the theoretical and the empirical level.

One of the included articles was presented, in an earlier version, at my two panels on 'Patronage and Corruption in New Democracies' at the Third ECPR Conference in Budapest, in September 2005. All but two articles were presented and discussed at a workshop entitled 'Political Parties and the State in Central and Eastern Europe', organized in Leiden in November 2005. I would like to thank the Department of Political Science at Leiden University for hosting the workshop, and the Netherlands Organization for Scientific Research (NWO) for providing financial assistance (Project No. 452-03-301). Several other colleagues – Ingrid van Biezen, André Gerrits, Imke Harbers, Paul G. Lewis, Yvette Peters, Maria Spirova and Frank de Zwart – accepted my invitation to the workshop, and provided valuable comments on our papers and contributed to the general discussion of party–state relationships. Special thanks go to Imke and Frank for their interesting workshop presentations on practices of patronage in, respectively, Mexico and India, and to Maria for her help with the editorial work. Finally, I would like to thank my contributors, for writing very interesting studies and for being willing to work under a series of tight deadlines.

NOTE

1. See Venelin I. Ganev, 'Postcommunism as an Episode of State-Building: A Reversed Tillian Perspective', *Communist and Post-Communist Studies*, Vol.38, No.4 (2005), pp.425–45; Conor O'Dwyer, 'Runaway State Building; How Political Parties Shape States in Postcommunist Eastern Europe', *World Politics*, Vol.56, No.4 (2004), pp.520–53; Anna Grzymala-Busse, 'Political Competition and the Politicization of the State in East Central Europe', *Comparative Political Studies*, Vol.36, No.10 (2003), pp.1123–47.

Petr Kopecký (Leiden University)
2006

Political Parties and the State in Post-Communist Europe: The Nature of Symbiosis

PETR KOPECKÝ

Political parties are conventionally thought of in societal terms. They are traditionally seen as representative agencies, giving a voice to well-established constituencies, and deriving legitimacy from their capacity to articulate their voters' interests and to aggregate their demands. This can easily be seen when we look at some initial categorization of party organizational types – cadre parties, mass parties, or catch-all parties – almost all of which derive from an analysis of the parties' linkage with the wider society. Most of the traditional party literature, especially that devoted to Western Europe, also compares parties on the basis of competing patterns of representation: workers' parties, religious parties, farmers' parties, or people's parties.

As far as most of this literature is concerned, parties are seen as an outgrowth of society, defined by, and best understood in terms of, their relationship with society.

Two developments have recently led to the questioning of these conventional views. First, parties in western democracies have changed. Their links with society have eroded,[1] and parties have become more dependent on the state, both for their resources and for their legitimacy. This is demonstrated by the now often-used categorizations of party organizational types – electoral-professional parties, parties as business firms, cartel parties, and modern cadre parties[2] – all of which emphasize parties' linkage with the state. Second, the third wave of democratization has drawn scholarly attention to parties in many non-western and non-European areas. There, from the very outset of democratization, political parties have been weakly anchored in society while at the same time they have strongly penetrated the state.[3] Therefore, as far as most of the contemporary literature is concerned parties are best understood in terms of their relationship with the state, rather than with society.

The patterns of party development in post-communist Europe broadly conform to these trends observed elsewhere. Indeed, if there is one element of party development on which most analysts of contemporary parties in Eastern Europe will agree, it is the parties' relatively weak position within (civil) society. Given the analytical biases in the traditional literature on parties, and given that much of this literature has become a reference point for the studies of parties in post-communist Europe, the party–society link is also an area of party development that is inevitably most researched and thus best documented. The precise dimensions of the weak social roots of contemporary Eastern European parties need not concern us in great detail here. Suffice it to say that it can be seen in a variety of indicators: comparatively low levels of popular party identification, high levels of electoral volatility, low levels of party membership,[4] declining voter turnout, and weak links between parties and collateral organizations.[5] Even taking into account cross-country and cross-party variation, these indicators all point in the same direction.

The reasons for the weak links between parties and society are manifold and, again, need not concern us in great detail here. Suffice it to say that the relatively high levels of socio-economic development, coupled with the legacies of the forced and extensive mobilization under the communist regime, have created an individualized social structure in which citizens are less likely to identify closely with partisan symbols and party ideologies, and indeed less likely to engage in conventional forms of politics. The traditional cleavages, in the sense of existing strong social divisions, pervasive collective identities and extended organizational networks, have virtually disappeared under the communist regime. Because of these social, cultural and economic conditions, contemporary parties in the Eastern European region are engaged in what Richard Rose aptly described as 'mobilizing demobilized voters'.[6]

A second trend that is often observed by students of the post-communist region is the parties' pronounced link with the state. Not surprisingly, the first to point out this feature are specialists on parties who employ the contemporary models of party organization to probe the organizational character of post-communist parties.[7] For most of these scholars, the parties' strong links with the state are both a consequence and a further cause of their thin presence on the ground. It is a *consequence* because parties need the state for material resources in the absence of strong roots in the wider society, and it is a *cause* because, once in possession of state resources, parties are significantly less compelled to engage in party-building strategies based on popular mobilization and extensive organizational development.

Political parties in Eastern Europe have been perfectly positioned to exploit the state for their purposes. There are several explanations for this. The first involves the fact that most parties in the region originated, and continue to originate even at present, as elite groups within parliaments and governments (that is, the party in public office), rather than as social movements outside the establishment (that is, the party on the ground). As a result, public office is what contemporary party-builders know best, and public offices are staffed by people who live *from* politics rather than *for* politics. Second, the principal task of post-communist parties and elites has been to rebuild the institutions of the state. In that sense, parties in post-communist countries have been in a unique and strong position to define the rules of the game so as to suit their private ends. Indeed, it may be argued that parties in the new democracies of Eastern Europe have enjoyed comparatively more leverage in determining their own environment than have parties in the contemporary established democracies.

Finally, it should be noted that a similar comparative advantage also relates to another important aspect of post-communist development, namely the nature of the post-communist state itself. Despite the appearance of the communist state as omnipresent and strong, many observers point out that the state structures carried over to the post-transition period are in fact quite weak.[8] The state appears weak in terms of its capacity to devise and implement policies, a feature that is often lamented by the European Union. However, the state also appears weak in terms of its ability to resist the rent-seeking behaviour by political parties. In other words, there are relatively few institutions within the post-communist state that are legitimate and strong enough to keep the partisan government in check and to limit the reach of partisanship within state structures. In this respect, again, the state structures in contemporary Eastern European states offer parties more possibilities for rent-seeking behaviour than similar structures in most contemporary West European countries.

All in all, what we observe in post-communist Europe is a potentially self-reinforcing process. Because political parties either cannot or do not wish to function as effective representative agencies, they are forced to seek their resources elsewhere. Because they originate within the state, and are endowed with the key task of reforming the state, they start to build up their role almost exclusively within state institutions. State structures in the post-communist period offer little resistance to party interference, so political parties, or elites associated with them, engage in mostly successful rent-seeking behaviour. And finally, because they can extract resources from the state, parties can afford to insulate themselves further from society.

However, this generally compelling logic suffers from at least two problems. First, it is unlikely that the self-reinforcing process of party- and state-building outlined above will produce identical outcomes across all post-communist Eastern Europe. To paraphrase Conor O'Dwyer,[9] post-communist states may be predisposed to party rent-seeking behaviour, but they are not predestined to it. For example, the state apparatus in one country may be much better placed to resist party colonization than that in another state. Some observers also point to the potentially constraining effects of a certain type of elite and party competition on the rent-seeking behaviour within the state, and thus to the possibility of very different outcomes of state-building processes within the post-communist region.[10] Second, it is not obvious what the relationship between political parties and the state actually involves. For example, students of parties usually write only about public party funding as a feature of this relationship. In contrast, scholars interested in questions of state-building, state capacity, and public administration reform often focus on corruption or the politicization of the state administration.[11] Thus, while both groups of scholars may observe a similar trend towards party penetration of the state, their observations are often predicated on the study of very different types of linkage and on different sets of empirical indicators associated with them.

The purpose of this collection of essays is to address precisely these complexities in the general study of party–state relationships, while focusing particularly on the post-communist states. This study offers both a conceptual and an empirical comparative examination of the linkage between political parties and the state in post-communist Europe. The first section focuses on conceptual issues. It outlines three different dimensions of party–state linkage – the dependence of parties on the state, the management of parties by the state, and the parties' colonization of the state – and discusses their operationalization. The second section provides an empirical analysis of the relationship between parties and the state in all electoral democracies in Eastern Europe. It draws on various sources of data, including the country-specific studies assembled in this collection, and probes the relevance and strength of each dimension in the post-communist context. I show that, on the whole, parties in post-communist Europe are financially dependent on the state and extensively managed by the state, and do not shy away from rent-seeking within the state. I also identify some important intra-regional variations in the predominant type of party–state linkage in the new post-communist democracies.

Three Dimensions of Party–State Linkage

As indicated above, the relationship between political parties and the state involves a number of elements, each of which could constitute a separate subject of inquiry. For the purposes of wider cross-regional analysis, here I use three dimensions of party–state linkage developed elsewhere.[12] These three dimensions include (1) the extent to which parties depend on the state; (2) the extent to which parties are managed by the state; and (3) the degree to which parties themselves colonize the state. I show below that these three dimensions actually cover most analytical and empirical categories used in various studies of party–state linkage. Moreover, in contrast to most studies that focus on only one or two dimensions, this analytical framework allows for a more integrated comparative analysis, including both cross-regional and cross-national analysis. It therefore allows highlighting potentially important similarities and differences in the type of party–state linkage.

Dependence of Parties on the State

The dimension referred to as 'dependence of parties on the state' captures the extent to which parties rely on the state for resources that facilitate, or even guarantee, their organizational survival. The public financing of political parties, perhaps the most-used indicator in the study of party–state linkage, is the key empirical indicator of this dimension here as well. Public funding for political parties is a relatively recent phenomenon: it was first introduced in Germany in 1959, and gradually spread to most West European democracies. Public funding has not entirely replaced other financial resources on which parties have traditionally relied, such as private donations or members' contributions.[13] However, many argue that the introduction of state subsidies to parties underlines the progressively strong interdependence between parties and the state and thus constitutes a critical turning-point both in the practice of party financing and in party development more generally. Indeed, it was the availability of public funds for parties that prompted Katz and Mair to advance the model of the cartel party;[14] it also encouraged much of the theorizing about the transformation of parties from private associations towards some form of public entities.[15]

The existing studies of post-communist Eastern Europe do provide a strong indication that the state has assumed a critical importance for the financing of political parties.[16] This involves not only direct funding but also, apparently, provisions that grant parties free political broadcasts in the media. Indeed, given the dependence of contemporary parties on modern means of mass communication in reaching their voters, and given the financial cost of publicity in the media, free broadcasts can in practice represent a subsidy as important as direct public funding itself. This is why free media access is the second key indicator used in the following empirical analysis to tap into the parties' dependence on the state.

The first key objective of this study is to investigate empirically the extent to which public subsidies and free media access have been universalized in contemporary post-communist democracies as a means of subsidizing political parties. If the expectations concerning the widespread dependence of parties on the state across post-communist Europe hold true, we should find few contemporary democracies in the region without public funding of political parties. Many of the essays presented in this collection ask similar questions with respect to individual East European countries, and further investigate the role of other state subsidies (tax relief, subsidies in kind and so on), and the amount of money derived from state resources in proportion to other sources.

Management of Parties by the State

The management of parties by the state – the second dimension of party–state linkage explored in this essay – refers to the extent of state involvement in internal party affairs. State control includes the regulation of party activities, financing, ideology and organization through public law, including the constitution. According to some observers, political parties in many contemporary liberal democracies have been progressively incorporated into the public domain, to the extent that party structures have become 'legitimate objects of state regulation to a degree far exceeding what would normally be acceptable for private associations in a liberal society'.[17] Post-communist Eastern Europe provides an interesting case in this respect. On the one hand, the over-regulated and over-bureaucratized nature of the communist one-party state could mean that post-communist elites will tend to adopt a very liberal approach to party regulation: namely, little or no regulation. On the other hand, if the preventive logic prevails among lawmakers, the parties could become subject to a host of laws and regulations on a hitherto unprecedented scale, as politicians try to avoid any abuses of power associated with the role of the communist party in the previous regime.

Which form of regulation will prevail is an empirical question, and its answer depends at least partly on what we consider to be public regulation. One of the key elements of public regulation of political parties involves the system of rules and regulations related to party financing. Indeed, in this essay I will use the existence or absence of a regulatory system of party finances as the first empirical indicator of parties' management by the state. The statutory control of party financing has obtained a strong stimulus with the introduction of public funding – so much so that any system of financial support for political parties by the state is very likely to be accompanied by a framework regulating party finances. In that sense, given the expectations concerning the widespread availability of direct public funding across post-communist democracies, we are unlikely to find many Eastern European countries without a regulatory system of party finances.

Moreover, regulations covering party finances have everywhere been part of the attempts to increase the transparency of parties' financial practices. This is especially true in the many regions where democracy has been established only recently, and where corruption has allegedly been endemic. Therefore, even when no public subsidies to parties exist, contemporary Eastern European democracies are likely to have drawn up a body of public law designed to regulate party finances, if only because it is a standard 'democratic formula' required by a host of international organizations and institutions that assist the process of democratization today.

In addition, public control also includes the constitutional recognition of political parties – the second empirical indicator of management of parties by the state that I shall use. Political parties have long been neglected in the constitutions of western liberal democracies. But with the restoration of democracy in Italy and Germany after the Second World War, parties' relevance for democracy became acknowledged more widely in political as well as constitutional terms. This practice has since been followed in constitutional revisions in many other polities, including many of the new democracies, to the point that pluralism, political participation and competition have come to be defined almost exclusively in terms of political parties in many contemporary democratic constitutions. As a result, the state management of political parties now often includes detailed regulation of party activities, ideology and organization through the constitution in addition to the body of law (special party laws, electoral laws or parliamentary rules). That being the case, the constitutional recognition of parties deserves special attention as a form of party–state linkage because it attests to a conception of democracy in which parties are seen as necessary and valuable institutions, and also because it can signal that the state has assumed a predominant role in the management of parties. Indeed, given the recent wave of constitution making and remaking in the region,[18] it is reasonable to expect the constitutional recognition of parties in Eastern Europe to be very widespread.

Party Colonization of the State

The third dimension of party–state linkage – party colonization of the state – refers to the rent-seeking behaviour of political parties within the state apparatus. It is a dimension that is most difficult to study, chiefly because data, and especially reliable cross-national data, are not readily available. If party finances, including the use of state subsidies or the parties' fund-raising activities, are often clouded in mystery, then the activities associated with rent seeking within the state are even less susceptible to systematic study. However, the problem is not only empirical. Party colonization of the state involves several related, but conceptually distinct, phenomena. Separating these different forms of rent-seeking behaviour from each other is the first step towards a more precise and reliable empirical inquiry.

The two most commonly mentioned forms of rent-seeking behaviour are patronage and clientelism. Patronage and clientelism are closely related in that both are forms of exchange relationships between patrons and clients in which state resources are traded for political support.[19] These exchange relationships have existed in various forms in both traditional and modern societies, in democratic and non-democratic regimes, in various types of organizations, and on local, regional, national or even supranational levels. However, one distinction to note immediately is the one between party patronage and party clientelism on the one hand, and patronage and clientelism more generally on the other hand. In the former, the party is the 'collective' patron in the exchange relations; in the latter case the patron is an individual (for example, a boss, or a local chief or notable). In the context of this study, and of this collection more generally, it is therefore party patronage and party clientelism that are the chief concerns.

Party patronage involves the allocation of jobs and other important public and semi-public positions, for example in the civil service, public sector companies, advisory boards, quangos, universities, and school and research institutes. In the European context, access to patronage resources provided party leaders with the means initially to build, and subsequently to maintain, party organizations by means of distributing 'selective incentives' to party activists and party elites in exchange for organizational (party) loyalty.[20] In this sense, party patronage is still likely to prove a valuable and effective strategy for dealing with problems of party organization and party building in many democracies today, including those in post-communist Europe. In fact, since the traditional representational links between parties and society are weak in Eastern Europe, and since party organizations often have to be built with little or no organizational and other resources available to party leaders, patronage may (when available, of course) become a key resource for anchoring the party within the political system. Patronage in this sense might compensate for underdeveloped organizational networks and the lack of party presence on the ground.

Party clientelism is a more penetrating phenomenon than party patronage. It is a form of representation based on selective release of a wide variety of public material resources – contracts, housing, subsidies, 'pork barrel' legislation – in order to secure electoral support, either from individuals or from selected segments of society. In that sense, clientelism is more a party–society than a party–state relationship. What is important to note, however, is that clientelism always involves patronage, for, without an ability to control appointments within the state institutions, political parties would not be in a position to distribute selective benefits. This is one reason why the two phenomena are so often treated synonymously, even though party patronage may conceivably develop and exist without clientelism.

In the context of established democracies, clientelism has arguably become unimportant as a mode of representation, for two reasons. First, the size and the scope of the state sector have been shrinking, which means that parties boast fewer resources to distribute among their potential clients. Second, because of the rising affluence of modern societies, traditional group identities and marginalized segments of population have disappeared. This has eroded constituencies needing selective material benefits in order to participate in the electoral process.[21] The same argument could be applied to post-communist Europe, certainly as far as the state's distributive capacity is concerned. The cash-strapped post-communist states have contracted greatly in terms of their ability and willingness to distribute welfare benefits and other public goods. However, it is possible that in at least some of the post-communist states the demand for clientelistic benefits will continue to be significant among the marginalized poor or among some of the secluded rural communities.

Finally, there is corruption – perhaps the most frequently used term when referring to rent seeking within the state. The distinction between party patronage and party clientelism, on the one hand, and corruption, on the other hand, becomes self-evident if we use the frequent definition of corruption as the exchange of money in return for favourable public decisions.[22] In the context of party politics, the common form of corruption is financial donations to party coffers in exchange for building contracts, arms contracts, or granting of licences. However, both patronage and clientelism in some sense also constitute corrupt practices. Both these forms of particularistic exchange distort the ideal form of democracy. For example, the exercise of patronage runs counter to the principles of job selection based on merit; clientelistic exchanges may be seen as a distortion of programmatic and ideological bases of political representation. So while neither of the two exchanges constitutes corruption proper, it is evident why a lot of the literature on party rent seeking often treats all three phenomena interchangeably.[23]

In any case, like party patronage and to a far lesser extent party clientelism, corruption of political parties is also likely to be rampant in post-communist Europe. First of all, state financing is unlikely to provide all funds necessary to run modern party organizations: it rarely does so. This means that parties will always be looking out for additional sources of money, potentially including illegal and corrupt sources, solicited from economic firms, for example. Second, although both communist and post-communist states have decidedly not suffered from a shortage of legal rules and party regulations, the enforcement of these rules and conventions is likely to be more nominal than real. In addition, as Venelin Ganev persuasively argues,[24] there is no obvious mobilized social constituency capable of monitoring and thwarting rent-seeking behaviour by political elites within the state.

Empirical Analysis

The empirical analysis in this section includes all current electoral democracies in Eastern Europe based on the 2004 ratings of Freedom House. Countries rated as an electoral democracy must have met certain minimum standards, including a competitive multiparty system and regularly contested fair elections based on universal adult suffrage. An 'electoral democracy' differs from a 'liberal democracy' in that the latter also implies the presence of a substantial array of civil liberties. Georgia is the only electoral democracy omitted from the empirical analysis because of the lack of data on most of the dimensions and indicators considered in this essay. Table 1 summarizes the relationship between political parties and the state in the post-communist democracies in all three dimensions outlined earlier. The precise indicators used for this assessment will be discussed in more detail below.

Public Funding and Free Media Access

The first two columns of Table 1 present information on the availability of direct public funding to political parties (thus not to individual candidates), and the availability of free media access to political parties. All other forms of indirect state support, such as special taxation rules, free transport or postage, are excluded. The data are taken from a comprehensive study of the Institute for Democracy and Electoral Assistance[25] on the financing of political parties and election campaigns, and complemented by three other authoritative surveys specifically focused on Eastern Europe.

The information in the first column of Table 1 shows that, on the whole, both state subventions of political parties and free media access have

TABLE 1
POLITICAL PARTIES AND THE STATE IN EASTERN EUROPE

	Dependence on the state		Management by the state		Colonization of the state	
	Availability of public funding for parties	Free media access	System of regulation of party finances	Constitutional recognition of political parties	Corruption of political parties	Impact of patronage on business (%)
Albania	Yes	Yes	Yes	Yes	2.9	40.5
Bulgaria	Yes	Yes	Yes	Yes	4.3	42.5
Croatia	Yes	Yes	No	Yes	3.8	37.8
Czech Republic	Yes	Yes	Yes	Yes	3.8	16.0
Estonia	Yes	Yes	Yes	Yes	3.5	34.8
Hungary	No	Yes	No	No	n.a.	5.5
Latvia	Yes	No	Yes	Yes	4.2	31.5
Lithuania	Yes	Yes	Yes	Yes	4.3	24.4
Macedonia	No	No	Yes	Yes	4.2	13.0
Moldova	Yes	Yes	Yes	Yes	4.0	38.7
Poland	Yes	Yes	Yes	Yes	4.2	27.5
Romania	Yes	Yes	Yes	Yes	4.0	41.8
Russia	Yes	Yes	Yes	No	3.9	30.7
Serbia and Montenegro	Yes	Yes	Yes	No	4.2	37.8
Slovakia	Yes	Yes	No	Yes	n.a.	32.6
Slovenia	Yes	n.a.	Yes	Yes	n.a.	11.3
Ukraine	No	Yes	Yes	Yes	4.1	24.5
East European democracies	Yes: 14 (82%) No: 3 (18%) (N = 17)	Yes: 14 (87.5%) No: 2 (12.5%) (N = 16)	Yes: 14 (82%) No: 3 (18%) (N = 17)	Yes: 14 (82%) No: 3 (18%) (N = 17)	Mean: 4.0 (N = 14)	Mean: 28.9 (N = 17)

Sources: 1. Classification of liberal democracies: Freedom House 2005, <www.freedomhouse.org>;
2. Party funding and regulation: IDEA (note 25); Vladimir Goati, 'Funding of the Political Parties in Postcommunist Country: The Case of Serbia', in *Political Party and Election Campaign* (note 27), pp.35–40; Ikstens, Smilov and Walecki (note 28); Toplak (note 29);
3. Constitutional recognition: country constitutions (various sources);
4. Political parties' corruption survey: Transparency International, TI Global Corruption Barometer 2004 and 2005, <http://www.transparency.org/surveys>;
5. Patronage: World Bank, The Business Environment and Enterprise Performance Survey 1999–2000, <http://info.worldbank.org/governance/beeps>.

become widespread in the new democracies of Eastern Europe. Both forms of
state subvention are available in 14 out of 17 countries (16 in the case of media
access); in other words, in more than 80 per cent of all post-communist
democracies. Latvia, Moldova and Ukraine are exceptions in that none of
these three countries provides direct funding to political parties, although all
three countries grant political parties free access to the mass media. Hence,
a first look at the table gives us a clear indication of considerable dependence
of parties on the state across the region. As elsewhere in the world, including
many regions with a recent history of democratization, some form of public
funding to political parties has been almost universalized.[26]

The key question nevertheless is how large the share of state-provided
money is in relation to the total party budgets. Large differences among
countries within one region can easily exist depending on the overall make-
up of the financing system. However, large differences can also exist among
parties within one country depending, for example, on whether the money
is granted primarily if not exclusively to the election winners (or parties
represented in parliament more generally), or whether smaller extra-
parliamentary parties also benefit from state subsidies.

Not surprisingly, available comparative studies indicate considerable
cross-national and inter-party differences. For example, Smilov[27] reports
that in Bulgaria, Russia and Ukraine, public funding is symbolic in comparison to the resources parties obtain from corporate donations.[28] The contribution of Oversloot and Verheul to this collection shows very clearly the
discrepancy between public and private money with reference to Russia. By
contrast, in the Czech Republic, Slovenia, Hungary and Estonia, the role of
state money looms much larger in the overall party budgets. This has been
verified by other reports: Toplak[29] argues that the state is crucial for party
coffers in both Slovenia and Croatia. For example, in Slovenia, funds from
the state budget represent up to 74 per cent of total funds during election
years and about 80 per cent in other years. Similarly, although to a lesser
extent than in Slovenia and Croatia, van Biezen and Kopecky[30] report that
the state provides nearly 50 per cent of all party income in the Czech Republic
and Hungary. Szczerbiak's contribution to this collection[31] shows that state
funding of parties has also gradually become critical for most parties
represented in parliament in Poland, especially after all the numerous parliamentary allowances are taken into consideration.[32] Finally, as Sikk argues
(also in this collection), the state in Estonia, too, provides a vital amount of
money to parliamentary parties despite a slight decrease in the share of
public donations in total party finances since 2003;[33] This trend may even
increase with the recent introduction of a ban on corporate donations.

To complicate matters further, significant differences exist among
individual parties within political systems, relating most notably to the

restrictiveness of state subventions. In Estonia, for example, extra-parliamentary parties are significantly disadvantaged in comparison with the parties already represented in parliament.[34] But differences also relate to the organizational origin of parties and their material endowment at the start of transition: as Lewis shows, Hungarian and Polish reformed post-communist parties enjoy significant material advantages unrelated to the level of state financing in comparison with the newly emerged (for example, post-Solidarity) parties.[35] Furthermore, the state appears relatively less important as the major source of party funds among parties that have had some experience in government compared with parties that have not.[36] A plausible hypothesis here could be that such parties are simply most attractive to large corporate donors, because of their recent or projected (or both) participation at the centre of decision-making authority.

All in all, sweeping generalizations are difficult to make, other than that state support to political parties in the form of direct subsidies and free media access is more or less the norm in post-communist Europe. However, there appears to be a division between Central European and the Baltic states, on the one hand, and the post-Soviet Republics and some of the Balkan countries, on the other. Among the former group, now all members of the EU, the principles of almost universal state support for political parties are endorsed much more strongly than in the latter group. This indicates a more egalitarian manner of distribution of state resources among the political parties, and hence also a more inclusive type of political competition.

Indeed, the lack of meaningful state funding may be pointing to a particular type of party–state linkage prevalent in different sub-regions of post-communist Europe. In the post-Soviet space, it may be illustrative of a system in which the sizeable benefits that parties gain from the state are almost solely derived from patronage, or even from corruption. As a consequence, state benefits are distributed in a highly unequal manner among political parties. Those who win elections control the state, and those who control the state are also in command of all resources necessary to sustain and promote their political organizations. The Russian case is illustrative in this respect. As Oversloot and Verheul argue below, the parties in Russia actually play only a marginal role in extracting resources from the state as they lack the autonomy to do so. Instead, it is the political and administrative elites, using the sizeable resources of the state, that invent parties, often only for a temporary period, in order to boost electoral and legislative support for the presidential administration, or to offset the challenge of other competitors.

Party Finance Regulations and Constitutional Recognition

The third and fourth columns in Table 1 deal with the management of parties by the state. Column 3 provides data on the regulations and enforcement rules related to the financing of political parties. The data are taken from the same sources as those on public funding and are based on whether there is a system of regulation for the financing of political parties. As can be seen from Table 1, the findings here are very similar to those described above in relation to the availability of public funding. A regulatory framework for the financing of political parties has been established in the large majority of post-communist democracies. Moreover, most countries that provide state support to political parties have also established a system of enforcement and regulation of party finances; only Latvia, Slovakia and Croatia appear as exceptions. However, even Slovakia now provides a certain regulatory framework; for example, it sets limits on campaign expenditures. Similarly, in Latvia parties are obliged to submit detailed annual financial declarations and face potential penalties if they fail to do so. In Croatia, finally, despite what is probably the most liberal approach to party finance regulations in the post-communist context, parties are at least obliged to declare intended expenditures and sources of income before the elections.[37] Similarly to state financing, the financial regulation of political parties has been nearly universalized in the post-communist region.

The fourth column in Table 1 contains information on the constitutional regulation of political parties, providing further evidence on the extent to which parties can be seen to be managed by the state. These findings are derived from a content analysis of the most recent constitutions. Constitutions contain very different types of references to political parties. Here, the constitutional recognition of political parties is acknowledged if the constitution contains one or more of the following three possible references to parties:

1. The constitution defines the democratic system itself, or electoral competition, in terms of political parties. A good example is the constitution of the Czech Republic, which states that '[The] political system is based on free and voluntary formation of and free competition between political parties' (Art. 5);
2. One or more pivotal democratic institutions are defined in such a way that they are of necessity composed of, or could not function without, political parties. A good example here is Article 61 of the Albanian constitution, which makes clear that it is necessary to form a party (or a coalition of parties) in order to be elected to the Assembly (parliament);
3. The activities of parties are regulated by the constitution, usually in order to mitigate their potential threat to democracy. A good example here is the Croatian constitution, which states that 'political parties shall be organized according to a territorial principle. The work of any political party which by its programme of activity violently endangers the democratic

constitutional order, independence, unity or territorial integrity of the
Republic of Croatia shall be prohibited' (Art. 6).

Countries were assigned a negative score if they lacked any references to
political parties whatsoever, or if they included a mention of parties but only
with reference to citizens' rights of expression or political association. While
this contains an important democratic entitlement of citizens to exercise their
political rights through parties, it cannot be seen as an indication of the
management of the place and role of parties in the political system.

With over four-fifths of post-communist democracies recording a positive
score on the constitutional recognition of parties, it appears that there is a
close relationship between parties and the state in this respect as well. The
proportion is in fact slightly higher if we consider that the data for Serbia and
Montenegro, one of the three exceptions in this respect, in fact refer to the
federal constitution: the constitution of the Serbian Republic does clearly recognize political parties. Therefore, only the Russian and Latvian constitutions do
not mention political parties other than with respect to the citizen's entitlement
to form and join them (Art. 102 of Latvian constitution), or with respect to the
very general recognition of the existence of political pluralism and the multi-
party system (Art. 13 of the Russian constitution). Post-communist Europe
differs substantially in this respect from old established democracies where
only about half of the countries with a written constitution recognize political
parties constitutionally.[38] This difference can most likely be accounted for by
the legacy of the historical conception of political parties as private and voluntary associations in the established liberal democracies, a conception that
largely disappeared after the Second World War.

It is also interesting to note the patterns in the way political parties are
constitutionally recognized in the post-communist world. Although a proper
discussion would require a separate and more detailed analysis, two points
are worth mentioning. First, there are very few post-communist countries
that do not issue some orders or instructions as to how parties should
behave or organize, or both. Most post-communist constitutions unquestion-
ably fall under what Janda calls the 'prescription model' of party regulation.[39]
The most frequent form of this prescriptive model is represented by constitutional formulas prohibiting parties from violating the constitutional order,
territorial integrity or independence (for example, Croatia and Macedonia).
Other formulas of this type include a ban on advocating totalitarian
methods of political activity (as in Poland and Albania), or dictating that
parties must be separated from the state (as in Bulgaria, Hungary and
Slovakia). In all likelihood, the regularity with which such prescriptive formulas feature in the post-communist constitutions is a reaction to the previous

one-party state, in which the single ruling party was instrumental in the establishment and maintenance of totalitarian rule.

Second, a significant number of post-communist constitutions appear to have elevated parties to a privileged position within the democratic system. Pluralism, political participation and competition in many of these documents have come to be defined almost exclusively in terms of party. Article 5 of the Czech constitution is mentioned above as a clear example, but many other East European countries, including Romania, Bulgaria, Hungary and Moldova, position parties as the key instrument of political expression and interest aggregation.[40] This is somewhat paradoxical. While the prescriptive feature of post-communist constitutions towards parties is understandable, this particular feature of post-communist constitutions is far less so, especially if we take into account the strong anti-party sentiments and the general distrust towards parties among both policy-makers and the population at large. Perhaps it shows that in Eastern Europe, as elsewhere in the democratic world, parties, though disliked and despised, do remain central in ideas about representative democracy.

Patronage, Clientelism and Corruption

As indicated above, both party patronage and party clientelism are notoriously difficult to investigate empirically. Proxy measures, such as the spending on personnel budgets of ministries,[41] or the changing size of the state administration,[42] are often employed in the empirical analysis. As Meyer-Sahling argues in this collection with special reference to the size of the state administration, these proxy measures carry considerable reliability problems. Corruption is also used on occasion as a proxy for patronage and clientelism,[43] despite the analytical and conceptual differences between these phenomena.[44]

This essay employs two measures that tap into the rent-seeking behaviour of political parties in the post-communist region. The first measure derives from a cross-nationally comparable survey data on corruption, using data from two special surveys – Global Corruption Barometer (GCB) 2004 and 2005 – of Transparency International (TI) focusing specifically on the corruption of political parties rather than on corruption *tout court*. The corruption as understood in the GCB surveys excludes practices of corruption unrelated to the political system, such as the business sector. Therefore, this data should give us a better idea about the role of parties as rent-seeking organizations than the widely used CPI Index of TI.

The data on the corruption of political parties in post-communist Europe are reported in the fifth column of Table 1. It reflects the score assigned to political parties (on a scale of 1 to 5) on the question to what extent they were perceived to be affected by corruption.[45] The data signal that, with a mean of 4.0, political parties in the region are seen to be quite corrupt.

Moreover, with the standard deviation value of 0.34, it appears that differences among the post-communist democracies are not very large. They are in fact much smaller than differences among the old established democracies on the same measure, indicating that the perception of parties as rent-seeking organizations is universally strong across the region.[46] Indeed, the GCB data shows that when compared to 14 other sectors and institutions (including parliament, the judiciary, the police, the business sector, the media and so on), political parties are clearly perceived as the most corrupt of all institutions in a majority of the post-communist countries. In eight out of the 13 countries in the sample for which information is available, parties are between the second and third most corrupt institutions, while in four countries, all new EU member states, parties come first as the most corrupt institutions.

The second measure of rent-seeking concerns practices of patronage. It is based on the data from the Business Environment and Enterprise Performance Survey (BEEPS) of the World Bank.[47] The data reported in the sixth column of Table 1 reflect answers from a sample of company leaders to the question, 'What impact does patronage (defined as public officials hiring friends and relatives into official positions) have on your business?' The figure reported is a sum of the percentages of those who classified the impact as either significant or very significant (as opposed to minor or no impact). The measure is only a proxy for *party* patronage, because the question as formulated in the survey asks about patronage in general, and about the impact of patronage on economic firms. However, these are the only cross-nationally available data that tap directly into the practices of patronage (that is, into the process of appointments within the state administration). It is therefore worth including in the analysis.

The data suggest that, in general, patronage does not appear to have a major impact in the post-communist countries: less than one-third of the respondents in the region (mean of 28.9 per cent) consider hiring of friends and relatives to official positions as having a significant or very significant impact. This finding stands in a stark contrast to the generally high perceptions of corruption of political parties presented above. Of course, what is measured here is the impact of patronage on companies. This is potentially very different from the impact of patronage on both political institutions and state administration, especially given the increasing withdrawal of the state from the economic sphere as a result of privatization and liberalization. Patronage can exist, but with few or no consequences for economic firms. However, the data do reveal some differences among post-communist countries. Indeed, with a standard deviation value of 11.50, it appears that differences among the post-communist democracies are rather significant in this respect, certainly more substantial than the differences among countries in the corruption of political parties. Hungary, the Czech Republic and Slovenia, for example, score very low on the impact of patronage, while more than

40 per cent of respondents consider patronage to have a significant (or very significant) impact in Albania, Bulgaria and Romania.

Again, these differences may well be accounted for by the fact that the former countries are front runners in the area of economic reforms among the post-communist countries. In these countries, state involvement in the economy has been the most reduced, and the general institutional and regulatory infrastructure of a market economy has been the best developed. However, these findings also reinforce the argument concerning the different types of party–state relationship prevalent in different parts of the post-communist region presented above: the division between those countries in which the party–state relationships are predominantly based on a nearly universal and inclusive system of state party financing and regulations, on the one hand, and countries in which the state resources are primarily accrued through the means of rent-seeking within the state institutions. Although this pattern is not entirely consistent across all indicators of party–state linkage presented in this study, it appears to represent a division between the Central European and Baltic countries, on the one side, and the post-Soviet Republics and some of the Balkan countries on the other.

Drawing on the other contributions to this collection, two substantive points concerning party patronage are worth highlighting. The first point concerns the resources of party patronage: that is, the positions that are habitually subject to party appointments. Although these resources inevitably vary among countries, many contributions to this collection seem to underline the importance of semi-state institutions, including advisory committees, various regulatory bodies, expert teams, governing boards of state-owned companies and public utilities, foundations and so on, as the important loci of patronage practices. For example, Roper shows that parties control appointments to both the state-run media and the bodies overseeing broadcast media in Romania. Similarly, Rybář alludes to the importance of governing boards of large energy utilities in this respect. In other words, it appears that patronage in post-communist countries is possibly located less in the core of the civil service (the ministerial bureaucracy) than in the other layers of public administration, which are often not subject to the legislation applying to civil servants.

Part of the explanation may involve the fact that many positions located outside the core civil service, such as advisory jobs or membership of the governing boards of state and semi-state companies, are financially more lucrative than regular bureaucratic jobs. This may well be relevant to the top echelons of party political elites used to comparatively high salaries and benefits at the national level of political office. Positions so distributed are thus true rewards for services rendered within political parties. None the less, other positions within the state administration, such as jobs in the state-owned media or the media-regulating boards, are controlled by parties for purely political reasons. Patronage, in that sense, is less a reward for organizational or personal loyalty than an instrument of party politics.

However, part of the explanation must also involve the gradual impact of administrative and civil service reforms on the sources of patronage in post-communist countries. These reforms, most notably the adoption of the Civil Service Laws, have largely been driven by the EU as part of the pre-accession negotiations. As both Meyer-Sahling and Rybář show (below) with respect to Hungary and Slovakia, the adoption of new civil service legislation has not completely insulated ministerial bureaucracies from political pressures. However, the civil service laws at least specified more clearly which positions within ministerial bureaucracies are subject to political (that is, government) appointment and which are to be filled on the basis of non-political criteria. In addition to creating a set of expectations and norms governing appointments within the state, as Roper shows in his study of the Romanian case (below), the civil service legislation has thus also empowered bureaucrats to challenge their eventual dismissal in courts.

The second point also relates to the location and scope of patronage within the public administration, but this time in terms of the division between the national level and the regional and local administrative levels. Many post-communist countries have recently embarked on institutional reforms aimed at state decentralization. These reforms have led to the creation (or reform) of regional and local administrations. As was the case with the civil service legislation, these reforms have been driven by the EU and often only reluctantly implemented by the candidate countries. However, numerous cases covered in this collection, most notably Slovakia, Estonia, Romania and Poland, seem to suggest that it is precisely in these newly created tiers of administration below the national level that party patronage is rampant. In other words, while civil service legislation may have decreased the scope for patronage on the national level, especially in the core of the civil service, decentralization has offered parties numerous new opportunities to reward party members and activists with jobs on the regional and local levels. As Rybář argues, patronage opportunities at those levels are a crucial incentive to mobilizing otherwise inactive party members.

Conclusion

There is a close symbiosis between political parties and the state in contemporary Central and Eastern Europe, along all three different dimensions of party–state linkage analysed above. First, parties are more and more financially dependent on the state, as shown in the increasing relevance of public state funding of parties across the region. Indeed, there is probably no Eastern European country that has reduced the amount of public money parties have been receiving since 1989, despite the existence of states where public funding still represents only a small portion of total party income. Together with the almost universal existence of free media access, this finding suggests that the state plays, and is expected to play, a vital role in providing resources needed to launch and run a political party. Second, parties are extensively managed by the state, as seen in the increasingly common regulation of their activities through public law and the constitution. States without a system of party finance regulation are an exception in the region, even though the enforcement of these rules in practice often leaves a lot to be desired. Similarly, many post-communist constitutions have *de jure* elevated parties to the position of an essential institutional infrastructure of democracy, even though parties are *de facto* neither particularly stable, nor highly valued or desired by either the elite or the citizens. Finally, the high scores of parties on indicators of corruption and, to a lesser extent, on practices of patronage suggest that parties in the region do not shy away from rent-seeking within the state in a quest to exploit state resources to their own advantage.

These general findings are not entirely surprising given the context of party formation in Eastern Europe. As other studies show, state financing of political parties is the norm in contemporary democracies, and is especially widespread among the new democracies.[48] Similarly, the high incidence of party recognition in constitutions is typical of new democracies; it reflects the contemporary conception of parties as indispensable public institutions for representative democracy. The high incidence of party rent seeking relates to a state-building process typical of new democracies in which state structures are less resistant to colonization by political parties.

However, the interesting phenomena are the differences among post-communist countries in the type of party–state linkage that exists. The empirical evidence presented above suggests a division between countries in which the party–state relationships are based on a nearly universal and relatively inclusive system of state party financing and regulations, and countries in which the state resources are primarily accrued through the means of rent-seeking within the state institutions, and in which therefore only those in positions of power command the resources necessary to sustain and expand their political organizations. Although this pattern is not entirely consistent across all indicators of party–state linkage, it appears to represent a division between Central European and Baltic countries, on the one side, and the post-Soviet Republics and some Balkan countries, on the other. This essay, and this collection, could not do much more than identify these different patterns, and point to some of the factors by which they are reproduced in some of the East European national contexts. Given that the state and the control of its resources are key instruments of power politics, a further, systematic, investigation of both the causes and consequences of these different forms of party–state linkage is certainly needed.

NOTES

1. See, for example, Russell J. Dalton, 'Political Support in Advanced Industrial Democracies', in Pippa Norris (ed.), *Critical Citizens* (Oxford: Oxford University Press, 1999), pp.57–77; Russell J. Dalton and Martin P. Wattenberg (eds.), *Parties without Partisans: Political Change in Advanced Industrial Democracies* (Oxford: Oxford University Press, 2000); Peter Mair and Ingrid van Biezen, 'Party Membership in Twenty European Democracies, 1980–2000', *Party Politics*, Vol.7, No.1 (2001), pp.5–21; Thomas Poguntke, 'Parties Without Firm Social Roots?: Party Organisational Linkage', in Kurt Richard Luther and Ferdinand Müller-Rommel (eds.), *Political Parties in the New Europe: Political and Analytical Challenges* (Oxford: Oxford University Press, 2002), pp.43–62.

2. See, respectively, Angelo Panebianco, *Political Parties: Organisation and Power* (Cambridge: Cambridge University Press, 1988); Jonathan Hopkin and C. Paolucci, 'New Parties and the Business Firm Model of Party Organization: Cases from Spain and Italy', *European Journal of Political Research*, Vol.35, No.3 (1999), pp.307–39; Richard S. Katz and Peter Mair, 'Changing Models of Party Organization and Party Democracy: The Emergence of the Cartel Party', *Party Politics* Vol.1, No.1 (1995), pp.5–28; Ruud A. Koole, 'The Vunerability of the Modern Cadre Party in the Netherlands', in Richard S Katz and Peter Mair (eds.), *How Parties Organize: Change and Adaption in Western Democracies* (London: Sage, 1994), pp.278–303.

3. See, for example, Ingrid van Biezen, *Political Parties in New Democracies: Party Organization in Southern and East–Central Europe* (London: Palgrave, 2003); Larry Diamond and Richard Gunther (eds.), *Political Parties and Democracy* (Baltimore, MD: Johns Hopkins University Press, 2001); Scott Mainwaring and Timothy R. Scully (eds.), *Building Democratic Institutions: Party Systems in Latin America* (Stanford, CA: Stanford University Press, 1995); Mohamed A. Salih (ed.), *Political Parties in Africa* (London: Pluto, 2003).

4. See, for example, Mair and van Biezen, 'Party Membership in Twenty European Democracies'.

5. See, for example, Jack Bielasiak, 'The Institutionalization of Electoral and Party Systems in Postcommunist States', *Comparative Politics*, Vol.34, No.2 (2002), pp.189–210. For an excellent review of party literature on post-communist Europe see Zsolt Enyedi, 'Party Politics in Post-Communist Transition', in William Crotty and Richard Katz (eds.), *Handbook of Political Parties* (London: SAGE, 2006), pp.228–38.

6. Richard Rose, 'Mobilizing Demobilized Voters in Post-communist Societies', *Party Politics*, Vol.1, No.4 (1995), pp.549–64.

7. See, for example, van Biezen, *Political Parties*; Karsten Grabow, 'The Re-emergence of the Cadre Party? Organizational Patterns of Christian and Social Democrats in Unified Germany', *Party Politics*, Vol.7, No.1, pp.23–44; Aleks Szczerbiak, *Poles Together: Emergence and Development of Political Parties in Post-communist Poland* (Budapest: CEU Press, 2001); Seán Hanley, 'Are the Exceptions Really the Rule? Questioning the Application of "Electoral–Professional" Type Models of Party Organisation in East Central Europe', *Perspectives on European Politics and Society*, Vol.2, No.3 (2001), pp.453–79; Hans Oversloot and Ruben Verheul, 'The Party of Power in Russian Politics', *Acta Politica*, Vol.35 (Summer 2000), pp.123–45; Petr Kopecký, 'Developing Party Organization in East–Central Europe: What Type of Party Is Likely to Emerge?', *Party Politics*, Vol.1, No.4 (1995), pp.515–34;

8. See Arista Maria Cirtautas, 'The Post-Leninist State: A Conceptual and Empirical Examination', *Communist and Post-Communist Studies*, Vol.28, No.4 (1995), pp.379–92; Venelin I. Ganev, 'The Separation of Party and State as a Logistical Problem: A Glance at the Causes of State Weakness in Postcommunism', *East European Politics and Societies*, Vol.15, No.2 (2001), pp.389–420.

9. Conor O'Dwyer, 'Runaway State Building; How Political Parties Shape States in Postcommunist Eastern Europe', *World Politics*, Vol.56, No.4 (2004), pp.520–53.

10. Venelin I. Ganev, 'Postcommunism as an Episode of State-Building: A Reversed Tillian Perspective', *Communist and Post-Communist Studies*, Vol.38, No.4 (2005), pp.425–45; Anna Grzymala-Busse and Pauline Jones Luong, 'Reconceptualizing the State: Lessons

from Post-Communism', *Politics and Society*, Vol.30, No.4 (2002), pp.529–54; O'Dwyer, 'Runaway State Building'.

11. See, for example, Jan-Hinrik Meyer-Sahling, 'Civil Service Reform in Post-Communist Europe: The Bumpy Road to Depoliticisation', *West European Politics*, Vol.27, No.1 (2004), pp.71–103.

12. Ingrid van Biezen and Petr Kopecký, 'The State and the Parties: Public Funding, Public Regulation and Party Patronage in Contemporary Democracies', paper presented at the conference on Political Parties and Development, National Democratic Institute (Washington, DC, 31 August 2005).

13. See Jon Pierre, Lars Svåsand and Anders Widfeldt, 'State Subsidies to Political Parties: Confronting Rhetoric with Reality', *West European Politics*, Vol.23, No.3 (2000), pp.1–24; Ingrid van Biezen and Petr Kopecký, 'On the Predominance of State Money: Reassessing Party Financing in the New Democracies of Southern and Eastern Europe', *Perspectives on European Politics and Societies*, Vol.2, No.3 (2001), pp.401–29.

14. Katz and Mair, 'Changing Models'.

15. Richard S. Katz, 'The Internal Life of Parties', in Kurt Richard Luther and Ferdinand Müller-Rommel (eds.), *Political Challenges in the New Europe: Political and Analytical Challenges* (Oxford: Oxford University Press, 2002), pp.87–118; Ingrid van Biezen, (2004). 'Political Parties as Public Utilities', *Party Politics*, Vol.10, No.6 (2004), pp.701–22.

16. Allan Sikk, 'Party Financing Regimes and Emergence of New Parties in Latvia and Estonia', paper presented at the ECPR Joint Sessions of Workshops (Uppsala, April 2004); Ingrid van Biezen, *Political Parties in New Democracies: Party Organization in Southern and East-Central Europe*; Steven D. Roper, 'The Influence of Romanian Campaign Finance Laws on Party System Development and Corruption', *Party Politics*, Vol.8, No.2 (2002), pp.175–92; Paul G. Lewis, 'Party Funding in Post-Communist East–Central Europe', in Peter Burnell and Alan Ware (eds.), *Funding Democratization* (Manchester: Manchester University Press, 1998), pp.137–57.

17. Katz, 'The Internal Life', p.90.

18. See, for example, Jan Zielonka (ed.), *Democratic Consolidation in Eastern Europe, Volume 1: Institutional Engineering* (Oxford: Oxford University Press, 2001).

19. See Wolfgang C. Müller, 'Patronage by National Governments', in Jean Blondel and Maurizio Cotta (eds.), *The Nature of Party Government: A Comparative European Perspective* (Basingstoke: Palgrave, 2000), pp.141–60; Simona Piattoni (ed.), *Clientelism, Interests, and Democratic Representation: The European Experience in Historical and Comparative Perspective* (Cambridge: Cambridge University Press, 2001); Luis Roninger, 'Political Clientelism, Democracy, and Market Economy', *Comparative Politics*, Vol.36, No.3 (2004), pp.353–75.

20. See Panebianco, *Political Parties*.

21. See, for example, Simona Piattoni, 'Clientelism, Patronage (and Corruption) in Modern Democracies: Reflections on Current Trends and Ways of Analysing Them', paper presented at the ECPR General Conference, Budapest, September 2005; see also Herbert Kitschelt, 'Linkages Between Citizens and Politicians in Democratic Polities', *Comparative Political Studies*, Vol.33 (2000), pp.845–79.

22. See Paul Heywood, 'Political Corruption: Problems and Perspectives', *Political Studies*, Vol.45, No.3 (1997), pp.417–35; Piattoni (ed.), *Clientelism, Interests, and Democratic Representation*.

23. For example, Jordan inserts 'patronage' into the title of his article, but the otherwise very interesting piece focuses almost solely on corruption scandals: see Jeffrey M. Jordan, 'Patronage and Corruption in the Czech Republic', *SAIS Review*, Vol.22, No.2 (2002), pp.19–52.

24. Ganev, 'Postcommunism as an Episode'.

25. IDEA, *Funding of Political Parties and Election Campaigns: Handbook Series* (Stockholm: Institute for Democracy and Electoral Assistance, 2003).

26. See van Biezen and Kopecky 'The State and the Parties'; Michael Pinto-Duschinsky, 'Financing Politics: A Global View', *Journal of Democracy*, Vol.13, No.4 (2002), pp.69–86.

27. Daniel Smilov, 'Comparative Party Funding and Corruption in Eastern Europe', in *Political Party and Election Campaign Financing in Southeastern Europe: Avoiding Corruption and Strengthening Financial Control* (Transparency International, 2002–2003), pp.22–30.
28. See also Janis Ikstens, Daniel Smilov and Marcin Walecki, 'Party and Campaign Funding in Eastern Europe: A Study of 18 Member Countries of the ACEEEO', paper presented at the ACEEEO annual conference on Transparent Election Campaign Financing in the 21st Century (Brijuni, 2001).
29. Jurij Toplak, 'Party Funding and Corruption in Balkan Countries – the Cases of Slovenia and Croatia', in *Political Party and Election Campaign*, pp.43–55.
30. See van Biezen and Kopecký, 'On the Predominance of State Money'.
31. See also Aleks Szczerbiak, 'Cartelisation in Post-Communist Politics: State Party Funding in Post-1989 Poland', *Perspectives on European Politics and Society*, Vol.2, No.3 (2001), pp.431–51.
32. See also Marcin Walecki, 'Money and Politics in Central and Eastern Europe', in IDEA, *Funding of Political Parties and Election Campaigns*, pp.71–93.
33. See also Sikk, 'Party Financing Regimes'.
34. See Sikk in this collection, and 'Party Financing Regimes'.
35. Lewis, 'Party Funding'.
36. See van Biezen and Kopecký, 'On the Predominance of State Money'; Walecki, 'Money and Politics'.
37. See Ikstens, Smilov and Walecki, 'Party and Campaign Funding'.
38. See van Biezen and Kopecký 'The State and the Parties'.
39. Kenneth Janda, 'Party Law and the Goldilocks Problem: How Much is Just Right?', paper presented at the National Democratic Institute for International Affairs (Washington, DC, 31 August 2005).
40. See also Sikk in this collection.
41. Jorge P. Gordin, 'The Political and Partisan Determinants of Patronage in Latin America 1960–1994: A Comparative Perspective', *European Journal of Political Research*, Vol.41, No.4 (2002), pp.513–50.
42. Anna Grzymala-Busse, 'Political Competition and the Politicization of the State in East Central Europe', *Comparative Political Studies*, Vol.36, No.10 (2003), pp.1123–47; O'Dwyer, 'Runaway State Building'.
43. See, for example, Philip Manow, 'Was erklärt Politische Patronage in den Ländern Westeuropas?', *Politische Vierteljahreszeitschrift*, Vol.43, No.1 (2003), pp.20–45.
44. However, Manow argues that the general Corruption Perception Index (CPI) of Transparency International, which reflects the perceptions (of business people and country analysts) of a wide variety of different types of corruption (including administrative and economic), constitutes a good proxy for party patronage. This is because the index actually taps into and measures aspects of patronage and it is likely that respondents in some of their answers had practices of party patronage in mind. In addition, Manow shows that the CPI correlates highly with various expert judgments and qualitative country rank orderings of patronage.
45. The figure for each country represents an average of scores in two consecutive years, 2004 and 2005. However, for Albania, Estonia, Latvia and Serbia and Montenegro, data were available for only one year.
46. The STD for older democracies is 0.60: see van Biezen and Kopecký 'The State and the Parties'.
47. The data come from the 1999–2000 survey; the World Bank repeated the survey in 2002, but unfortunately the question concerning patronage and its impact was not asked in the 2002 survey.
48. See van Biezen and Petr Kopecký 'The State and the Parties'.

The Rise of the Partisan State? Parties, Patronage and the Ministerial Bureaucracy in Hungary

JAN-HINRIK MEYER-SAHLING

Research on the transformation of the post-communist state argues that the intertwining of party building and state building in post-communist Europe provides 'ideal conditions for party patronage'.[1] Hungary is commonly cited as an outlier in the region in that it has experienced the least patronage, operationalized as the number of public administration personnel and its rate of increase over time. The negative growth of state personnel and thus the apparently negligible relevance of patronage for Hungary is related to factors such as the country's status as a front runner in the area of public administration reform, in particular the adoption and implementation of civil service legislation shortly after the change of regime, the presence of a 'critical opposition', and the early institutionalization of 'responsible party government', all of which are said to have prevented the use or abuse of the state apparatus for the provision of jobs to party supporters.[2]

This study re-examines the arguments surrounding the relationship between political parties and the state in post-communist Hungary. It examines to what extent, in what ways and why patronage matters for the ministerial bureaucracy. Patronage is understood as the staffing of public offices – here the ministerial bureaucracy – on the basis of political criteria. This definition differs from the broader understanding of patronage as the distribution of specific goods in exchange for political support, in that jobs form but one kind of special benefit that can be handed out to party supporters.[3] At the same time, the focus on patronage as the provision of jobs in the ministerial bureaucracy overlaps with usage of the concept of 'politicization' in comparative public administration research. Politicization is typically referred to as 'the substitution of political criteria for merit criteria in the selection, retention, promotion, rewards and disciplining of members of the public service'.[4] The terms 'patronage' and 'politicization' are therefore used interchangeably in this essay.

Taking issue with the results of recent research, this study presents a three-fold argument on party patronage and the politicization of the ministerial bureaucracy in post-communist Hungary. First, it argues that civil service legislation has not provided an effective constraint against the politicization of the ministerial bureaucracy in Hungary. Rather, governing parties can potentially control the staffing of the entire ministerial bureaucracy. The presence of civil service legislation is therefore not sufficient to infer that the post-communist state is not politicized nor can it be considered to be a sufficient brake on the politicization of the state. Second, the politicization of the ministerial bureaucracy in Hungary is, and over time has become, far more extensive and intensive than has hitherto been appreciated. The politicization of the ministerial bureaucracy has been especially important for the senior ranks, as evidenced by large turnover after changes of government and by the obvious political connections of appointees to positions that are nominally part of the permanent civil service. At the same time, the core structures of the central government ministries have generally been less subject to politicization below the senior level, but there are signs that the politicization of the ministerial bureaucracy is creeping downwards, increasingly involving the wider, non-managing civil service.

Third, it is argued that the politicization of the ministerial bureaucracy in Hungary results less from the logic of building and maintaining party organizations than from the attempts of governing parties to address problems of governance under conditions of polarized political competition between former communists and anti-communist parties. Under these conditions, new governing parties have an incentive to initiate personnel turnover in the ministerial bureaucracy and to insert officials who combine political loyalty and expertise for the sake of initiating and implementing public policy change and of conceivably managing the distribution of particularistic goods – patronage understood broadly – to party supporters. The consolidation of party organizations of parties both on the left and on the right has facilitated the politicization of the state, in that it has enhanced the access of parties to politically associated experts, promoting the rise of the partisan state in post-communist Hungary. In contrast to the literature on patronage in Central and Eastern Europe, this study therefore concludes that the polarization of political competition and party strength rather than party weakness and the absence of a critical opposition produce the politicization of the post-communist state.

Public Administration Reform and the Parties' Reach into the Ministerial Bureaucracy

In Hungary, governing parties have the possibility of reaching deeply into the ministerial bureaucracy. They can potentially exercise political discretion over the staffing of the entire ministerial bureaucracy. Hungary is the front runner in the area of public administration reform in post-communist Europe, in particular civil service reform.[5] This record is usually assumed to create conditions that limit party patronage and the politicization of the state.[6] Hungary was indeed the first country of Central and Eastern Europe to adopt and implement civil service legislation in 1990 and 1992. Subsequently, Hungary has passed three more civil service reforms, in 1997, 2001 and 2002–3, each of which led to the revision of the formal–legal basis governing personnel policy in the ministerial bureaucracy. This legislation has gradually institutionalized rules and procedures that reduce the possibilities for governments and their ministers to staff the ministerial bureaucracy on the basis of political criteria.[7] State secretaries and senior and higher civil servants are required to hold a university degree; higher civil servants have to be recruited on the basis of a formal procedure for open competition, and they have to pass a basic examination upon entry to the civil service; senior civil servants and state secretaries have to pass a special examination after taking up their post; the political rights of civil servants are restricted in that they may not hold posts in a political party and are obliged to resign from the civil service if they run for elections at the national level; civil servants at all levels generally enjoy permanent tenure; they can be dismissed only in exceptional circumstances; and they have a prospect of pursuing a career in the civil service that takes into account criteria for merit and seniority.

It is, however, problematic to relate the degree of politicization to the adoption of civil service legislation because the formal–legal framework incorporates a number of discretionary instruments that ministers can use to politicize personnel policy. Even if state secretaries have to meet certain criteria upon their appointment, members of the government have the authority to select and de-select them at all times. The assignment and reassignment of officials to positions at the rank of senior civil servant, representing levels 3 to 5 in the ministerial hierarchy and responsible for managing ministerial departments and divisions, are also subject to the discretion of the minister of the day. Ministers and the prime minister can set up ministerial cabinets with ministerial and political advisers up to five and ten per cent respectively of the overall ministerial staff. Members of the government can also freely appoint and dismiss titular state secretaries and government commissioners for the sake of performing specific tasks in the interest of ministers, the prime minister or the government. Finally, civil service legislation also provides ministers with possibilities to intervene in the appointment, promotion, transfer and dismissal of civil servants in higher, middle and lower-ranking positions. In Hungary, these personnel decisions are formally taken by administrative state secretaries as professional heads of the ministerial organization, and not by an independent civil service commission. Because the appointment of administrative state secretaries may be politicized by the governing parties, incumbent ministers may exercise indirect political discretion through the administrative state secretary.[8] As a consequence, civil service legislation in Hungary provides enough political discretion for governments to influence the staffing of both the senior and the non-managing ranks of the ministerial bureaucracy, suggesting that the presence of civil service legislation is generally not sufficient to prevent the politicization of the state.

When the Party Never Stops: Patronage and the Growth of the Ministerial Bureaucracy

In Hungary, the politicization of the ministerial bureaucracy has been intense but it has been concentrated in the senior ranks. However, there are signs that politicization is creeping downwards into the non-managing ranks. Patronage is generally difficult to identify and measure. Eschenburg emphasizes that the essence of patronage is found in the motive or intention of the appointing authority.[9] Patronage occurs when the motive for the appointment of a person is incompatible with the official function of the office, for instance the appointment to a public position on the basis of partisan, special interest criteria. In order to estimate the precise extent of patronage in the ministerial bureaucracy, it would be necessary to identify the motive of the person who took the personnel decision, or the person on whose behalf the personnel decision was taken, for each and every position in the ministerial bureaucracy.

Even if this were possible, for instance, on the basis of an endless number of interviews, one would still have to address the problem that interviewees have good reason to conceal their true intention, because this would entail the confession that they have not acted in accordance with the official and functional requirements of the office but with special interests in mind. Similar to corruption, patronage therefore belongs to the realm of 'covert politics'.[10]

In an attempt to develop indicators to capture the extent of patronage, recent research examines the size of public sector employment or a particular category of public sector employment, its growth over time, and the growth of government wage bills.[11] To the extent that these studies refer to Eastern Europe, Hungary is usually identified as the case that has experienced the least patronage since the number of public administration personnel is said to have even contracted during the 1990s, while other countries have experienced positive – in some cases excessive – growth.

However, the rate of growth of administrative personnel is a problematic indicator of the measurement of patronage. First, the growth or reduction of administrative personnel over time is not necessarily the product of party patronage but may result from the reform and reorganization of public administration, or public sector restructuring more broadly. In Hungary, for instance, the greatest drop in state administrative personnel occurred between 1995 and 1997 as a result of the Bokros austerity programme, which included the goal of cutting back the personnel of administrative institutions by 15 per cent in order to reduce the government wage bill. Conversely, the biggest increase in the size of the central state administrative personnel occurred in 1999 after the self-governing social security organs were recentralized and as a result were transferred and reclassified from their former status as a public corporation at the local government level. In both cases, personnel fluctuations were thus unrelated to the presence or absence of party patronage.

Second, studies of patronage usually assume that parties turn to public sector jobs as a reward and selective incentive for their supporters.[12] The assumption that the growth in administrative personnel indicates patronage implies that parties hire new personnel but do not fire the personnel recruited by their predecessors in government, and that they therefore feed the supporters and organization of their political competitors. When taking office, parties should therefore have a strong incentive to dismiss officials who are associated with the opposition parties, and the discussion (above) of Hungary's civil service law suggests that governing parties in Central and Eastern Europe do in fact have the discretion to do so. As a result, they can save budgetary resources for purposes that correspond more closely to their interests. This consideration is especially relevant when taking into account that public finances were under severe pressure in most countries during the first decade after the change of regime.[13]

Third, the size of administrative personnel is a contingent indicator for patronage in that it depends to a large extent on the countries under scrutiny, the portion of public sector employment examined and the period of time studied. When looking at the size of the ministerial bureaucracy, here without the prime minister's office, Table 1 shows that during the period 1993–2003, the size of the civil service in general and the ministerial bureaucracy in particular did indeed shrink until 1998 and 1997 respectively but has since grown, exceeding its original 1993 level. Moreover, Table 1 reveals that the staff trajectory of different ministries has taken very different directions. On the one hand, the ministry of economic affairs and its predecessors shrank by 45 per cent until the end of 2000. On the other hand, the ministries of cultural heritage, education, and youth and sports, as the successor ministries of the ministry of culture and education, grew by 62 per cent during the 1990s. In both cases, the staff trajectories reveal at best half the story in so far as patronage is concerned.

TABLE 1
DISTRIBUTION OF CIVIL SERVANTS BY EMPLOYING MINISTRY

	1993	1994	1996	1997	1998	1999	2000
Interior	594	569	549	526	648	640	538
Health						309	335
Welfare	438	477	427	344	381		
Agriculture	478	495	440	437	451	608	727
Economic Affairs						805	755
International Economic Relations	424						
Industry & Trade	652	1,369	1,087	1,005	677		
Defence	120	124	111	135	131	143	191
Justice	315	267	335	318	283	297	321
Environment	383	374	381	370	464	454	528
Transport	389	337	342	342	301	331	378
Foreign Affairs	1,633	1,618	1,745	1,578	1,772	1,835	1,887
Cultural Heritage						241	253
Education						458	653
Youth and Sport						89	117
Culture and Education	630	696	584	506	551		
Finance	579	569	591	572	620	576	520
Social and Family Affairs						324	252
Labour	237	225	236	286	318		
Total Ministries	*6,872*	*7,120*	*6,828*	*6,419*	*6,597*	*7,110*	*7,455*
Total Civil Service	*n.a.*	*104,092*	*107,061*	*104,646*	*103,296*	*108,249*	*111,746*

Source: Ministry of Interior.

At first glance, the contraction of the ministry of economic affairs suggests that patronage has been irrelevant in this sector and that the state is indeed retreating 'from rowing to steering', in that the transition to a market economy has led to the redundancy of many administrative functions and units.[14] On the one hand, the figures for the ministry of economic affairs, and for several other ministries, hide that staff changes have resulted from the reorganization of ministries. For instance, the ministry of economics received units responsible for labour market policy and vocational training in 1998 from the former ministry of labour. By contrast, in 2001, departments dealing with research and development were shifted to the ministry of education, and the departments for international trade were transferred to the ministry of foreign affairs, causing continuous fluctuations in staff across ministries. The figures also conceal that the ministry of economic affairs is usually identified as a central player in the provision of party patronage broadly understood, including the provision of contracts, services and funds. In 2000, for instance, the ministry developed and subsequently managed the so-called Széchenyi Plan. The Széchenyi Plan was originally launched by the Orbán government as a development programme for the revitalization of the small and medium-sized business sector in Hungary, one of the core constituencies of the centre-right parties. However, the opposition parties charged the government that the programme allows the governing parties to direct public money to 'associated businesses' because of the application of soft eligibility criteria for the allocation of grants.

On the other hand, there are good grounds to relate the staff increase in the successor ministries of culture and education to party patronage. Here, the increase in the size of the ministries can indeed capture some degree of party patronage but also indicates more broadly that reorganizations provide excellent opportunities to dismiss unwanted personnel and to hire 'friendly' staff into new units or new ministries such as the ministry of youth and sports, controlled by Fidesz (Alliance of Young Democrats) between 1999 and 2002, or the ministry of informatics, under the control of the SZDSZ (Alliance of Free Democrats) since 2002. Second, what is not visible in Table 1 is that party patronage in terms of providing jobs to party supporters is often concentrated in the back offices of the ministries, such as newly established marketing offices or research centres, leading one observer to the cynical comment that 'for these guys, the party never ends'. All these examples suggest that, if staff numbers and evidence from interviews are valid indicators, there are signs of an increase rather than a decrease, or a stabilization on a low level of party patronage in the ministerial bureaucracy as well as in the periphery of the ministries.

Finally, aggregate figures on the size of the state cannot capture the extent to which different positions within the state bureaucracy are affected by party patronage. For Hungary, the politicization of the senior ranks of the civil service and the identification of an appropriate dividing line between politics and administration has been a matter of continuous debate.[15] In particular, administrative and deputy state secretaries, who are nominally the top two ranks of the senior civil service, have been subject to politicization. Four features of politicization stand out. First, Figure 1 shows that the number of positions available for the appointment of state secretaries has increased by more than 30 per cent, from fewer than 60 in the early 1990s to more than 80 since the Socialist–Liberal government under Prime Minister Medgyessy took office in 2002. Second, the changes of government in 1990, 1994, 1998 and 2002 each triggered a large turnover among state secretaries, as new governments replaced the state secretaries they inherited from their predecessors in government. Turnover rates varied from more than 90 per cent under the

FIGURE 1
TURNOVER AMONG STATE SECRETARIES

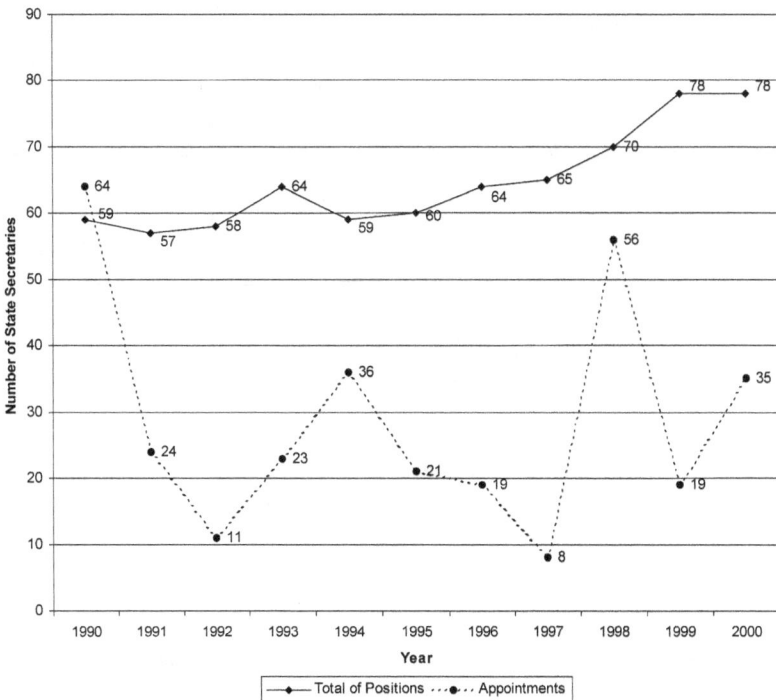

Source: Compiled by author.

Note: Elections were held in 1990, 1994 and 1998.

Antall government that took office in 1990 and roughly 60 per cent during the Horn government (which took office in 1994), while both the Orbán (1998) and the Medgyessy governments (2002) replaced about 70 per cent of the state secretaries who had served the previous government.[16] Because the replacement and new appointment of state secretaries clearly peak in the aftermath of political leadership changes, this kind of turnover can be taken to indicate the use of political criteria in staffing state secretary positions. However, Figure 1 also shows that turnover and appointments are not restricted to periods of political change but persist – though at lower levels – during a government's term in office.

The third feature concerns the career pathways of newly appointed state secretaries. In Hungary, state secretaries are primarily recruited from outside the ministerial bureaucracy such as other organs of public administration, academia, the private sector, interest groups and non-governmental organizations. Moreover, it is not unusual to find state secretaries with some kind of political background such as a former position in government as political state secretary, or a career as member of parliament, or a party functionary, employee or activist. In fact, the civil service law forbids the simultaneous holding of party or elected office and a post in the civil service but considers it sufficient that new state secretaries resign from their political position upon their appointment to a state secretary post. Governing parties are therefore confronted with very few effective constraints upon the use of partisan criteria to staff positions of state secretary.

The most striking features of the politicization of state secretaries in Hungary, however, is not simply their recruitment from settings other than the ministerial bureaucracy, and thus a personnel policy that contradicts the principles of a professional and politically neutral civil service as well as the most common modes of senior personnel politicization in West European countries.[17] Rather, the politicization of the senior civil service is characterized by the appointment of state secretaries who are returnees, in the sense that these officials have earlier been appointed to senior positions of the ministerial bureaucracy under governments formed by parties from the same political spectrum; they leave the ministries when their party is voted out of office and work in the private sector or academia or at a political party; and they return to the senior ranks of the ministries when their party or bloc of parties is voted back into government.

For instance, when taking office in 1994, the Horn government appointed state secretaries who had already served in the senior bureaucracy during the last socialist government led by Prime Minister Németh. These officials left the state administration in 1990 or shortly afterwards, mostly to take jobs in the private sector rather than at the MSZP (Hungarian Socialist Party), and they were 'invited' to return to the ministries when the MSZP won the elections in 1994. These 'new' state secretaries did not work as party officials during their period outside government office, but their career background inevitably associates them with the MSZP. Most of these state secretaries were representatives of the 'late Kádárist technocracy' who gained growing influence over government management from the early 1980s and began to dominate the ruling communist MSZMP (Hungarian Socialist Workers' Party) in the late 1980s.[18]

Similar patterns of recruiting a large proportion of returnees into state secretary positions reproduced themselves after the 1998 and the 2002 elections. When the coalition of Fidesz, the MDF (Hungarian Democratic Forum) and the FKGP (Independent Smallholders, Agrarian Workers and Civic Party) took office in 1998, it appointed state secretaries who had already served in senior positions during the first centre-right government between 1990 and 1994, in particular officials who had been recruited late in the term and thus closer to the 1994 elections. In 2002, when the second Socialist–Liberal coalition took office, the ministries witnessed another influx of state secretaries whose faces were well known from the Horn – and often even the Németh – years. This 'mode of partisan politicization', that relies on the replacement of inherited officials by returnees, partisans and outsiders after changes of government, has therefore become increasingly stable in post-communist Hungary.[19] While hard data for the comparison of governments and ministries is unavailable for the turnover of senior officials below the state secretary ranks, there are signs that the politicization of the senior civil service has begun to reach deeper into the service, in particular at the level of head of department, and it increasingly follows the same mode of politicization as that of state secretaries.

The exception to the mode of partisan politicization to the senior bureaucracy was the first democratically elected government, formed in 1990 by parties of the former democratic opposition under Prime Minister Antall. In contrast to its successors, the Antall government recruited its senior officials primarily from the lower managing ranks of the ministerial bureaucracy and thus from among the officials who had pursued careers during the communist regime. This initially friendly takeover of the senior bureaucracy after the change of regime was a short-lived pheno-menon, however, as the Antall government soon adopted a far more asser-tive approach to senior personnel policy. In sum, a closer look at the ministerial bureaucracy reveals that patronage and politicization have indeed been very important in post-communist Hungary. The politicization has been concentrated at the top of the ministerial civil service but it has changed its defining features from the Antall government to its successors, suggesting an intensification of the use of political criteria for the staffing of the senior bureaucracy. Moreover, there is a trend that political parties are tightening their grip on the ministerial bureaucracy in that the politicization of the civil service is expanding downwards.

In the Hungarian case, the approach of political parties to governing the state has therefore come to look quite similar to the approach of the communist party before the change of regime. Political reliability and party control have again become virtually necessary conditions for an appointment or promotion to the senior ranks of the ministerial bureaucracy. At the same time, appointees are required to possess policy and administrative expertise, suggesting a preference for the selection of red-and-expert officials that was characteristic of personnel policy during the late-communist regime.[20] The striking difference from the communist regime, however, is that the new centre-right parties that emerged from the former democratic opposition seem to have successfully emulated their political 'competitor' from before the change of regime as regards governing the state bureaucracy. To be sure, the democratic alternation of parties in government implies that post-communist parties cannot maintain long-term control over the ministerial bureaucracy. But for the time they form the government, the mode of senior personnel politicization in Hungary suggests that parties of both the right and the left approach the governance of the state in ways that are very similar to the ruling communist parties before the change of regime.

The Structure of Political Competition and the Politicization of the Ministerial Bureaucracy: Towards an Explanation

The discussion of patronage and politicization in the ministerial bureaucracy suggests that, contrary to the findings of earlier research, it is problematic to classify Hungary as a case of low or no patronage. Rather, patronage has been important and it has grown in terms of both extent and intensity, casting doubt on the arguments brought forward by Grzymala-Busse that the politicization of the state is a function of the 'absence/presence of a critical opposition' or by O'Dwyer it reflects that the 'institutionalization and robustness of post-communist party systems'.[21] This section briefly examines how these arguments fare when applied to the ministerial bureaucracy in Hungary. Subsequently, the section explores an alternative explanation of state politicization in Hungary. It argues that it is problematic to assume that political parties turn to the provision of jobs in the ministerial bureaucracy for the sake of ensuring their organizational survival. Instead, it is argued that the politicization of the ministerial bureaucracy is driven by the attempts of governing parties to enhance political control over policy making and implementation under conditions of polarized party competition between ex-communist and anti-communist political forces.

First, by the conceptual standards of Grzymala-Busse, Hungary has had a 'critical opposition' only since the elections of 1998 and not before.[22] After the

1998 elections, the centre-right Fidesz–MPP (Alliance of Young Democrats – Hungarian Civic Party) formed a coalition with the agrarian FKGP and the conservative MDF, while the socialist MSZP and the liberal SZDSZ went into opposition. The MSZP–SZDSZ opposition can be classified as 'credible' in the sense that both parties had been in government; they had a clear 'profile' in that they had not dramatically altered the ideological appeal over the previous years nor did the opposition leaders regularly change their partisan affiliations; and, finally, the opposition was to become 'contentious' in the sense that it would vigorously monitor and criticize the governing coalition. Under these circumstances, we should expect less politicization and thus a stabilization or conceivably even the contraction of the size of administrative personnel. However, as shown above in Table 1, this is exactly the time when the ministries started to grow. Moreover, the crucial change from a more moderate 'mode of bounded politicization' to a mode of partisan politicization occurred after the change of government in 1994, not in 1998.

At the same time, it is more problematic to classify the pre-1998 opposition as a *critical* opposition. Between 1994 and 1998, the MSZP and the SZDSZ ruled in an oversized coalition commanding 71 per cent of the seats in parliament. At the same time, the centre-right opposition underwent a process of restructuring.[23] The centre-right parties certainly provided a contentious and vocal opposition, but the Fidesz only 'grew into' the dominant party of the centre right party during this period: it had not yet acquired the credibility of a former governing party, and it had only just completed an ideological reorientation from a radical liberal, anti-communist party into a liberal, national, conservative party of the centre-right. In these circumstances, the MSZP and the SZDSZ would therefore have found ideal conditions for the politicization of the state, but this is also the period when state employment in general decreased most radically. Moreover, the explanation is doubtful when examining the politicization of the senior civil service because a very different type of government–opposition relationship in 1998 returned the same mode of politicization as in 1994. Finally, the presence of a critical opposition is doubtful for the period before 1994, when the MDF ruled in coalition with the KDNP (Christian Democratic People's Party) and the FKGP because the MSZP, which could have qualified as a critical opposition, remained small, with only 8.6 per cent of the parliamentary seats, and, as Ágh argues, 'for two years, it was forced into a political ghetto' before emerging as the main force on the centre-left of the party system.[24]

O'Dwyer's argument, that the 'institutionalization of party systems' and the 'robustness of party competition' prevent the growth of administrative personnel, encounters similar problems when applied to the ministerial bureaucracy in Hungary.[25] When party competition started to show most signs of institutionalization, namely in 1998 and subsequently, the state administrative personnel began to grow, while periods with lower levels of party system institutionalization witnessed the negative growth of ministerial personnel. To be sure, these reflections on the staff development in Hungary do not refute the argument that a critical opposition and the institutionalization of party systems reduce the possibilities and incentives for political parties to use the state for the provision of patronage jobs. However, they question the suitability of the indicators of party patronage and state politicization and possibly the applicability of the arguments to the ministerial bureaucracy.

So how can we explain the politicization of the ministerial bureaucracy in post-communist Hungary? First, in contrast to the literature on party patronage in Central and Eastern Europe, I argue that the incentive of political parties to supply jobs for their supporters in order to ensure their organizational survival does not apply well to the logic of personnel policy at the level of ministerial bureaucracies. Rather, the appointment of potentially incompetent partisan officials to senior ranks in the ministerial bureaucracy may be entirely dysfunctional. Not only does it have the potential to weaken the general policy-making capacity of the government but it may even undermine the capability of governing parties to pursue a patronage strategy and thus to distribute particularistic goods such as contracts and services to their supporters. The costs of appointing an incompetent partisan official to the senior ranks of the ministerial bureaucracy may therefore far outweigh the benefits of having satisfied the office-seeking aspirations of one party supporter. At the level of central government ministries, I therefore follow the executive politics literature and argue that the logic of personnel policy is instead primarily driven by the desire of governing parties to control the bureaucracy and to make use of the expertise of ministerial bureaucrats for the sake of preparing and implementing public policies.

Second, in accordance with the literature on party patronage, I argue that the structure of political competition is indeed central to the explanation of state politicization in Central and Eastern Europe. Yet I argue that it is especially the polarization of political competition between former communist parties and their political allies, on the one side, and anti-communist parties, on the other, that creates pressure for the politicization of the ministerial bureaucracy in post-communist Europe. In conditions of political polarization, changes of government do generally imply major ideological reorientations of government policy. On the one hand, new governing parties are therefore in need of technical and procedural expertise in order to develop new policies and to effect changes in the management of existing policies. On the other hand, principal–agent analysis suggests that governments and their members will be reluctant to rely on the expertise of ministerial bureaucrats who are associated with their political competitors and predecessor in government, bearing in mind that bureaucrats may have an incentive to use their superior expertise strategically, misrepresent it or hide it altogether. If a change of government takes place in a context of polarized party competition, the members of the new government can therefore be expected to face problems of trust *vis-à-vis* the ministerial bureaucracy, which will create an incentive for the new governing parties to replace inherited officials with trusted appointees.[26] However, new governing parties will be able to replace inherited officials only if there is a supply of suitable personnel alternatives that promise a mix of political responsiveness and governmental expertise, because otherwise they could fall into the potentially costly patronage trap outlined above. Governing parties therefore need to have developed the capacity to access personnel alternatives, be this within their own party organization, in the private sector, in academia, or inside the ministerial bureaucracy itself.

While political polarization can generally be expected to create pressures for the politicization of the ministerial bureaucracy after changes of government, I assume here, in accordance with Frye, that in Central and Eastern Europe the polarization of political competition is especially 'atrocious' when former communist parties and anti-communist parties are divided into two ideological camps.[27] As a result, the politicization of the ministerial bureaucracy in post-communist settings can be expected to rise if two conditions are met: first, the structure of political competition is characterized by a polarization between former communist forces and their political allies on the one side and anti-communist parties on the other; and, second, governing parties can rely on the supply of personnel that combines political loyalty and governmental expertise to fill ministerial posts.[28]

Two alternative constellations can also be derived from the 'politicization hypothesis' presented here. First, irrespective of the structure of political competition, the politicization of the ministerial bureaucracy will necessarily be limited if governing parties lack a supply of personnel alternatives. Second, irrespective of the supply of alternative personnel, the politicization of the ministerial bureaucracy can be expected to be lower if the political competition for government formation is less polarized; this is because new governments will find it less difficult to trust the ministerial bureaucracy and will thus lack an incentive to initiate major personnel changes in the first place.

These hypotheses can be examined by tracing the politicization of the ministerial bureaucracy in Hungary. Our discussion compares the four governments that have held office since 1990 and concentrates on the senior ranks of the ministerial bureaucracy. In particular, the theoretical perspective must be able to explain why the first freely elected government formed by three centre-right parties of the former democratic opposition opted for the more moderate politicization involving the promotion of officials from the lower ranks of the ministerial bureaucracy, while subsequent governments have consistently opted for far more intense, partisan politicization. However, the discussion also shows that the politicization hypothesis and its alternatives gain support when examining the politicization differences at lower levels of aggregation, such as differences between governing parties of the same coalition.

The Polarization of Political Competition and the Politicization of the Ministerial Bureaucracy in Hungary

At first glance, we would expect that the Antall government, formed by parties of the former democratic opposition, faced the most serious problem of trust because the change of government was embedded in a change of regime and the new government was facing the remnants of the communist cadre administration. The Antall government should have had a clear incentive to replace the officials inherited from the communist regime with trusted officials from its own circle. However, it appears that the Antall government took office in a politically much less polarized context than its three successor governments, providing conditions for the formation of relations of mutual trust between the members of the new government and the ministerial bureaucracy. Moreover, the Antall government differs from subsequent governments in that it was unable to turn to an alternative administrative elite to replace the inherited communist bureaucracy. In other words, even if the Antall government had wanted to initiate major personnel changes it would have hardly had the means to do so.

The origins of the friendly takeover of the ministerial bureaucracy by the Antall government in the summer of 1990 can be traced to the events surrounding Hungary's transition to democracy. First, the legacy of the late communist regime, in particular the personnel policy and the public policy record of the Németh government, facilitated the formation of trust between the senior bureaucracy and the members of the Antall government. Political hardliners among senior bureaucrats were effectively forced to leave the administration during the Németh years, while reform-oriented officials were promoted or brought into the administration from academia, for example. Moreover, the Németh government pursued economic policy reforms that sought to pave the way for the establishment of a market economy. This helped senior officials to start developing a reputation of support for the objectives of the 'dual transformation'.

Second, the round table talks of Hungary's pacted transition provided an opportunity for the Antall government to mitigate problems of trust in relation to the ministerial bureaucracy. At the time of their appointments in 1990, most of the administrative state secretaries, for example, were well known by the new Prime Minister Antall and, to a lesser extent, by the new ministers.

Many of them had represented the ministries at the national round table talks in the spring of 1989. During the negotiations, this new generation of senior officials was able to signal to the representatives of the parties of the democratic opposition that they supported the change of regime and associated policy changes.

Third, the Antall government lacked access to alternative personnel with governmental expertise to fill the posts in the ministerial bureaucracy. The lack of a sufficiently large pool of experts associated with the former democratic opposition at the time of government and regime change meant that the new governing parties effectively lacked the possibility of initiating a large-scale purge of the ministerial bureaucracy. The first generation of ministers themselves lacked experience in government. They had entered the political scene shortly before or during the period of regime change, and none had previously worked in a government ministry close to political power. The three governing parties also lacked an infrastructure that could provide specialist support for the development of policies outside the ministries. Even if some academics were recruited into the ministerial bureaucracy, ministers were almost completely dependent on their ministerial staff in the policy-making process. In these circumstances, Prime Minister Antall recognized that it was impossible to replace the entire ministerial bureaucracy after the change of regime. Instead, it was considered necessary to work with those senior officials who were expert staff but had not held formal positions in the MSZMP in order to make the far-reaching reform ambitions of the first government work.

This is not to say that the government was exposed to no politicization pressures. The parliamentary factions of the governing parties, in particular the MDF parliamentary faction, exerted pressures on Antall to assert more control over the staffing of the senior bureaucracy. The MDF was founded in 1987 by populist writers and intellectuals as a political movement rather than a political party. Adopting the image of a 'rightist-centrist people's party' during the 1990 election campaign, the MDF continued to accommodate several political currents under its roof including a moderate-pragmatic, a conservative and a radical-populist wing.[29] The members of the Antall government represented the moderate-pragmatic strand of the MDF, whereas radical-populist and conservative factions were underrepresented in the cabinet. The approach of the latter two factions to Hungary's bureaucracy was based on the radical anti-communist assumption that the completion of the change of regime requires a 'thorough cleansing' of the bureaucracy from all connections to the former ruling party, MSZMP.[30] Such ideological considerations of some parts of the governing parties prevented the formation of trust. In consequence, the anti-communist factions within the MDF questioned Antall's approach to senior personnel policy, calling for the exclusion from the policy-making process of senior officials associated with the communist regime and the insertion of trustworthy officials into the senior ranks of the ministerial bureaucracy.

The position of the anti-communist factions within the MDF does therefore also support the politicization hypothesis formulated above at a lower level of aggregation, in that it demonstrates that individual factions within governing parties can demand the tightening of political control and so push for the politicization of personnel policy. As long as Antall's position was largely uncontested within the governing coalition, he could contain these pressures for politicization. However, during the first parliament the party system moved from a tripolar to a bipolar structure of political competition. The rapprochement between the MSZP and the SZDSZ after 1991–92 pulled the MSZP out of its 'political ghetto' and, as a result, the ideological division of the regime over how to deal with the communist past no longer cut across the historically dominant socio-cultural divide but reinforced it.[31] Ágh, for instance, argues that under these conditions the Hungarian party system began to exhibit the 'permanent marks of a polarized pluralism'.[32] The growing polarization of political competition during the first parliament, together with the fading popularity of the governing parties in the context of political and economic crisis, the gradual disintegration of the governing parties, and Antall's deteriorating health condition, weakened his position within the governing coalition while strengthening the influence of the anti-communist wing. As a result, the government gradually stepped up the level of political control over the ministerial bureaucracy and, by the time the second parliamentary elections approached in the spring of 1994, most of the first generation of state secretaries had been replaced by appointees who were politically sympathetic to the centre-right parties.

In contrast to the Antall government, all subsequent governments took office in circumstances that created pressure for and facilitated the politicization of the ministerial bureaucracy. All three governments were formed in a climate of political polarization that created demand for personnel change in the managerial ranks of the ministerial bureaucracy, in particular, and all three governments were formed by political parties that had developed the capacity effectively to bring their own administrative elite to government to prepare and manage public policies.

The remainder of this section briefly looks at each of the three subsequent governments that were in office from 1994 to 1998 (Horn government), 1998 to 2002 (Orbán government) and since 2002 (Medgyessy/Gyurcsány) before discussing the facilitating role played by ministerial bureaucrats themselves in the politicization game in Hungary.

First, in 1994, the Horn government took office in a context of polarization between the MSZP and its political ally SZDSZ, on the one side, and the anti-communist centre-right parties, on the other. This created an incentive for the new government to initiate personnel changes. In particular, the Horn government had an incentive to replace the state secretaries who were appointed by the Antall government. The state secretaries who were appointed by the Antall government owed their careers to the former government, and their loyalty to the MSZP–SZDSZ government was therefore called in question. Accordingly, the main victims of the 1994 senior personnel turnover were the state secretaries recruited by the Antall government to the ministries only after 1990, whereas state secretaries who had been continuously employed in the administration since the late 1980s had a higher chance of survival.

Second, the MSZP sought to distinguish itself from the centre-right parties by stressing its policy achievements and its experience in running the state and the economy before the change of regime.[33] In the 1994 elections, the MSZP became the largest party, with the slogan 'Let Competence Govern'. Márkus argues that 'the vote contained a twofold message: a refusal of ideologically determined policy-making ... and moderate support for Westernization. ... The well-known faces and familiar style of the ex-Communists offered a sense of stability and security, after the turmoil of the first post-89 government and its policies'.[34] Accordingly, the MSZP promised not only a 'government by experts' but, as Bozóki argues, more precisely a government by those experts who had handed over the country 'in good order' (the Németh government) in the spring of 1990.[35]

As a consequence, the MSZP was effectively able to bring back its own administrative elite – officials who had already been appointed to senior positions under Németh and earlier. MSZP ministers also benefited from their past experience. All MSZP ministers had gathered experience in the administration or in government before 1990, giving them a good prior knowledge of senior officials' professional capabilities, preferences and political orientations. In addition, ministers could take advantage of the rather well-developed national organization of the MSZP and its broad-based social networks, both in policy development and in their search for appropriate candidates.[36] In contrast to the centre-right parties in 1990, the MSZP was therefore not constrained by a lack of supply of personnel with adequate governmental expertise, and this facilitated the shift towards a partisan mode of politicization in 1994.

Third, there were considerable differences in the politicization of ministries led by the MSZP and those that were under the control of the small coalition partner SZDSZ, providing evidence that the hypotheses formulated above can also account for differences across political parties within governing coalitions. Like the MSZP, the SZDSZ had an incentive to initiate changes in the senior ranks of the ministries; however, it was far more constrained in tackling problems of political trust than the MSZP. SZDSZ ministers shared many of the problems that had already puzzled Antall's ministers in the early 1990s. They were largely dependent on the ministries for the development and drafting of policies, as they lacked both experience in government and the opportunity to rely on a party infrastructure that could provide policy-making support from outside. SZDSZ ministers were also exposed to pressures from the parliamentary faction to avoid the promotion of senior civil servants to state secretary ranks because senior civil servants were associated with the political views of the MSZP, potentially creating an opposition to the ministers within the ministries. As a result, the culture and education ministers tapped the backbone of SZDSZ support to staff the state secretary ranks of the ministry: the intelligentsia of the capital city Budapest. By contrast, for the SZDSZ ministers heading the ministries of interior and transport, it became a matter of necessity to seek co-operative relations with the inherited senior officials of the ministries, as the SZDSZ had difficulties in recruiting suitable staff from the wider social environment of the party that could have been appointed to state secretary ranks.

Fourth, the approach of the centre-right parties that formed the Orbán government in 1998 shares many more similarities with the MSZP in 1994 than with the centre-right parties of the Antall government in 1990. These similarities and differences across governments suggest first of all that the politicization of the ministerial bureaucracy is not driven by the ideology of governing parties but by other factors. Indeed, the impetus for the politicization of the ministries came again from the heightened polarization between ex-communist political forces and radical anti-communist forces on the right of the political spectrum. Fidesz and its political allies regarded the Horn government essentially as a reincarnation of a pre-transition socialist government, especially owing to the appointment to the helm of government and administration of personnel who had already been in senior positions during the Németh administration. The radical anti-communist stance of the centre-right parties led them to associate virtually the entire ministerial bureaucracy with the former communist regime. The governing parties therefore had a motive to initiate personnel turnover even further down the ministerial ranks and they had little faith in promoting officials from within the ministries to state secretary ranks.

At the same time, the Orbán government had access to a pool of politically associated personnel with governmental expertise who could fill the vacant posts in the ministerial bureaucracy, and it took the opportunity to reactivate many state secretaries who had already acquired experience in government in the early 1990s under Antall. Moreover, the government could tap a far larger pool of potential appointees from other sectors of society than the Antall government could in 1990, since Fidesz in oppposition had invested in the formation of social networks.[37] Hence there was no necessity for the Orbán government to pursue a gradual takeover of the senior bureaucracy as the

Antall government had done in the early 1990s. Instead, the personnel policy legacy of the Horn government, the continuous political polarization between left and right and the organizational development of the centre-right parties reproduced the personnel policy features of the Horn years.

Finally, the change of government in 2002 indicates the stabilization of a mode of politicization that relies on large turnover and the appointment of returning officials, party affiliates and outsiders to the senior ranks of the ministerial bureaucracy. The Socialist–Liberal government under the leadership of Prime Minister Medgyessy took office in a climate of again intensified political polarization between left and right, which created pressures for politicization. Yet both the MSZP and, by 2002, the SZDSZ were able to turn to a pool of politically sympathetic appointees to staff the senior ranks of the ministries, many of whom had already gathered experience in the administration at an earlier point of their career. As a result, the 2002 change of government reproduced a mode of politicization very similar to the changes of government in 1994 and 1998.

Since the two camps – ex-communist MSZP plus the liberal ally, SZDSZ, on the one side, and the anti-communist Fidesz plus the smaller parties of the right on the other – have consolidated, political competition has increasingly taken on a friend-and-foe logic that leaves little room for non-affiliates. In particular, in government and politics, and hence also in the ministerial bureaucracy, officials are effectively forced to take sides if they seek to advance. During the mid- and late 1990s, it was still very common that ministerial bureaucrats below approximately the top three ranks would try to stay outside the political games in order to secure the longer-term security of tenure. With the increasing stabilization of a mode of politicization that relies on the appointment and reappointment of politically associated experts from outside to the senior ranks of the ministerial bureaucracy, higher and middle-ranking officials have started to read the writing on the wall, which indicates that career progress requires political commitment to either of the two sides. One of the most recent products of this politicization of careers within ministries is the establishment of a new platform, the 'Third Wave', associated with the MSZP party organization. This loose grouping consists exclusively of people from the 'apparatus', that is, the various public sector organizations, in particular the central state administration. Members tend to be young, and the Third Wave considers itself to stand outside or cut across the traditional, ideologically defined platforms within the MSZP. Again, these kinds of development look very familiar when compared with the communist state bureaucracy before the change of regime.

As a result, the politicization of the ministerial bureaucracy is indeed creeping downwards. However, the downward politicization is not simply a product of party incentives for political control: it is reinforced by bureaucratic responses to a changing structure of career incentives. The adaptation of civil servants to these changing incentives also indicates that the politicization of the ministerial bureaucracy in general, and a mode of partisan politicization in particular, are effectively being institutionalized, for by the time officials have reached a certain level they almost inevitably join the troops of politically associated experts who switch between the ministries, the private sector, academia and politics, the highest prize being the appointment as a minister and not as an administrative state secretary. Quite clearly, the conclusion therefore is that the politicization of the state has become – again – a central feature of Hungarian political life.

Conclusion

This study has taken issue with claims that post-communist Hungary has successfully contained pressures for the politicization of the state. Concentrating on the ministerial bureaucracy, it has shown that governing parties have a deep reach into the ministries, in that they can potentially exercise political control over the staffing of the entire ministerial civil service. It has also shown that patronage and politicization have been concentrated in the senior ranks of the ministerial bureaucracy, although there are signs that the politicization is increasingly affecting the non-managing ranks of the civil service.

Finally, in seeking to trace the politicization of the ministerial bureaucracy in post-communist Hungary, the study has argued that the politicization of the ministerial bureaucracy has primarily been driven by the polarization of political competition between the ex-communist MSZP and its political ally SZDSZ, on the one hand, and the anti-communist parties, in particular Fidesz, on the other. In these circumstances, new governing parties have been confronted with major problems of political trust *vis-à-vis* the ministerial bureaucracy because they associate ministerial bureaucrats with the policies and interests of their political competitors. Governing parties therefore have an incentive to replace ministerial bureaucrats with their own trusted appointees, but the extent to which they can do so depends on their capacity to recruit officials who combine political loyalty and governmental expertise. As parties of both the left and the right have gradually developed this capacity, the Hungarian trajectory suggests that the partisan politicization of the ministerial bureaucracy remains stable, at least so long as the political competition is dominated by the divide between ex-communist and anti-communist parties. The argument presented here therefore turns the dominant explanations of the literature on party patronage in Central and Eastern Europe on their head: the polarization of political competition and party strength, rather than party weakness and the absence of a critical opposition, produces the politicization of the post-communist state.

NOTES

1. See Conor O'Dwyer, 'Runaway State Building: How Political Parties Shape States in Postcommunist Eastern Europe', *World Politics*, Vol.56 (2004), pp.520–53 (p.521).
2. As argued by Anna Grzymala-Busse, 'Party Competition and the Pace of State Reform', paper prepared for presentation at the Annual Meeting of the American Political Science Association, Philadelphia, PA, 27–31 Aug. 2003; Anna Grzymala-Busse, 'Political Competition and the Politicization of the State in East Central Europe', *Comparative Political Studies*, Vol.36, No.10 (2003), pp.1123–47; O'Dwyer, 'Runaway State Building'.
3. See Martin Shefter, 'Party and Patronage: Germany, England and Italy', *Politics and Society*, Vol.7, No.4 (1977), pp.403–52.
4. Quoted from B. Guy Peters and Jon Pierre (eds.), *Politicization of the Civil Service in Comparative Perspective* (London: Routledge, 2004), p.2.
5. See Jan-Hinrik Meyer-Sahling, 'Getting on Track: Civil Service Reform in Post-communist Hungary', *Journal of European Public Policy*, Vol.8, No.6 (2001), pp.960–79.
6. See Grzymala-Busse, 'Party Competition and the Pace of State Reform'; Grzymala-Busse, 'Political Competition and the Politicization of the State'; O'Dwyer, 'Runaway State Building'; Antoanetta Dimitrova, 'The Europeanization of Civil Service Reform in Central and Eastern Europe', in Frank Schimmelfennig and Ulrich Sedelmeier (eds.), *The Europeanization of Central and Eastern Europe* (Ithaca, NY: Cornell University Press, 2005), pp.71–90.
7. For the further empirical analysis and conceptual foundation of the argument, see Jan-Hinrik Meyer-Sahling, 'The Institutionalization of Political Discretion in Post-Communist Civil Service Systems: The Case of Hungary', *Public Administration*, Vol.83, No.3 (2006), pp.693–716.
8. See László Vass, 'Politicians, Bureaucrats and Administrative Reform in Hungary: Who Stops Whom?', in B. Guy Peters and Jon Pierre (eds.), *Politicians, Bureaucrats and Administrative Reform* (London: Routledge 2001), pp.83–92.
9. Theodor Eschenburg, *Ämterpatronage* (Stuttgart: Curt E. Schwab, 1961).
10. See, for example, Wolfgang Müller, 'Patronage by National Governments', in Jean Blondel and Maurizio Cotta (eds.), *The Nature of Party Government: A Comparative European Perspective* (Basingstoke: Palgrave 2000), pp.141–60.
11. See, for example, Jorge Gordin, 'The Political and Partisan Determinants of Patronage in Latin America 1960–1994: A Comparative Perspective', *European Journal of Political Research*, Vol.41 (2002), pp.513–49; Grzymala-Busse, 'Party Competition and the Pace of State Reform'; Grzymala-Busse, 'Political Competition and the Politicization of the State'; O'Dwyer, 'Runaway State Building'.
12. See Miriam Golden, 'Electoral Connections: The Effects of the Personal Vote on Political Patronage, Bureaucracy and Legislation in Postwar Italy', *British Journal of Political Science*, Vol.33 (2003), pp.189–212.
13. See, for example, Martin Brusis and Vesselin Dimitrov, 'Executive Configuration and Fiscal Performance in Post-Communist Central and Eastern Europe', *Journal of European Public Policy*, Vol.8, No.6 (2001), pp.888–910; Vesselin Dimitrov, Klaus Goetz and Hellmut Wollmann (eds.), *Governing After Communism* (Lanham, MD: Rowman & Littlefield, 2006).
14. See Barbara Nunberg (ed.), *The State After Communism: Administrative Transitions in Central and Eastern Europe* (Washington, DC: The World Bank 1999).
15. Discussed in András Körösényi, 'A közigazgatás politikai irányítása és a patronázs', *Valóság*, Vol.40, No.12 (1997), pp.46–71; István György, 'The Civil Service System of Hungary', in Tony Verheijen (ed.), *Civil Service Systems in Central and Eastern Europe* (Cheltenham: Edward Elgar, 1999), pp.131–58; Zoltán Szente, 'Közigazgatás és politika metszéspontján: a miniszterek és az államtitkárok rekrutációja Magyarországon, 1990–1998', *Századvég*, Vol.13 (1999), Summer, pp.3–52; László Andor, *Hungary on the Road to the European Union: Transition in Blue* (Westport. CT: Praeger, 2000); László Vass, 'Politicians, Bureaucrats and Administrative Reform in Hungary: Who Stops Whom?', in Peters and Pierre (eds.),

46   POLITICAL PARTIES & THE STATE IN POST-COMMUNIST EUROPE

Politicians, Bureaucrats and Administrative Reform, pp.83–92; Tamás Fricz, 'Kormányváltások vagy "rendszerváltások"'?! Az eddigi kormányváltások személyi és szervezeti következményei Magyarországon, 1990–2003', in Péter Sándor, László Vass, Ágnes Sándor and Ágnes Tolnai (eds.), *Magyarország politikai évkönyve* (Budapest: Democrácia Kutatások Magyar Központja Alapítvány, 2004), pp.122–39.

16. In 1990, the number of appointments is higher than the number of positions because a few positions experienced two personnel changes within about six months or even less. For the other election years, the values represent the appointments within the entire year of 1994 and 1998. Because new governments took office in the summer, in both cases a few appointments were still made by the outgoing government in the first half of the year.

17. See, for example, Edward C. Page and Vincent Wright, 'Conclusion: Senior Officials in Western Europe', in Edward C. Page and Vincent Wright (eds.) *Bureaucratic Élites in Western European States* (Oxford: Oxford University Press 1999), pp.266–79.

18. See Erzsébet Szalai, *Post-Socialism and Globalization* (Budapest: Új Mandátum Könyvkiadó, 1999).

19. The mode of partisan politicization is one of four modes of politicization that indicate correspondence to different western modes of politicization and divergence from western traditions of politicization. Partisan politicization points to a distinctive, post-communist mode of politicization: see Jan-Hinrik Meyer-Sahling, 'The Changing Colours of the Post-Communist State: The Politicization of the Senior Civil Service in Hungary', *European Journal of Political Research* (2007 forthcoming).

20. The similarities can be drawn further. For instance, the mobility between the ministerial bureaucracy, the party (headquarters), the economy, and what is now referred to as the third sector, are more common career paths of senior appointees than careers that are limited to the ministerial bureaucracy alone.

21. See Grzymala-Busse, 'Party Competition and the Pace of State Reform'; Anna Grzymala-Busse, 'Political Competition and the Politicization of the State in East Central Europe'; O'Dwyer, 'Runaway State Building'.

22. Grzymala-Busse provides several criteria to distinguish a critical opposition: see her 'Party Competition and the Pace of State Reform', p.10.

23. See Ágnes Batory, *Hungarian Party Identities and the Question of European Integration*, Sussex European Institute Working Paper No.49 (Brighton: University of Sussex, 2001).

24. See Attila Ágh, 'Defeat and Success as Promoters of Party Change: The Hungarian Socialist Party after Two Abrupt Changes', *Party Politics*, Vol.3, No.3 (1997), pp.427–44.

25. O'Dwyer, 'Runaway State Building'.

26. See Jan-Hinrik Meyer-Sahling, 'Civil Service Reform in Post-Communist Europe: The Bumpy Road to Depoliticization', *West European Politics*, Vol. 27, No.1 (2004), pp.69–101.

27. Timothy Frye, 'The Perils of Polarization: Economic Performance in the Post-Communist World', *World Politics*, Vol.54 (2002), pp.308–37. This is not to say that other political divides do not matter for the politicization of the bureaucracy, but the pressure can be expected to be particularly serious if former communist and anti-communist forces face each other.

28. Obviously, a third condition is that the formal-legal basis of personnel policy makes possible the politicization of the bureaucracy. However, we can consider the formal-legal basis to be endogenous to the politicization hypothesis. If governments feel constrained by civil service legislation because they are troubled by problems of trust *vis-à-vis* the ministerial bureaucracy, they can amend the law in order to increase the 'degree of political discretion' built into legislation and thereby increase their opportunities to politicize civil service policy: see Shefter, 'Party and Patronage'; Meyer-Sahling, 'Civil Service Reform in Post-Communist Europe' and 'The Institutionalization of Political Discretion'.

29. See András Körösenyi, *Government and Politics in Hungary* (Budapest: Central European University Press, 1999), p.36.

30. See Miháhly Bihari, 'Change of Regime and Power in Hungary', in Sándor Kurtán, Péter Sándor and László Vass (eds.), *Magyarország Politikai Évkönyve* (Budapest: Ökonómia Alapítvány, 1991), pp.32–47.

31. Herbert Kitschelt, Zdenka Mansfeldova, Radoslav Markovski and Gábor Tóka, *Post-Communist Party Systems: Competition, Representation, and Inter-Party Cooperation* (Cambridge: Cambridge University Press 1999); Batory, *Hungarian Party Identities*.

32. Attila Ágh, 'The Year of Incertitude', in Sándor Kurtán, Péter Sándor and László Vass (eds.), *Magyarország Politikai Évkönyve* (Budapest: Demokrácia Kutatások Magyar Központja Alapítvány 1994), pp.16–37.

33. See Anna Grzymala-Busse, *Redeeming the Communist Past: The Regeneration of Communist Parties in East Central Europe* (Cambridge: Cambridge University Press, 2002).

34. Quoted from György Márkus, 'Cleavages and Parties in Hungary after 1989', in Kay Lawson, Andrea Römmele and Georgi Karasimeonov (eds.), *Cleavages, Parties, and Voters: Studies from Bulgaria, the Czech Republic, Hungary, Poland, and Romania* (Westport, CT: Praeger, 1999), pp.141–57 (p.148).

35. See András Bozóki, 'The Ideology of Modernization and the Policy of Materialism: The Day after the Socialists', *Journal of Communist Studies and Transition Politics*, Vol.13, No.3 (1997), pp.56–102 (p.78).

36. See Attila Ágh, 'Partial Consolidation of the East–Central European Parties: The Case of the Hungarian Socialist Party', *Party Politics*, Vol.1, No.4 (1995), pp.491–514.

37. See Tamás Fricz, 'Democratization, the Party System and the Electorate in Hungary', in Mária Schmidt and László Gy. Tóth (eds.), *Transition with Contradictions: The Case of Hungary 1990–1998* (Budapest: Kairosz Publishing, 1999), pp.93–124.

State Party Funding and Patronage
in Post-1989 Poland

ALEKS SZCZERBIAK

This study examines the role of the state as a source of funding and patronage for political parties in post-communist Poland. It begins by examining the way in which direct state party funding in the form of election refunds and continuing state subventions has developed during the post-communist period. It then considers indirect forms of state party funding, notably the resources made available to parliamentary caucuses and individual parliamentarians. Third, it considers the extent to which parties control appointments to state bodies and use this as a form of patronage. Fourth, it discusses the implications of this increase in state funding and patronage for the party system and functioning of democracy in post-communist Poland.

The argument presented is that the widespread practice of state financial support has become increasingly important to Polish parties and that both its level and its scope have been expanded progressively. In terms of direct state party funding, this began in 1993 with a system of one-off election refunds, and was then extended to include regular donations to cover parties' day-to-day 'statutory' activities. This culminated in the 2001 amendments to the party and electoral laws that substantially increased the scope of state financing and placed restrictions on parties obtaining income from other sources. This has made state party funding the main source of income for a number of parties. Polish parties' dependence upon and interest in exploiting the financial resources provided by the state becomes even more evident when one considers the numerous forms of indirect state subsidies that parties receive. The most important of these are the various forms of allowances that are paid to the party-based parliamentary caucuses and parliamentarians, but are often overlooked in accounts of state party funding. Finally, data – admittedly rudimentary – reveal that appointments to state and quasi-state bodies, particularly in public administration and in state-owned or partially owned companies, also appear to be an important source of patronage for parties in post-communist Poland. The Polish party funding regime and state patronage opportunities clearly favour 'insiders', and have further centralized power in party leaderships. However, the Polish party system remains too unstable to conclude that a party 'cartel' of privileged insiders is emerging, while state party funding has, at most, simply reinforced existing trends in terms of party leader-orientation and anti-party and anti-elite sentiment among Polish citizens.

Direct State Party Funding

Until 1993 there was no provision for any form of state party funding in Poland. Indeed, the 1990 law establishing the new legal framework within which parties in the post-communist system would operate explicitly prohibited it.[1] The 1993 law on elections was the first step towards introducing state party funding by establishing a system of one-off donations from the state budget to refund expenses incurred during a parliamentary election campaign. These refunds were paid only to those election committees (comprising parties or electoral coalitions) that secured parliamentary representation, in proportion to the total number of seats won in the Sejm and Senate, the two chambers of the Polish parliament. Receipt of these refunds was dependent upon the election committees publishing a financial report of their campaign accounts within three months of the election. Although the refund went only to those parties that won parliamentary seats, it was paid directly to party central offices via the electoral committees submitting the candidate lists from which the Sejm deputies or senators were elected. In the September 1993 election these were either single parties – the Polish Peasant Party (Polskie Stronnictwo Ludowe: PSL), Democratic Union (Unia Demokratyczna: UW), Labour Union (Unia Pracy: UP), Confederation for an Independent Poland (Konfederacja Polski Niepodległej: KPN), and the Non-party Bloc for Supporting Reforms (Bezpartyjny Blok Wspierania Reform: BBWR) – or electoral coalitions comprising a number of organizations such as the Democratic Left Alliance (Sojusz Lewicy Demokratycznej: SLD) led by the communist successor party Social Democracy of the Polish Republic (Socjaldemokracja Rzeczpospolitej Polskiej: SdRP), which, once expenses had been covered, then divided any surplus from the refund between their members.

The amount available for campaign refunds was set at 20 per cent of the total expenditure assigned in the state budget to cover the costs of organizing, preparing and conducting the election. This sum was divided by 560 (the total number of parliamentarians) and then multiplied by the number elected from that election committee. In 1993 this meant that every eligible party or political grouping received 14,500 zlotys for every seat won in either of the two chambers. There were considerable variations in the amounts paid to each of the groupings, with the victorious parties receiving significant sums of money, while those parties with only a few parliamentarians barely covered the repayment of the loans they had taken out to finance their campaigns. The Democratic Left Alliance and Peasant Party, for example, secured refunds of 3 million and 2.4 million zlotys that easily covered their expenditure. The Democratic Union's 1.1 million refund virtually covered the loans and credit that they took out to finance the campaign, as did the Non-party Bloc's 260,000-zloty refund, while the Confederation for an Independent Poland's 319,000-zloty refund just covered the party's expenditure shortfall. The Labour Union, on the other hand, covered its election costs through other sources of income, and its 623,000-zloty refund therefore represented pure 'profit'.[2]

Without access to sets of properly audited party accounts, it was impossible at this point to make any firm judgements as to how much importance each party attached to these refunds compared with other, internally generated sources of revenue. Unfortunately, even though the principle of transparency of funding was built into the original 1990 law on political parties, detailed information on Polish party funding was extremely patchy and difficult to obtain until the passage of the replacement law of 1997. These refunds, and the interest accrued from them, appeared to be highly significant for the one party that did publish its accounts during this period, the Labour Union.[3] However, this was a party with a very small membership and no significant assets or obvious access to income from large private sponsors.

Until the passage of the 1997 law on political parties, therefore, direct and continuing state party funding did not formally exist in Poland, and the reimbursement of election campaign expenses was the one possibility for financing political parties and groupings directly from the state budget. The 1997 law introduced three significant changes to the Polish state party funding regime that affected parties participating in that year's parliamentary election. First, it supplemented the 1993 law by establishing a new system of regular state donations – known as 'objective' donations [*dotacje celowe*] – to be paid to those election committees that specifically registered themselves as political parties (and not electoral coalitions) as a contribution towards funding these parties' statutory activities. These new subventions were to be paid in addition to the one-off election refunds – henceforth known as 'subjective' donations [*dotacje podmiotowe*] – that continued to be paid to all eligible electoral committees to cover election expenses on the basis of the number of seats won. Second, although the level of election refunds and donations paid to each party was still determined by its electoral performance, the regular donations were to be allocated in proportion to the number of votes obtained rather than seats won. Third, the regular donations were paid to all parties that won more than three per cent of the valid votes 'cast for all political parties' candidates' lists across the whole country' in the Sejm election and not just, as was the case with election refunds, those whose electoral committees crossed the five per cent threshold for parliamentary representation. The total budget for state subventions remained unchanged, with the new regular donations accounting for 60 per cent of the total, paid in four annual instalments: 40 per cent for the first year and 20 per cent in the three subsequent years (adjusted in line with inflation).

Following the 1997 parliamentary election, the total amount allocated to all the election committees that qualified for refunds and regular donations was more than 14 million zlotys. As electoral coalitions, Solidarity Electoral Action (Akcja Wyborcza Solidarność: AWS) and the Democratic Left Alliance were not entitled to regular donations and received only one-off election refunds worth approximately 25,000 zlotys for each parliamentarian elected, with Solidarity Electoral Action earning 6.3 million and the Democratic Left Alliance 4.8 million. Meanwhile, those election committees that registered as political parties shared a total of 2.725 million zlotys, 25,000 per parliamentary seat multiplied by the 109 seats won by the three political parties that crossed the five per cent threshold for parliamentary representation: the Freedom Union (Unia Wolności: UW), Polish Peasant Party and Movement for Poland's Reconstruction (Ruch Odbudowy Polski: ROP). These three parties also received one-off donations but worth only 10,000 zlotys per seat, having to share the remainder set aside for regular, 'subjective' donations with those parties that had not won any seats but still obtained more than three per cent of the vote. This meant that, in total, the Freedom Union received 1.3 million zlotys (680,000 refund and 630,000 in donations), the Peasant Party 640,000 (300,000 refunds and 340,000 donations) and the Movement for Poland's Reconstruction 370,000 (110,000 refunds and 260,000 donations).[4]

Originally, it was assumed (and this was probably the intention of those parties who framed the legislation) that these regular donations were payable only to those parties that won more than three per cent of the total number of votes cast for *all election committees*. In 1997, therefore, only the Labour Union (which won 4.74 per cent of the votes) would have been eligible among those parties that failed to cross the five per cent threshold. However, it emerged subsequently that the three per cent figure related only to the number of votes cast for election committees that were *specifically registered as political parties*, without taking into account the votes cast for electoral coalitions such as Solidarity Electoral Action or the Democratic Left Alliance. This made the *de facto* threshold for regular donations just over one per cent and meant that the two pensioners' parties – the National Party of Retirees and Pensioners (Krajowa Partia Emerytów i Rencistów: KPEiR) and the National Agreement of Retirees and Pensioners of the Polish Republic (Krajowe Porozumienie Emerytów i Rencistów Rzeczpospolitej Polskiej: KPEiR RP) – that won 2.18 per cent and 1.63 per cent of the votes respectively in the 1997 election were also eligible. The Labour Union, therefore, received 220,000 zlotys in donations while the two pensioner parties received 100,000 and 80,000 respectively. This new system of regular donations was (in theory, at least) accompanied by much greater financial transparency, with parties obliged to submit annual financial reports on 'expenditure undertaken on their statutory objectives' or face the risk of losing their entitlement to receive further donations. Moreover, all parties (even those that did not receive any election refunds or state donations) also had to submit details of any donations to their election funds that were ten times greater than the forecast average public sector salary for that year, together with a more general set of financial accounts. Failure to do so could result, respectively, in the party's election fund being frozen or the party's deletion from the official register of political parties. The more rigorous requirements to publish annual accounts placed on parties by the 1997 party law meant that a somewhat clearer picture of the relative importance of state party funding began to emerge slowly. However, as Table 1 shows, the first set of published party accounts for 1997–2000 revealed that state subsidies and refunds played a significant role in the finances of only the two smaller parties that benefited from state party funding: the Movement for Poland's Reconstruction and the Labour Union. On the other hand, state funding appeared to play only a marginal or virtually insignificant role in the income streams of the two more significant parties, the Freedom Union and Peasant Party.

However, these figures were somewhat misleading and tended to underestimate the importance of state party funding. The two most significant beneficiaries from state party funding arising from the September 1997 parliamentary election were the Solidarity Electoral Action and Democratic

TABLE 1
PROPORTION OF PARTY INCOME DERIVED FROM STATE PARTY FUNDING,
1997–2000 (%)

Party	1997	1998	1999	2000
Polish Peasant Party	4.75	4.44	0.68	0.54
Freedom Union	0	11.63	4.52	3.16
Labour Union	73.33	100	33.78	13.21
Movement for Poland's Reconstruction	N/A	66.99	63.98	N/A

Source: Author's calculations based on party accounts submitted to the Warsaw Regional Court;
and Marcin Walecki, *Money and Politics in Poland* (Warsaw: Institute of Public Affairs,
2005), p.113.

Left Alliance electoral coalitions. Only a very small proportion of the electoral refunds that these coalitions received found their way back to the coffers of the parties that formed them once the costs of election expenses had been covered (none in the case of Solidarity Electoral Action), with the balance retained by the election committees. In other words, virtually none of this – more significant – flow of income from state funding was reflected in party financial statements.

In fact, the role of state party funding in Poland was transformed by the new 2001 election law that contained important amendments to the 1997 party law, as we shall see, making it, in effect, the main form of funding for some of the major parties. In the first place, only registered political parties, coalitions of parties or 'committees of electors' (referred to hereinafter as 'civic' election committees) could contest elections and not, for example, trade unions; an amendment that was to have significant implications for Solidarity Electoral Action, spearheaded by the Solidarity union. All election committees continued to be eligible to receive the one-off *post hoc* election refunds, and this was still based on the number of seats won in the election in the first and second chambers. However, the 2001 law also introduced a new provision for a maximum expenditure limit and stipulated that the total level of refund paid to any election committee could not now exceed the actual total amount that it incurred as set out in its financial report.[5] The level of refund paid to each election committee was the amount of election expenditure incurred by all election committees winning at least one seat in parliament divided by 560 (the total number of seats in the Sejm and Senate) and then multiplied by the number of seats won by that party. In the case of election committees comprising coalitions of parties the refund was divided proportionately among those parties on the basis of the agreement that these parties reached at the time that their committee was established. Election refunds were supposed to be paid six months after the announcement of the validity of the elections, although the refund for the 2001 election was actually paid in two instalments in 2002 and 2003 (see below).

The total refund allocated to all electoral committees participating in the 2001 election was 62.5 million zlotys, with just over 111,000 zlotys paid out per parliamentarian.[6] As Table 2 shows, the Democratic Left Alliance–Labour Union coalition obtained a full refund for the 27 million zlotys that it incurred on election expenditure. Of this, the Democratic Left Alliance received just over 21 million and the Labour Union 3 million, with the remainder divided between the other parties constituting the coalition according to a formula contained in the July 2001 coalition agreement between these parties.[7] The Law and Justice party (Prawo i Sprawiedliwość: PiS) received a 4.8 million-zloty refund that fully covered its expenses, while Civic Platform (Platforma Obywatelska: PO) obtained 7.3 million zlotys, and incurred a shortfall of 9 million. The Peasant Party (1.3 million zlotys) and League of Polish Families (Liga Polskich Rodzin: LPR – 129,000 zlotys) both had their refunds reduced by 75 per cent, and Self-Defence's (Samoobrona) refund was reduced by 65 per cent (to 184,000 zlotys) owing to irregularities in their campaign financial statements.[8]

The 2001 Law also stipulated that parties winning at least 3 per cent of the total votes cast (not just those cast for parties, as stipulated in the 1997 law) continued to receive state subventions for their statutory activities. However, these subventions would also be paid to parties that formed electoral coalitions and obtained at least 6 per cent of the total vote and would not be paid to 'civic' electoral committees, which would be eligible for only the one-off election refunds. As a result of the 2001 law there was, therefore, also a massive increase in the level of these subventions. Rather than all the eligible parties and coalitions of parties sharing a specified total, the precise

TABLE 2
2001 ELECTION REFUNDS (IN ZLOTYS)

Party/committee	Seats	Expenditure	Refund
Democratic Left Alliance-Labour Union	291	26,992,002	26,995,002
Civic Platform	65	16,319,018	7,258,628
Law and Justice	44	4,820,840	4,820,840
Polish Peasant Party	46	9,369,290	1,284,218*
Self-Defence	55	534,957	184,629**
League of Polish Families	40	514,841	128,710***

Notes: * Refund reduced by 75 per cent (3,852,656 zlotys) owing to irregularities in its financial report.
** Refund reduced by 65 per cent (350,328 zlotys) owing to irregularities in its financial report.
*** Refund reduced by 75 per cent (386,131 zlotys) owing to irregularities in its financial report.

Source: Polish State Electoral Commission (<http://www.pkw.gov.pl>).

sum to be paid to each party was based on a sliding scale that linked the level of subvention to the number of votes won: 10 zlotys per vote for parties winning 3–5 per cent of the total vote; 8 zlotys for 5–10 per cent; 7 zlotys per vote for 10–20 per cent support; 4 zlotys per vote for 20–30 per cent; and 1.5 zlotys per vote for more than 30 per cent. By increasing the proportional share of the subsidies paid to smaller parties, the new law recognized that some party running costs were fixed regardless of the size of the party. These state donations were to be paid in four annual instalments, adjusted in line with inflation, throughout the four-year term of the Sejm.[9]

In fact, in November 2001, two months after the election, the incoming government proposed a 50 per cent reduction in all direct state funding to parties and election committees, including a 75 per cent reduction in annual subventions, in order to help tackle the spiralling budget deficit.[10] Opposition parties protested at this, arguing that the government could not reduce the level of election refunds retrospectively as some parties had taken out bank loans to finance their campaigns using the prospect of refunds as collateral, and threatened to refer any amendment to the new law that limited them to the constitutional court. In the event, the government secured parliamentary approval for a modified proposal. First, as noted above, it introduced temporary new regulations stipulating that election refunds would be paid in two instalments, spreading their cost over two years.[11] Second, annual subventions were reduced for these first two years by between 25 and 50 per cent depending on the proportion of votes gained by a party: from 10 zlotys to 8, from 8 zlotys to 4, from 7 zlotys to 3, from 4 zlotys to 1.5, and from 1.5 zlotys to 0.5. This meant that, for these two years, the Freedom Union received 80 per cent of its allocation, the League of Polish Families 70.94 per cent, Law and Justice 67.44 per cent, Self-Defence 66.29 per cent and the Democratic Left Alliance 51.03 per cent.[12] Therefore, as Table 3 shows, in 2002 the Democratic Left Alliance received 11.2 million zlotys subvention, Law and Justice 7.5 million, the League of Polish Families 5.8 million, Self-Defence 5.3 million, the Freedom Union 3.2 million, the Labour Union 1.6 million, the Peasant Party 1.3 million, the National Party of Retirees and Pensioners 700,000 and the Democratic Party and Peasant–Democratic Party 200,000 each. However, in 2003 the Peasant Party, Labour Union and Democratic Party lost their right to subventions for the next three years when the State Election Commission rejected their 2002 annual reports.[13] The other parties received broadly the same sums as in 2002: Self-Defence's subvention increased to 7.5 million and the Peasant–Democratic Party to 290,000. However, in 2004 eligible parties were to receive the full level of subventions. This meant that the Democratic Left Alliance was expected to receive 22 million zlotys, Self-Defence 11.5 million, Law and Justice 11 million, the League of Polish Families 8.6 million, Freedom Union four million, National Party of Retirees and Pensioners two million and the Peasant–Democratic

TABLE 3
STATE SUBVENTIONS FOR 2002–4 (IN ZLOTYS)

Party	2002	2003	2004 (estimate)
Democratic Left Alliance	11,222,165	11,222,165	21,989,418
Law and Justice	7,550,732	7.550,732	11,196,088
Self-Defence	5,276,542	7,537,917	11,546,617
League of Polish Families	5,813,450	5,813,450	8,612,250
Freedom Union	3,232,592	3,232,592	4,040,740
Polish Peasant Party*	1,273,688	0	0
Labour Union*	1,582,613	0	0
Retirees and Pensioners Party	704,982	1,007,117	1,937,409
Peasant-Democratic Party	201,424	287,748	563,831
Democratic Party*	201,424	0	0

Note: * These parties lost subventions for the next three years after the State Electoral Commission rejected their 2002 annual financial reports.

Sources: Polish State Electoral Commission (<http://www.pkw.gov.pl>).

Party 560,000. Depending on the rate of inflation, the figures for 2005 were likely to be broadly similar. Following the September 2005 election, it was estimated that the following annual subventions would be paid in the 2005–9 parliament: Law and Justice 22.186 million zlotys, Civic Platform (since 2002 registered as a political party) 20.84 million, Self-Defence 11.792 million, the Democratic Left Alliance 11.707 million, the League of Polish Families 8.706 million, the Polish Peasant Party 7.753 million and Polish Social Democracy (Socjaldemokracja Polska: SdPl) 4.593 million.[14]

At the same time, the 2001 law prevented parties from obtaining income from any sources other than: membership subscriptions, small donations from individuals (none to exceed 15 times the minimum wage),[15] wills and bequests, and interest on savings.[16] Parties were forbidden to engage in business activity, derive income from office rental, sell party bulletins, organize public collections and sell 'bricks' (a form of anonymous campaign donation), or obtain money from foreigners or individuals not living in Poland.[17] In order to prevent them from circumventing these regulations by deriving income in kind, parties had to receive income paid by cheque, money transfer or credit card to the party's bank account.[18]

The scale of the increase in direct party funding can be seen in the total amounts that election committees received in refunds and donations from approximately eight million zlotys in 1993, and 14 million in 1997, to a massive 257 million 2001. As Table 4 shows, a combination of the substantial increase in the level of state party funding and the new restrictions on obtaining income from other sources has made the income from the state much more significant in terms of its proportion of party income, making the state the

TABLE 4
PROPORTION OF PARTY INCOME DERIVED FROM STATE FUNDING, 2002–3
(INCOME FIGURES IN ZLOTYS)

Party	2002		2003	
	Income	State funding (%)	Income	State funding (%)
Democratic Left Alliance	50,842,000	37.3	33,584,000	64.8
Polish Peasant Party	109,886,000	1.5	8,043,000	11.9*
Self-Defence	4,544,000	89.1	7,533,000	93.8
League of Polish Families	4,446,000	99.5	5,962,000	98.6
Law and Justice	9,069,000	89.0	4,523,166	90.1
Freedom Union	3,236,000	75.6	3,797,695	85.1
Labour Union	3,236,000	82.6	2,396,077	78.5

Note: * 51.5 per cent if asset sale income is excluded.

Sources: 'Kasa partyjna, pieniądze państwowe', *Polityka*, 26 April 2003; 'Dwa krezusy', *Gazeta Wyborcza*, 2 July 2003; and author's calculations based on State Electoral Commission figures (<http://www.pkw.gov.pl>).

main income source for a number of parties.[19] For Self-Defence, the League of Polish Families, Law and Justice, the Freedom Union and the Labour Union, state party funding made up between 75.6 and 99.5 per cent of their income in 2002 and 2003. For the Democratic Left Alliance state subventions made up 37.3 and 64.8 per cent of the party's income in 2002 and 2003 respectively. Civic Platform did not receive any continuing state party funding as it fought the 2001 election as a 'civic' election committee rather than as a party. The only real exception to this pattern was the Peasant Party for which state party funding made up only 1.5 per cent of its income in 2002 and 11.5 per cent in 2003. This stemmed from the fact that the party owned a large amount of real estate property from which it derived rental income.[20] Amendments to the party law passed in 2001 forbade parties from obtaining funding from this source, forcing the Peasant Party to divest itself of these assets; hence asset sales made up a large proportion of its income in 2002 and 2003. Without these asset sales, for example, state party funding would have comprised 51.5 per cent of the party's 2003 income. In fact, as noted above, the party has not received any state subventions since 2003, partly because the assets were sold to a trust whose board consisted mainly of Peasant Party leaders, which led to rejection of the party's financial statements.

Indirect State Party Funding

However, even though parties are now required to submit financial statements and to be open and transparent about their sources of funding, these are not necessarily a completely reliable expression of the true state of party accounts. For a start, the state election commission, responsible for approving or rejecting them, lacks the resources to conduct proper audits.[21] Perhaps even more significantly, the figures in party accounts do not include the numerous forms of indirect state subsidies, notably the funds channelled to parties by the Sejm and Senate Chancelleries for various forms of support for parliamentary fractions (comprising parties in most cases), together with the salaries, expenses and material resources provided to help individual parliamentarians perform their parliamentary duties, at both national and constituency level. These grants are another, equally important source of state party funding.

An important element of this was the standard monthly payments that parliamentary clubs and circles received to finance their activities. These were paid per deputy and senator according to the size of the parliamentary fraction and reduced as the size of the parliamentary grouping increased. For example, in 2001 parliamentary fractions with more than 100 members received 1,073 zlotys per deputy, those with 50–100 received 1,145 and those with fewer than 50 deputies obtained 1,221.[22] Walecki estimated that the total budget allocated to parliamentary parties in 2001 alone was 55.75 million zlotys.[23]

At the beginning of every parliamentary term, deputies and senators also received a one-off payment to help them set up their offices and purchase office equipment: furniture, a computer and printer, photocopier, telephone and fax. In 2001 this was 5,000 zlotys for new parliamentarians and 3,000 for re-elected ones.[24] In addition, they also received help with a substantial general expense allowance to run parliamentary offices in their local electoral districts. For example, in 2001–2 each deputy received a monthly allowance of 9,320 zlotys to cover rent, staff wages, telephone bills, the purchase of materials and petrol.[25] In 2003 alone Sejm deputies received 56 million zlotys to run their offices, 53.5 million of which was spent: on staff expenses (18.2 million), car travel (9.8 million), material services including office rental (8 million) and phone bills (7.6 billion). In 2004, the Sejm and Senate spent some 70 million on the running of parliamentary offices.[26]

These sums are often overlooked when discussing state party funding and it is, of course, questionable whether they can all be included within this broad definition. They are formally intended to be used on parliamentary rather than strictly party activities and do not appear in party accounts. Parliamentary directives insist that these office expenses should, in theory, 'not be used to finance the activity of political parties, social organizations, foundations or charitable activity nor the activity of the parliamentary club'.[27] Moreover, ultimately, of course, it is up to the individual parliamentarian, and not the parliamentary party leaderships, to decide how this particular allowance should be allocated. Indeed, the wages paid to full-time 'professional' deputies on top of their allowances, in the form of a so-called *ryczalt*, are paid as parliamentarians' personal income.[28]

In practice, however, it is impossible to distinguish between the two types of activity, parliamentary and strictly party, and parliamentary salaries and allowances have been very closely linked with, and inevitably shaded into, the general question of parliamentary club and party funding in general. Many deputies and senators regularly passed on part of their salaries and expense allowances for the needs of the parliamentary club as a whole, or even the party central office, as an established procedure, and the so-called 'party tax' that parliamentarians had to pay formed an important source of income for many parties.[29] Similarly, the practice has developed whereby local parliamentary offices, which they obtained from local authorities at greatly reduced rents, often doubled up as local party offices and performed a crucial role in their local organizational infrastructure such that it was often difficult to distinguish between the funds spent on constituency work and those used to promote local party activity. In 2004, there were 460 'basic' (primary) Sejm deputies offices and a further 482 'secondary' (branch) offices. Sejm deputies employed 848 staff and there were 2,671 others working for them on a voluntary basis.[30] It is no exaggeration to say that the local parliamentary office has been the *de facto* basic organizational unit for the most important Polish parties.[31] These parliamentary party offices should, therefore, properly be regarded as a de facto form of backdoor state financing for parties as a whole rather than for the individual parliamentarian. In the same way, parliamentary fractions often used their allowances from the Sejm and senate chancelleries to employ officials who were party activists, or to provide paid work to those closely allied to the party by ordering expert analyses and studies.[32]

The total amount allocated to support the activities of parliamentary clubs (mostly party-based), together with the individual parliamentarians' allowances and expenses, should not be regarded as a form of marginal funding. Indeed, until the 2001 amendments to the law on political parties, this source of income represented a considerably larger share of state party funding than the election refunds and subsidies. In 1995, for example, the Democratic Left Alliance parliamentary club received a total of 9.8 million zlotys, the Peasant Party 7.9 million, Freedom Union 3.7 million and Labour Union 1.9 million to fund their activities *for that year alone*.[33] In comparison, as noted above, the refund that the party central offices received after the 1993 election to cover *four years* of activities was: 3 million zlotys for the Democratic Left Alliance, 2.4 million for the Peasant Party, 1.1 million for the Freedom Union and 600,000 for the Labour Union.[34] In other words, the four largest parliamentary parties in the 1993–97 parliament actually received more than three times as much funding in the form of various parliamentary allowances as their respective party central offices received in their entire one-off refund for the September 1993 election. The expansion of direct state party funding that resulted from the 2001 law has increased the relative importance of this form of income, but none the less parliamentary allowances remain a highly significant source of indirect income for Polish parties.

Party Appointments to State Bodies

Finally, there are the various appointments to state and quasi-state bodies that are in the gift of Polish parties. Although no in-depth empirical research has been undertaken on this subject,[35] and it is unclear quite how widespread the phenomenon is, party appointees appear to play a prominent role in Polish public administration at every level. Every incoming government appoints ministers who in turn appoint political cabinets, directors-general and directors of central government departments, central government press officers and the main appointments in the diplomatic corps. New governments also make appointments to central administrative agencies and quasi-central institutions and so-called 'objective' funds. In 2002, it was estimated that there were 100 of these institutions and funds, including: 40 central agencies (such as the Main Customs Office, the Office of Physical Culture and Sport, the National Labour Office), 24 quasi-central institutions (various agencies and inspectorates such as the Government Centre for Strategic Studies, the Agricultural Market Agency, or the State Treasury Ownership Agency) and 27 so-called 'objective' funds, such as the National Insurance Agency which alone has 250 directors' posts at its disposal.[36]

At the regional level, an incoming government appoints 16 regional governors and their deputies, the regional directors-general and departmental directors, local press officers and regional office heads. The party-nominated regional governors and their deputies can then appoint the heads of the 11 local services and inspectorates, while the heads of the local police and fire brigades are appointed by the ministry of internal affairs. In sum, there were 13 such agencies in every region, making a total of 208 offices across the country.[37]

Public television and radio also provided many opportunities for party-linked appointments at both national and local level, although, given the different terms of office of governments and the various boards and supervisory councils, public sector broadcasting has not always been controlled by the governing party in Poland.[38] All of this does not include all the various public service appointments in the gift of local authorities that are now elected in three tiers (regional, county and parish). As one commentator put it, 'In Poland there is little chance of getting a post as the director of a cultural centre, hospital manager or head of social services without the support of a party apparatchik'.[39] Indeed, the local government and health service reforms introduced by the Solidarity Electoral Action–Freedom Union government in 1998 created a whole new sphere of potential party appointments by establishing two new tiers of local government at the regional and county levels and the so-called local health funds.[40]

There have been various estimates of how many such appointments are controlled by political parties. The 1997 Polish civil service law identified 1,700 'politically sensitive' posts in government ministries, central and local administration.[41] Although the intention of the civil service law was actually to 'departify' the state, a 2003 report from the Batory Foundation accused the Democratic Left Alliance-led government of circumventing the law, purging these senior positions in the public administration of representatives from the previous administration, and filling many of these posts with party-nominated appointees.[42] One estimate put the total number of party-linked officials in public administration as high as 200,000, arguing that up to two-thirds of 300,000 posts in the central, local and quasi-government sector were party-linked appointees.[43] Indeed, Jan Pastwa, head of the Polish civil service under the Solidarity Electoral Action-led governments, argued that the effect of patronage on Polish state administration has been to replace a communist 'monoparty nomenklatura' with a post-communist 'multi-party nomenklatura'.[44]

Finally, one of most important sources of party patronage in Poland is the supervisory councils of state treasury and 'communal' companies. The 1993–97 Democratic Left Alliance–Peasant Party government increased the number of these (from 723 in 1994 to 1,498 in 2000) by creating hundreds of publicly owned but 'commercialized' companies, intended as a precursor to their eventual privatization, although in most cases this did not happen.[45] One analysis conducted in 1997 estimated that there were some 20,000 appointments linked to the 3,600 state-owned and 2,000 para-state (commercialized) companies, although it was only really straightforward to remove those employed in wholly treasury-owned companies.[46]

Implications of State Party Funding and Patronage

In this section, I examine the implications of this substantial, and increasing, level of state party funding and patronage, and the form of this financing, for the party system and the functioning of Polish democracy by considering three questions. First, has it led to the emergence of a privileged and self-sustaining group of 'insider' parties as envisaged in, for example, Katz and Mair's cartel party model? Second, how has it affected the distribution of power within Polish parties? Third, has it led to parties becoming more alienated from the citizenry and produced an 'anti-party backlash' in Poland? In their cartel party model, Katz and Mair argue that a pattern of increased party dependence on the state for funding and patronage would lead to inter-party collusion in the division of state resources in such a way that a group of 'insider' parties could be seen to be laying the basis for their own joint survival. Given that state subventions and access to state appointments were generally tied to previous party performance or position (whether defined in terms of electoral success or parliamentary representation), they would thereby privilege insiders and help existing parties to resist challenges from those on the margins, thus limiting the scope for the emergence of 'new entrants'.[47]

There was some evidence to support the notion that such a party cartel might be developing in post-communist Poland. Polish legislation certainly provided greater access to certain financial and material resources to those parties that achieved the greatest electoral success and parliamentary representation. As noted above, the most successful parties in the 1993, 1997 and especially 2001 elections received a handsome financial premium for their electoral victories. Moreover, the various, extremely generous additional forms of funding for parliamentary clubs and individual parliamentarians provided those parties represented in parliament with a further obvious advantage over those that were excluded, and thereby gave election winners a further premium for victory. To some extent, then, the existing rules for state access to parliamentary resources limited the scope for new entrants by discriminating against parties that emerged between elections unless they were formed on the basis of existing parties with parliamentary representation. Together with the system of electoral refunds, they represented a clear move towards the creation of a party cartel in Poland. Similarly, party patronage was, obviously, a preserve of electorally successful parties.

However, there was other evidence suggesting that the Polish party system remained relatively fluid and unstable, exemplified by the very high levels of electoral volatility and party system instability in post-1989 Poland. The level of net electoral volatility calculated according to the Pederson index was 38.78 per cent in 1993, falling to 19.9 per cent in 1997 and then increasing to a massive 49.3 per cent in 2001.[48] The new system of election refunds, introduced in 1993, did not prevent the formation and entry into parliament in 1997 of both the Movement for Poland's Reconstruction and Solidarity Electoral Action (the latter, admittedly, under the aegis of the Solidarity trade union). Similarly, the 2001 election saw the election to parliament of four new parties and political groupings: two of them (Civic Platform and Law and Justice) based on the existing decomposing parliamentary formations (Freedom Union and Solidarity Electoral Action), and a further two that emerged as 'externally created' parties (Self-Defence and the League of Polish Families).[49] Indeed, in 2001 both governing parties, Solidarity

Electoral Action and the Freedom Union, that between them won 47.2 per cent of the vote in 1997, actually failed to cross the thresholds for parliamentary representation.

If a party system is characterized by a relatively stable pattern of inter-actions among its constituent units, then the Polish one has manifested a rather low level of such systemic qualities. In other words, the development of state party funding and patronage appears not to have prevented the emer-gence of new entrants. Indeed, the prospect of party funding may, ironically, in some ways have actually reduced barriers to entry. Parties that emerge from within existing parliamentary parties have automatic access to the range of resources available to parliamentarians. These and other parties can also secure loans to finance election campaigns on the strength of electoral refunds that will be paid subsequently and can then maintain themselves on the basis of subventions. This makes it problematic to talk of the 'fixed menu of parties', envisaged in the cartel party model, from which Polish voters choose.

The September 2005 parliamentary election provides some tentative counter-evidence that the Polish party system may be stabilizing. On the one hand, by European standards, the level of electoral volatility remained extremely high at 35 per cent, exemplified by the fact that the vote the govern-ing Democratic Left Alliance saw a massive slump in support, from 41.03 per cent to 11.31 per cent.[50] On the other hand, this level of electoral volatility represented a fall from its 2001 peak of 49.3 per cent and, perhaps most impor-tantly, the same six parties and political groupings that secured election in 2001 were re-elected in 2005. If this becomes a trend, it suggests that the huge increase in state party funding introduced in 2001 may be starting to create a cartel of insiders, but it is far too early to draw any long-term con-clusions from this, particularly given the continuing high levels of electoral volatility.

As far as the shifting balance of power within parties is concerned, the various state subsidies and parliamentary allowances and concomitant rules governing their allocation, and access to party patronage, have certainly made the position of the party leadership considerably more important and influential, to the emphatic detriment of the 'party on the ground'. Until 2001, the generous and weakly controlled system of parliamentary allowances ensured that most state party funding was actually directed to the parlia-mentary party fractions and individual parliamentarians.[51] Given that it was the party central office that benefited from – and determined the allocation of – both election refunds and the flow of donations, the substantial increase in direct state party funding paid to party headquarters that occurred in 2001 should have centralized power within parties even more. In particular, it should have led to an increase in the power of the leadership of the party central office at the expense of both the party on the ground and the parliamentary party. In fact, given that party financing was highly centralized even before the rise of state party funding, the post-2001 reforms merely reinforced an already well-established trend. Moreover, the parliamentary party still retained an overwhelming share of the state funding, even in the post-2001 funding regime, as well as control over most state patronage. Research conducted by the author has also found that, as far as parties with parliamentary representation are concerned, there is considerable overlap between the leadership of the party in public office and that of the party on the ground, to the extent that in some parties they are virtually indistinguishable, making it difficult to identify the 2001 reforms as indicating any shift in power between these two party 'faces'.[52]

The corollary of the high level of party orientation towards the state is the fact that Polish parties are seen as remote and somewhat distant. Poland is certainly characterized by very weak links between parties and their electorates, and this often finds expression in the form of anti-party sentiments. This can be seen in a number of ways. Polish parties have very low levels of social implantation, exemplified by the fact that they have extremely low memberships. According to comparative data produced by Mair and Van Biezen, Poland had the lowest level of party membership at the end of the 1990s among the 20 countries surveyed, at only 1.15 per cent as a proportion of the electorate (326,5000) compared with the average of 4.99 per cent.[53] Similarly, according to the 1999–2000 European Values Survey, party membership in Poland was the lowest in Europe at only 0.7 per cent of the population.[54] Indeed, survey evidence also suggested that Poles had extremely negative attitudes towards parties, so that even if party strategists actively sought to recruit substantially more individual members (which they rarely do), their prospects for success would be slim.[55] Eurobarometer data from 2004 showed that only three per cent of Poles expressed trust in political parties, the lowest of any EU member state and compared with an average of 14 per cent, also making them by far the least-trusted institution in post-1989 Poland.[56] This was reflected in Polish survey data. For example, an April 2003 survey conducted by the CBOS polling agency found that 87 per cent of respondents felt that Polish politicians only looked after their own interests, 78 per cent that they were not credible, and 77 per cent that they were dishonest. When asked what motivated someone to become a politician, 52 per cent said it was a desire to make money and 30 per cent that they wanted to acquire power; these figures contrasted with only nine per cent who said that they wanted to realize some idea and six per cent that they wanted to do something for others.[57] Weak social implantation and high levels of alienation from political (and, therefore, party) elites, even by post-communist standards, is a plausible explanation for the extraordinarily low levels of parliamentary election turnout in post-1989 Poland, even compared with the rest of the region, where turnout is low by West European standards.[58] Indeed, the fact that average turnout for post-1989 presidential elections – focused on individual candidates rather than parties – is consistently higher (58.4 per cent) than that for parliamentary elections (46 per cent) also appears to offer tentative support for this hypothesis.[59]

However, it is also the case that anti-party sentiment has always been high in Poland, and it is unclear by how much state party funding and patronage has contributed to, or led to an increase in, it. Certainly, there has always been substantial public opposition to both the principle of state party funding and its extension. For example, a March 2001 CBOS survey found 71 per cent of respondents opposed state party funding.[60] There is also clear evidence of some political groupings using the issue of state party funding as a campaign issue, most notably Civic Platform, which, from its formation in 2001, has made opposition to state party funding a key plank of its electoral platform.[61] Moreover, much of the enormous backlash against party and political elites that has emerged in Poland, particularly since the start of 2003, is rooted in concerns about the abuse of state power linked to corrupt connections between private business interests and parties, exemplified by the so-called Rywin affair, which in many ways set the process in train when it came to light at the end of 2002.[62]

However, interestingly, this concern was not necessarily linked directly to the issue of state party funding. Indeed, state party funding was increased so substantially in 2001 precisely in order to address growing concerns about the perceived role of private money in the Polish political process that preceded the Rywin affair. This suggests that state party funding, together with an increase in openness and transparency and restrictions on other forms of funding, was actually seen by the Polish political elite (if not the citizenry), as part of the solution to growing anti-party and anti-elite sentiment rather than part of the problem.[63]

Conclusion

The widespread practice of state financial support has become increasingly important for Polish parties and both its level and its scope have been expanded progressively. In particular, the new 2001 election and party law, which massively increased the amounts that election committees received in refunds and donations, transformed the role of direct state party funding. A combination of this substantial increase in the level of state funding and the new restrictions on obtaining income from other sources has made the income from the state a much more significant proportion of party income, so the state is now the main source of income for several parties. Polish parties' dependence upon and interest in exploiting the financial resources provided by the state becomes even more evident when one considers numerous and substantial forms of indirect state subsidies that parties receive, particularly in the form of various forms of allowances paid to support the activities of the party-based parliamentary caucuses and individual parliamentarians' allowances and expenses, as well as party appointments to state and quasi-state bodies. The expansion of direct state party funding that resulted from the 2001 law increased the relative importance of this form of income; none the less, parliamentary allowances remained a highly significant source of indirect income for Polish parties.

So what are the implications of this substantial and increasing level of direct and indirect state party funding and patronage? Polish legislation certainly provides greater access to funds for parties that achieve electoral success and obtain parliamentary representation. Substantial increases in state subsidies paid directly to party central offices and other factors have also boosted the position of party leadership at the expense of party organization in the country. Moreover, the corollary of the high party orientation towards the state is the fact that Polish parties appear remote. Poland is characterized by very weak links between parties and their electorates, and this often finds expression in the form of anti-party sentiments. However, the Polish party system remains extremely fluid, and the development of state party funding and patronage appears not to have created a 'party cartel' by preventing the emergence of new entrants. Party financing was highly centralized even before the rise of state party funding, and the post-2001 reforms reinforced an established trend of centralizing power in the party leadership. In any case, anti-party sentiment has always been high in Poland, and it is unclear how far state funding and patronage has contributed to it or led to an increase.

NOTES

1. Walecki argues that this was due partly to the widespread public anger that greeted the revelations by the new Solidarity government of the existence and amount of the budget subsidies allotted to the communist party and its allies in 1989, a year of severe economic crisis: see Marcin Walecki, *Money and Politics in Poland* (Warsaw: Institute of Public Affairs, 2005), p.134.
2. See Aleks Szczerbiak, 'Cartelization in Post-Communist Poland: State Party Funding in Post-1989 Poland', in Paul Lewis and Paul Webb (eds.), *Pan-European Perspectives on Party Politics* (Leiden: Brill, 2003), pp.127–49 (p.145). Although the surplus from the refund was supposed to be assigned to 'publicly beneficial purposes', parties discovered various ways to circumvent this provision. The party could also, of course, earn bank interest on any excess sums, and this could then, quite legally, be spent on *strictly* party activities. For more on this see Paul G. Lewis and Radzisława Gortat, 'Models of Party Development and Questions of State Dependence in Poland', *Party Politics*, Vol.1, No.4 (1995), pp.599–608 (p.606).

3. See P.G. Lewis, 'Party Funding in Post-communist East–Central Europe', in P. Burnell and A. Ware, *Funding Democratization* (Manchester: Manchester University Press, 1998), pp.137–57 (p.139).
4. See Szczerbiak, 'Cartelization in Post-Communist Poland', p.145.
5. See Dominika Wielowiejska, 'Wypłata za wybory', *Gazeta Wyborcza*, 29–30 Sept. 2001. As noted above, in the past, election committees could claim a refund in excess of their actual expenditure and therefore make a profit on the election; they could then use this (or the interest accrued on it) to fund future activities.
6. See 'Miliony za wybory', *Rzeczpospolita*, 24 May 2002.
7. The National Party of Retirees and Pensioners received 1.9 million and the Democratic Party (Stronnictwo Demokratyczne: SD) and the Peasant–Democratic Party (Partia Ludowo-Demokratyczna: PLD) 540,000 each.
8. See Dominika Wielowiejska, 'Partyjne pieniądze', *Gazeta Wyborcza*, 24–26 Dec. 2001.
9. See Żaneta Semprich, 'Metodą Satine-Lague, bez listy krajowej', *Rzeczpospolita*, 9 March 2001. As a further innovation, 5–15 per cent of this subvention was to be earmarked for the party's know-how fund, known as the Party Foundation, to cover the costs of legal, social, political and economic expertise and publishing activities.
10. See Walecki, *Money and Politics in Poland*, p.138.
11. See Wielowiejska, 'Partyjne pieniądze'.
12. See Walecki, *Money and Politics in Poland*, pp.139–40.
13. The Peasant Party ended up losing this subvention because it had been depositing money in the wrong account and, instead of selling its real estate, it passed it over to a foundation whose leadership was almost identical to that of the party; the party had already seen its 2002 subvention reduced owing to irregularities in its 2001 financial statement: see 'Jak finansują się partie', *Rzeczpospolita*, 21 June 2004.
14. See 'Subwencje dla partii: 22 mln zł dla PiS; 20 dla PO', *Gazeta Wyborcza*, 30 Sept. 2005, at <http://www.wiadomosci.gazeta.pl/wybory2005/2029020,67805,2943176.html>, accessed on 30 Sept 2005.
15. However, separate donations could also be made to a party's election fund.
16. Parties that broke the rules or failed to submit accurate annual financial statements or accounts of their election expenses faced reductions in their refunds and donations, as was the case with the Peasant Party, Labour Union and Democratic Party.
17. See 'Ordynacja wyborcza bez listy krajowej', *Rzeczpospolita*, 8 March 2001.
18. See Semprich, 'Metodą Satine-Lague'.
19. These figures only include income to cover the party's statutory activities that they undertake between elections, and they exclude money paid into the party election funds: see Marek Henzler, 'Kasa partyjna, pieniądze państwowe', *Polityka*, 26 April 2003.
20. These were partly from assets that it inherited from the communist-era satellite United Peasant Party (Zjednoczone Stronnictwo Ludowe: ZSL), of which it was the direct organizational successor, and partly resulted from its use of its 1993 election refund to purchase a large number of buildings.
21. See Marcin Walecki. 'Kto płaci za wybory', *Gazeta Wyborcza*, 20 Sept. 2005, at <http://www.wiadomosci.gazeta.pl/wybory2005/2029020,67805,2925845.html>, accessed on 21 Sept. 2005.
22. See Walecki, *Money and Politics in Poland*, p.145. Parliamentary parties' specialist and expert reports are largely paid for from these funds, although Sejm deputies and senators who chair parliamentary committees can also obtain additional assistance; this can, of course, be utilized indirectly for party purposes.
23. See ibid., p.143.
24. See Frederyk Frydrykiewicz, Beata Kopyt and Eliza Olczyk. 'Grunt to dobry adres', *Rzeczpospolita*, 8 Jan. 2002.
25. See Walecki, *Money and Politics in Poland*, p.144.
26. See Marek Henzler, 'Pan poseł przymuje', *Polityka*, 24 April 2004.
27. See Ania van der Meer-Krok-Paszkowska and Marc van der Muyzenberg, 'The Positions of Parties in the Polish and Hungarian Parliaments', paper prepared for the Fourth

Workshop on 'Transformation Processes in Eastern Europe', The Hague, 1–2 Feb. 1996, p.8.

28. See Janina Paradowska, 'Lewa Kasa, Prawa Kasa', *Polityka*, 22 Jan. 2000. This term is, somewhat confusingly, also used sometimes to simply describe parliamentarians' office expense allowances.
29. See 'Na własny rachunek', *Rzeczpospolita*, 10 Dec. 2001.
30. See Henzler, 'Pan poseł przymuje'.
31. See Aleks Szczerbiak, 'Testing Party Models in East–Central Europe: Local Party Organization in Postcommunist Poland', *Party Politics*, Vol.5, No.4 (1999), pp.523–37; and Janina Paradowska, 'Drogie partie', *Polityka*, 3 March 2001. On other occasions, Sejm deputies and Senators rented out rooms for their offices in party-owned buildings, thereby using state money to supplement the party's income, although the 2001 party law should put an end to this practice: see Frydrykiewicz et al., 'Grunt to dobry adres'.
32. See Paradowska, 'Drogie partie'.
33. See Stanisław Gebethner, 'Problem Finansowania Partii Politycznych a System Wyborczy w Polsce w Latach 90', in Franciszek Ryszka et al. (eds.) *Historia–Idee–Polityka* (Warsaw: Wydawnictwo Naukowe Scholar, 1995), pp.425–34 (p.431). Gebethner's calculation included: the financial resources passed on directly to the parliamentary clubs and circles themselves, Sejm deputies and senators' personal expense allowances, and the total amount allocated to parliamentary deputies to maintain their offices. Only the *ryczałts* (the lump sums paid to 'professional' parliamentarians who had given up all paid employment to devote themselves to full-time parliamentary work) was excluded, since this was supposed to replace income forgone. Even these calculations did not include the various services-in-kind enjoyed by Polish deputies and senators (such as free public transport by land or air and the free use of hotel accommodation in Warsaw) of which it was impossible to calculate the exact value.
34. See Szczerbiak, 'Cartelization in Post-Communist Politics', p.145.
35. Compare Connor O'Dwyer, 'Runaway State Building: How Political Parties Shape States in Postcommunist Eastern Europe', *World Politics*, Vol.56 (2004), pp.520–33.
36. See Dorota Macieja, 'Rzeczpospolita nomenklaturowa', *Wprost*, 5 Aug. 2002.
37. Ibid.
38. See A. Szczerbiak, 'Polish Parties and the Media: The Politics of Public Broadcasting in Post-communist Poland', *Wrocławskie Studia Politologiczne*, Vol.1 (2001), pp.47–65.
39. See Macieja, 'Rzeczpospolita nomenklaturowa'.
40. See Ryszard Kamiński, 'Paraliż Państwa', *Wprost*, 1 April 2001. On the general growth of the public sector in post-1989 Eastern Europe, see O'Dwyer, 'Runaway State Building'.
41. See Kamiński, 'Paraliż Państwa'.
42. See 'Działacze partyjni zamiast urzedników', *Rzeczpospolita*, 25 June 2003.
43. See Macieja, 'Rzeczpospolita nomenklaturowa'.
44. Cited in O'Dwyer, 'Runaway State Building', p.539.
45. See 'Rzeczpospolita nomenklaturowa'.
46. See Mariusz Janicki and Wiesław Władyka, 'Wielki przeciąg', *Polityka*, 11 Oct. 1997.
47. See Richard S. Katz and Peter Mair, 'Changing Models of Party Organizations and Party Democracy: The Emergence of the Cartel Party', *Party Politics*, Vol.1, No.1 (1995), pp.5–28.
48. However, the 2001 figure for gross volatility is considerably lower (28.66 per cent) and the net volatility figure can also be reduced (to 19.25 per cent) if one makes certain assumptions about some of the 'new' parties simply being continuations of the old: see Radosław Markowski and Mariusz Cześnik, 'Polski system partyjny: dekada zmian', in Radosław Markowski (ed.), *System Partyjny i Zachowanie Wyborcze: Dekada Polskich Doświadczeń* (Warsaw: ISP PAN, 2002), pp.17–47 (pp.26–7). For more on Polish electoral volatility, see Mariusz Cześnik and Radosław Markowski, 'Ewolucja polskiego systemu politycznego', in Irena Jackiewicz and Krzysztof Murawski (eds.), *Rozwój instytucji demokratycznych w Polsce 1989–2001* (Warsaw: Wydawnictwo Sejmowe, 2002).

49. The League also comprised some existing parliamentarians elected in 1997 on the Solidarity Electoral Action and Movement for Poland's Reconstruction tickets.
50. Even though it fought the 2001 in coalition with the Labour Union which joined a Democratic Left Alliance breakaway, Polish Social Democracy, which won 3.98 per cent of the vote.
51. See Szczerbiak, 'Cartelization in Post-communist Politics'.
52. See Aleks Szczerbiak, *Poles Together? The Emergence and Development of Political Parties in Post-communist Poland* (Budapest: Central European University Press, 2001), pp.42–6.
53. See Peter Mair and Ingrid van Biezen., 'Party Membership in Twenty European Democracies, 1980–2000', *Party Politics*, Vol.7, No.1 (2001), pp.5–21 (p.9).
54. See Loek C.J.M. Halman, *The European Values Study: A Third Wave*, source book of the 1999/2000 European Values Study Surveys (Tilburg: EVS, WORC, Tilburg University, 2001); available at <http://spitswww.uvt.nl/web/fsw/evs/documents/Publications/Sourcebook/EVS_SourceBook.pdf>, accessed 15 May 2006.
55. See Aleks Szczerbiak, 'The New Polish Parties as Membership Organizations', *Contemporary Politics*, Vol.7, No.1 (2001), pp.57–69.
56. See European Commission, *Candidate Countries Eurobarometer 2004.1, Feb.–March 2004* (Brussels: European Commission, 2004), p.21.
57. See CBOS, *Opinie o polskiej klasie politycznej* (Warsaw: CBOS, June 2003); data for April 2003.
58. See Susanne Jungerstam-Mulders, 'Parties and Party Systems in Post-Communist EU Member States: Comparative Aspects', in Susanne Jungerstam-Mulders (ed.), *Post-communist EU Member States: Parties and Party Systems* (Aldershot: Ashgate, 2006), p.14.
59. Author's calculations.
60. See CBOS, *Finansowanie partii politycznych* (Warsaw: CBOS, March 2001); data for March 2001.
61. See, for example, 'Z czego pozyją partie', *Gazeta Wyborcza*, 6 March 2001.
62. This centred on allegations that individuals linked to the Democratic Left Alliance, including the media mogul and film producer Lew Rywin, demanded payment from the newspaper publisher Agora in return for favourable changes to the government's media regulation law.
63. See, for example, Ludwik Dorn, 'Finansowanie działalności politycznej w Polsce. Obecna praktyka i jej reforma', in Marcin Walecki (ed.), *Finansowanie polityki. Wybory, pieniądze, partie polityczne* (Warsaw: Wydawnictwo Sejmowe, 2000), pp.141–78.

Powered by the State: The Role of Public Resources in Party-Building in Slovakia

MAREK RYBÁŘ

Political parties are at the core of modern government and politics. Nevertheless, their role has changed over time. It is argued, for example, that the functional position of political parties has shifted from being the agents of society to representing effectively and managing the institutions of the modern state.[1] Similarly, the principal functions of parties tend to revolve around the recruitment of new political leaders, and the building and maintaining of governments, while their representative functions are in decline.[2]

The proximity of parties and the state is well illustrated in the new democracies of post-communist Europe. There are several reasons for this. First, the previous non-democratic regime was characterized by the ruling communist party's excessive control of society and, especially, of the state. The party dominated the state apparatus through the system of *nomenklatura*, whereby appointments to all important positions within the state apparatus were subjected to vetting by the party leadership. Pre-communist patterns of party–state relations are less telling because of the limited experience of Eastern and Central European countries with democracy before the Second World War. Hence, if past patterns of behaviour have any impact on the post-communist practice, they may suggest extensive control of parties over state institutions.

Second, in the aftermath of the regime change of the late 1980s, political parties found themselves in a privileged position to shape the rules of the new political game. In the absence of a significant opposition to their dominant position, they forged the institutional environment in a manner that was clearly beneficial for partisan interests.

Third, most political parties in the post-communist region emerged from within the institutions of the state itself. Political parties were often set up by ambitious individuals within the national parliaments, and there are also examples of parties originating in the executive. Thus, political parties in Eastern and Central Europe emerged within the state institutions, and their leaders exploited this opportunity to endow their organizations with strategically important resources. There are two main ways through which they did that: the provision of state financing of political parties, and the practice of patronage.

Contrary to the practice in established western democracies, where state subsidies to parties were introduced at a later stage of party system development, in the new democracies of post-communist Europe state subsidies were available from the very beginning of democratic party competition. Because links between parties and society tend to be underdeveloped, at least at this stage of post-communist development, the availability of state resources suggests a systematic shift of parties towards the state, with important consequences for the organizational development and party-building strategies of political parties.

The practice of patronage was also a way to link political parties with the state. In this essay, patronage is used to refer to the ability of political parties to control appointments in various state and semi-state institutions. State subsidies to parties are typically distributed on the basis of parties' electoral performance in the previous elections and in order to secure the organizational and financial sustainability of party-based political activities; subsidies tend to have long-term implications for the ways parties function and organize. In contrast, the effects of patronage on parties are immediate, normally rather short-lived and usually confined to periods when parties occupy important executive positions. Hence, state subsidies to parties and patronage opportunities are complementary resources with different functional logics but with similar consequences for party–state relations.

The analysis of the nature of party–state relations cannot be complete, however, without a consideration of formal and informal rules governing the consumption of these two resources. What I mean here is that we need to take into account how strict the formal regulations and rules regarding party finance and patronage are, and whether they represent a serious *de facto* constraint on the ways parties act. In cases where there are strict formal regulations as well as effective enforcement mechanisms limiting party activities, parties' control over the state is naturally lower than in situations where strict regulations are absent or cannot be enforced in practice.

This contribution aims to highlight the role played by the state and its resources in the process of forming and maintaining political parties in post-communist Slovakia. It addresses three interrelated questions. First, how are Slovak political parties maintained financially, and what role have state subsidies played in the process of their formation and development? Second, how strict are the rules on the disclosure of party finance and how far has the nature of party finance regulations contributed to the penetration of parties into the state apparatus? Third, to what degree do parties control the state institutions through the system of patronage? It is argued that in the early stage of party system development, governing parties used the system of patronage as the principal tool to boost their organizational development and, to some extent, their electoral support; state financing of parties was less consequential. Since the late 1990s, however, the importance of state subventions has increased dramatically. Parties still widely enjoy the benefits brought by patronage; however, compared with previous practice, patronage has either decreased or is being used more proportionally. Important distinctions are found between patronage practices within the vertical and horizontal state administration. I argue that this is mostly because parties need to strengthen their regional party organizations by allocating positions within the vertical (regional) state administration to their representatives. Moreover, some of the patronage practices used by parties in the horizontal state administration in the 1990s have been discredited and are now considered to be illegitimate. Parties therefore largely refrain from using them. By making direct state subsidies the main resource extracted from the state, parties compensated themselves collectively for a declining availability of alternative resources, whether state or private.

Access to State Resources and Party Competition

In contrast to the process of democratization in Western Europe in the late nineteenth century, the advent of democracy in Slovakia gave citizens equal political rights at the same time as it allowed for party competition. The simultaneity of liberalization and democratization influenced the character of party formation and shaped the functional position of parties in linking state institutions and society. Most political parties in Slovakia are products of the post-1989 political development. The only exception was the Party of the Democratic Left (SDL) which had genuine personal and organizational continuity with a pre-1989 political party: its organizational predecessor, the Communist Party of Czechoslovakia,[3] was the hegemonic party in pre-1989 Czechoslovakia. A significant anti-communist political opposition emerged only during the process of regime decay in the late 1980s. The Public Against Violence (VPN) in Slovakia and the Civic Forum (OF) in the Czech lands, two principal opposition forces of the anti-communist Velvet Revolution in 1989, formed as elite circles articulating political demands of the 'masses in the streets'. Even before the first competitive elections were held, the VPN and OF representatives joined the federal as well as national governments and their nominees became members of the legislative assemblies.[4] These developments brought about a situation where new political parties were being created internally by ambitious members of parliaments, a behavioural pattern replicated by many parliamentarians in subsequent electoral cycles.

The share of parliamentarians who left their original parliamentary party group between two consecutive parliamentary elections is a good proxy for the fragmentation of the party system during this period. Between 1990 and 2005, between one-tenth and one-third of all MPs defected from their original parliamentary group in each parliament. Moreover, there seems to be no trend towards a more stable parliamentary environment over time. The largest number of parliamentarians changed political affiliation in the first parliamentary term (1990–92) when it was reasonable to expect that party loyalties and party system stabilization would be not be very high.[5] Between 1992 and 1998 there appeared to be less instability of the parliamentary party groups, but since 1998 there has been an upsurge in the 'volatility of parliamentarians', as a fourth to a fifth of members of parliament left their original parliamentary caucus. The increase in the absolute number of parties represented in the parliament is even more revealing: this rose from nine after the 1990 elections to 12 two years later, and from six in 1998 to 16 at the time of the 2002 elections; after these last elections the number of parties with parliamentary representation rose from seven to 14.

Politically, parliamentarians leaving their parliamentary party group have three options. They may join an existing political party, whether a parliamentary or an extra-parliamentary entity. Second, they may set up a new political party and run in the next parliamentary elections. Third, they may use the social capital acquired in parliament and launch a new career outside politics. The second option is the most relevant in the context of the present enquiry.

Two of Slovakia's most prominent parties, the Movement for a Democratic Slovakia (HZDS) of the former prime minister, Vladimír Mečiar, and the Slovak Democratic and Christian Union (SDKÚ) of the current prime minister, Mikuláš Dzurinda, were created as breakaway factions from the largest parliamentary party groups. In 1991, the HZDS was formed by a group of two dozen parliamentarians, originally elected to the parliament on the Public Against Violence party list. In 2000, the SDKÚ was created by the leading representatives of the Slovak Democratic Coalition (SDK), a formation set up by five parties in 1998 to compete effectively with the HZDS. Both parties were therefore internally created. What distinguishes the HZDS from the SDKÚ, however, is the extent of state resources that their founders could rely upon when setting up their organizations. The founding fathers of the HZDS relied primarily on parliamentary resources, whereas the SDKÚ leaders could also use the executive and patronage resources (see Table 1).

Table 1 presents a categorization of political parties based on their access to three types of state resources and the level of the resources available. As direct state subsidies are available to political parties only on the basis of their electoral performance (see below), newly formed parties normally try to exploit indirect state resources. 'Executive resources' refers to benefits that political parties and their representatives enjoy by virtue of holding executive offices. These include, among other things, privileged access to important information, capacity to influence key policy decisions, extensive media coverage, and the use of government infrastructure and financial resources for *de facto* party activities. Patronage resources usually go hand-in-hand with control of executive offices and are therefore enjoyed only by those newly formed parties that participate in the government from the beginning of their existence. Finally, parliamentary resources available to members of parliament include access to information, influence over policy making, and media coverage (usually less extensive than is the case with the executive). Moreover, since 2000, members of parliament in Slovakia have had at their disposal financial resources to pay for their assistants and for their regional offices. Typically, these resources have been used by the MPs-turned-party-leaders to establish a network of *de facto* regional party centres, and as such they represent significant resources for party-building activities.

TABLE 1
ACCESS OF NEWLY FORMED PARTIES TO STATE RESOURCES

	Executive resources	Patronage resources	Parliamentary resources	Examples
High	Yes	Yes	Yes	SDKÚ, DÚ
Medium	No	No	Yes	HZDS
Low	No	No	No	KSS, ANO

The case of the SDKÚ is particularly illustrative of a party that had access to high levels of all three kinds of resources. The party was created by seven out of eight cabinet members (including the prime minister) nominated by the SDK. They were joined by about half of the SDK members of parliament and also by all five SDK nominees to head the state administration at the regional level. Hence, the SDKÚ was a creation of politicians who held key positions within the institutions of the state (in the cabinet, parliament and top state administration). Similarly, the Democratic Union (DÚ) was set up in 1994 by members of parliament and cabinet (again including the prime minister, Jozef Moravčík) who were originally elected to parliament on the party lists of the HZDS and the Slovak National Party. Control of executive positions combined with the availability of patronage resources in the state administration and substantial parliamentary resources boosted the organizational development of both the SDKÚ and the DÚ and helped to consolidate their respective party organizations.

A second category, parties with medium access to state resources, comprises parties that were formed within the institutions of the state but without access to executive positions. Most parties that were formed internally belong to this group, including the HZDS in 1991, the Association of Slovak Workers (ZRS)[6] in 1994, the Real Slovak National Party in 2001 (PSNS) and the Free Forum (SF) in 2003.[7]

A third category – new parties with a low level of access to state resources – consists of parties that were formed outside parliament and hence had to mobilize alternative (non-state) resources to secure electoral success. Hence, however important indirect state resources are for the initial success of the new parties, there have been examples of newcomers whose electoral fortunes were not conditioned by their access to state resources. Examples of political parties that managed to secure considerable political power and influence without initial access to state resources include the unreformed Communist Party (KSS), re-established in 1992; the Party of Civic Understanding (SOP), formed shortly before the 1998 elections;[8] and the New Citizen Alliance (ANO), founded in 2001. The electoral success of new political parties obviously cannot be attributed to the availability of state resources as a single cause: alternative resources may be crucial for some new parties in attaining parliamentary seats. However, indirect state resources represent a powerful factor in parties' organizational and mobilization strategies. Hence, the state indirectly supplies political leaders with important tools that have a very strong impact on the course and character of political competition and electoral mobilization.

At the same time, privileged access to state resources does not guarantee the survival of political parties. In fact, the relatively short life-span of most relevant political parties is one of the chief characteristics of Slovak politics.

Among the parties represented in the 2002 parliament, only two have an unequivocal record of parliamentary presence in all legislatures since the first free elections of 1990: the Christian Democrats (KDH) and the HZDS. Representatives of the Hungarian minority have also been present in all post-1989 parliaments; however, the original three independent formations merged in 1998 into a single party (the SMK). Two parties that had been the cornerstones of Slovak party politics throughout the 1990s – the Party of Democratic Left and the Slovak National Party – split in early 2000s; their remnants did not manage to clear the five per cent threshold required to enter parliament in the 2002 elections. Three of the seven parties elected to the National Council in 2002 did not even exist at the time of the previous parliamentary elections; similarly, in 1998, three out of six successful parties did not contest the previous parliamentary elections. Because of this, the analysis of party finances is confined to parties represented in the parliament since the 1998 elections.

Party Financing

Legislation governing the state financing of political parties in Slovakia was enacted a few months before the first free elections in June 1990. At that time, only the communist party had substantial organizational and financial resources, equipment and experienced personnel at its disposal. This was because of the party's leading role before 1989 which was both a constitution-ally entrenched principle and a matter of fact. After the regime change the parliament adopted a law requiring the communist party to return a substantial part of its property, especially immovable assets, to the state. There have been suggestions that, because of the rapid and unexpected pace of the communist breakdown in Czechoslovakia, the communist party was unable to take defensive action against confiscation of its assets;[9] in fact, however, there are many examples of local and regional communist party officials selling party property before the law took effect, thus securing important financial resources for their political activities.[10] Consequently, even after confiscation, the communist party possessed substantially more property than all the other political parties combined. The disadvantaged position of the other political parties explains in part why state funding of political parties in Slovakia was introduced at the early stage of party (and party system) development. However, it remains unclear how newly formed political parties managed to sustain their activities before the 1990 parliamentary elections. Clearly, various western political foundations and political parties played an important role: Pridham lists various examples of direct and indirect funding, material support, and training of political personnel provided as aid to the new political parties in Eastern Europe.[11]

In Slovakia, the main principles of state funding of political parties have not been changed since 1990. First of all, eligibility for state subsidies is tied to electoral performance in parliamentary elections. Since only parties and alliances (electoral coalitions), and not individuals, can run for parliamentary seats, independent candidates are by definition not eligible to receive state funding. Independents can run for the directly elected presidential office and also for positions in the local and regional governments. However, neither parties nor individuals can claim public subsidies on the basis of their performance in these second-order elections. Similarly, no public funding is available on the basis of the European Parliament elections where, again, only political parties have the right to nominate candidates.

State funding of political parties has two major forms: reimbursement of election expenses, and contributions to parties' annual running costs. In practice, however, both are calculated in the same way and the only difference rests in the timing of the payments. In 1990, all parties that received more than two per cent of the vote were entitled to state subsidies. For each vote that they had won, the party received ten Czechoslovak crowns, payable a few weeks after the general election as a reimbursement of electoral expenses. The same amount was paid to the parties annually – in four instalments – during the four years of the parliamentary term as running costs. In 1992, the amount per vote was increased to 15 Czechoslovak crowns. Between 1990 and 1992, when Slovakia was part of the Czechoslovak Federation, successful political parties received state subsides on the basis of their performance in the elections to the national parliament as well as to the two chambers of the Federal Assembly. To compensate for the financial losses following the break-up of Czechoslovakia (when the federal parliament was dissolved), in 1994 the Slovak parliament increased the amount per vote to 60 Slovak crowns. At the same time, the eligibility threshold was increased: to receive state funding parties had to win at least three per cent of the votes in the parliamentary elections. The way contributions to parties' annual running costs were calculated was not affected.

In 2000, the parliament adopted a modification to the system of state subsidies. The existing components remained intact but a new source of money was made available to parliamentary parties. For each member of parliament a party had, it received an additional 500,000 Slovak crowns annually. Consequently, in terms of state funding to political parties, three categories of political parties are defined:[12] first, a group that did not compete in the parliamentary elections, or received less than three per cent of the vote: these parties are not entitled to receive state subsidies; second, a group of parties that gained more then three per cent of the vote but did not clear the five per cent threshold needed for parliamentary representation; third, the parties represented in parliament. The system of state funding is most generous to the third group, while parties of the first group (including parties created internally between elections) receive no direct state funding. This mechanism of state funding is similar to ones observed in established democracies, where new or small parties, or both, do have access to state money but the parties already in parliament receive even more direct state funding.[13]

In 2004, the parliament unanimously changed the amount of state money parties receive per vote. Instead of a fixed sum, the contribution was set as one per cent of the average nominal wage in the national economy in the previous year. The provision actually meant an increase from 60 to 144 Slovak crowns in 2004.[14] The last change to the system was adopted in early 2005. The new amendment changed the sum that parties annually receive for each member of parliament elected on their list. Here, the amount was also tied to the average nominal wage. Instead of 500,000 crowns per seat, each parliamentary party will receive a sum equivalent to 30 times the current national average monthly wage, and for each additional seat a sum to the amount of 20 times the current national average monthly wage. The measure will cause a modest drop in income compared with the status quo; in relative terms the most affected will be the strongest parliamentary parties. In the long run, however, parties will not need to change the previously fixed contribution per seat, thus securing a continuous rise in the amount of the subsidy.

To sum up, over the past ten years political parties gradually increased the amount of direct subsidies they received from the state budget. Since only parliament is entitled to change the legislation, and only political parties can nominate candidates for the positions in parliament, political parties used their strategic position within the political system to endow themselves collectively with financial resources crucial for their organizational survival. Characteristically, changes to the system of state subsides were passed by overwhelming parliamentary majorities that included all relevant political parties. Only the 2005 amendment was opposed by the HZDS; it is unclear whether their attitude was motivated by disagreement with financial aspects of the proposal.[15]

Naturally, there are other sources of income besides state subsidies, and membership fees and donations constitute the lion's share of the non-state financial resources of Slovak political parties. The share of state subsidies in their total income serves as a good proxy for the degree of dependency of parties on state resources. However, the general picture, as presented in Table 2, may be somewhat misleading since five of the seven parties were not eligible to receive any direct state subsidies in the period immediately before the 2002 parliamentary elections.

Hence, if we take into account only periods after parties did become eligible for state funding (namely, since 2002; or, in the case of the HZDS and the SMK, since 1998) their dependence on state money rapidly increases.

TABLE 2
STATE SUBSIDIES AS PERCENTAGE OF TOTAL PARTY INCOME, 1998–2004
(PARLIAMENTARY PARTIES SINCE 2002)

	1998	1999	2000	2001	2002	2003	2004
ANO				0	28.84	33.88	15.41
Smer		0	0	0	47.98	81.94	59.14
KSS	0	0	0	0	80.09	60.51	74.59
KDH	47.59	0	0	0	47.18	68.70	50.60
HZDS	63.15	36.24	37.31	58.98	82.65	83.10	81.57
SDKÚ			0	0	56.50	39.84	71.65
SMK	85.92	66.71	74.19	93.11	82.62	74.04	90.28

Source: Annual reports of political parties and author's own calculations.

For example, the average share of state subsidies in the annual income of the SMK is 81 per cent, and for the HZDS and Smer the share is over 63 per cent. The New Citizen Alliance (ANO) has been the least dependent on state money, with an average of 26 per cent of its income derived from state subsidies. The ANO is also the only parliamentary party whose share of non-state money has been lower than 50 per cent. Table 2 also shows that parties' ability to secure non-state money increases in the year of parliamentary elections (2002). In general, however, public subsidies represent the most crucial and therefore indispensable resource for parties' activities. Political parties, by virtue of electing their representatives to parliament, have systematically increased the amount of money available to them from the state budget since 1990.

Direct state subsidies represent the most important but not the only form of state resources that flow to parties' coffers: their parliamentary party groups also receive money and staff support from the parliamentary budget. Even though they are less significant than direct subsidies, they represent an important 'start-up' source for parties created between elections.[16] Since 1998, three parties have secured financial support in this way: the KDH, re-established as a party group in 2000,[17] the Real Slovak National Party (in 2001 and 2002), and a group of deputies who left HZDS and set up a new party in 2003.

Moreover, since 2000, all members of parliament receive about 300,000 crowns a year as compensation for the rent they pay for their regional offices. Even though systematic data are not available, anecdotal evidence suggests that most parliamentarians rent offices from their regional party headquarters or from companies that give donations to their party. Consequently, the money reserved to support the activities of parliamentarians often ends up in the bank account of their party. Unlike parties created without any significant personal anchor in parliament, political parties elected to parliament, or created internally between the elections, benefit financially from this access to state resources.

A Weak System of Party Management by the State

Assessing the role state money plays in the financial matters of political parties is only half the story. It is equally important to find out how strict regulations of party finances are and how effectively the rules are enforced. Moreover, party finance regulations are only one component of what Kopecký calls the management of parties by the state.[18] The character of party–state relationships is also shaped by the extent to which other aspects of the internal life of political parties are regulated by the state. Following Kopecký's suggestions in the introductory contribution to this collection, the state management of parties is assessed on the basis of the existence of mechanisms and principles of intra-party democracy, the constitutional status of political parties, and the regulation of party finances.

As in most democracies established after the Second World War, the Slovak legal system recognizes the importance of political parties for a democratic political regime. The Constitution emphasizes the importance of political parties and political movements, and also stresses their separation from the state. Parties may organize only on a territorial principle: no other forms of party organization are allowed. An authoritative interpretation of the Constitution stresses that such a provision was a reaction to the experience with the pre-1989 communist party, which had organizations in the workplace and an armed militia as an integral part of its organization.[19]

The statute on political parties explicitly mentions that a crucial function of parties is to participate in the working of the parliament and of the elected authorities at the sub-national level. The legislation only allows the existence of political parties that comply with the Constitution and other laws, observe principles of intra-party democracy, and do not seek the elimination of the democratic regime and free political competition. Leaders of breakaway factions from all Slovak political parties have often accused the party leaders of widespread manipulation, undemocratic behaviour and abuse of leadership powers. However, no single case of charges against a political party occurred from 1991, when the law on parties was enacted, until early 2006, when a case was brought against the politically insignificant extreme right party, the Slovak Community, which was dissolved by the Supreme Court on the grounds that it did not conform to democratic norms. The regulation of party financing has undergone some changes since the early 1990s. However, even though the state now requires parties to submit more information on their financial situation and transactions than in the early 1990s, in reality enforcement has not changed much. Until 2000, for example, all registered political parties had been obliged to submit an annual financial report to parliament. Parties were required to disclose the amount of money they received from membership fees, donations, and their own entrepreneurial activities. The reports were also to contain information on the type of activities parties spent their money on (such as campaigning, political education, personal expenses, and so on). However, the regulatory framework did not contain any major sanctions against parties that did not comply with the regulations. The only sanction that could have been imposed on them was the withholding of funds from parties eligible for state funding. The 1992 law required them to submit a report stating how they spent the money they received from the state budget in the previous year as a precondition for receiving state subsidies in the following year. However, in 1998, for example, 52 out of 95 registered political parties did not submit their reports.[20] In addition, even though the financial reports contained only minimal relevant information, parties were not obliged to release these documents to the public.

Amendments to the law adopted in 2000 increased the requirements of what parties had to make publicly available. First, they were obliged to publish their reports. Second, the reports had to disclose basic identification information on donors to political parties; in previous years donations to parties could remain anonymous. Third, all reports had to be certified by a randomly selected licensed auditor. Finally, the amendments also introduced the possibility of sanctioning political parties that did not submit annual reports by a fine of up to 100,000 crowns. Critics of the law pointed out that, even though parties were obliged to disclose more information, the principles of transparency concerned only one source of income (direct donations), while other sources (*de facto* indirect donations, such as loans) could remain anonymous. The main criticism, however, stressed that it was the representatives of political parties themselves (a parliamentary committee) who were to review the reports. Hence, control over party financing remained in the hands of political parties.[21] It therefore comes as no surprise that since 2000 the parliamentary committee has approved – without a single exception – all financial reports, and no sanctions have been imposed on parties. Further minor changes to the system were introduced in early 2005. The law now requires donors to confirm their donation to political parties in written form; in addition, membership fees exceeding 25,000 crowns per year must also be identifiable. However, the absence of changes to the enforcement mechanism led critics to point out that the new legislation will not guarantee more transparency of party finances.[22]

It is interesting to note that tightening the control over parties' finances, however ineffective, has occurred simultaneously with a major increase in state subsidies to parties. The introduction of contributions to parties per parliamentary seat was accompanied by changes to the regulatory framework, and so were the amendments of 2004–5. Political parties at least symbolically acknowledged the need for a stricter regulation of their finances, even though in fact they preserved a largely ineffective system of financial control. It has been observed that major reforms of party finance regulations usually take place only after financial scandals involving major parties force politicians to react because of critical public opinion.[23] However, scandals surrounding party finances in Slovakia did not lead to comparable results. In 2003, for example, a Slovak daily newspaper revealed that some people whom the Slovak Democratic and Christian Union had claimed as donors in 2000–2 denied giving money to the party; yet neither the parliamentary committee responsible for reviewing financial reports nor the ministry of finance (in charge of administering the state subsidies to parties) took any formal action, thus effectively refusing to deal with the problem.[24] The same party claimed in its 2001 financial report that it had received 12 million crowns in state subsidies even though at that time the party was not even eligible to receive state money. By and large, party finances in Slovakia remain outside the effective control of the state. An acknowledgment that the state has no effective tools to manage party finances came in 2005, when the new law on parties abolished the campaign spending limit. Since 1994, parties had been limited to spending 12 million crowns in the parliamentary election campaign. Only in 2001, however, did the state introduce the possibility of sanctions against parties that did not comply with the rules. Even after that change it remained very easy for parties to bypass the limit, since it applied only to money parties paid within the official 30-day campaign before the elections. Most parties started campaigning much earlier, and some claimed that expenses related to their activities were paid several months in advance.[25] Even though there were several proposals for making the spending limit regulation enforceable, parliament decided to abolish the limit completely.

Parties and Patronage

Rent-seeking behaviour by political parties within the state administration is notoriously difficult to prove, and any effort to document this aspect of party activities necessarily involves the use of 'soft' data and incomplete information.[26] In the rest of this study I provide a tentative and exploratory account of the patronage practices of Slovak political parties. Patronage is understood here as 'a divisible benefit that politicians distribute to individual voters, campaign workers, or contributors in exchange for political support'.[27] These benefits may be of various types. I am concerned here primarily with the distribution of posts within the civil service. This is an important limitation on the scope of the analysis, for party patronage often affects other sectors and layers of the administration. Party patronage frequently flourishes in various regulatory bodies, expert teams and advisory committees set up by national ministries. Similarly, the governing boards of state-owned companies are often filled with state representatives nominated in practice by political parties. Láštic, for example, quotes a leading representative of the Christian Democrats (KDH) who in 2002 acknowledged that the parties in government nominated their representatives to the governing board of the energy utility Slovenské elektrárne.[28] Unfortunately, information of this sort is rather scarce and the available data are insufficient to provide conclusive answers. Hence, the following account of the changes in patronage practices in Slovakia should be read with this important caveat in mind.

The post-communist political context is especially conducive to the frequent use of patronage. First, party systems have often been in flux, with new successful parties regularly emerging in parliamentary elections. Because post-communist countries are by and large characterized by 'demobilized societies', where citizens distrust political parties and do not frequently engage in partisan activities, party leaders need to use selective incentives such as patronage positions to stimulate their party-building purposes. Second, the post-communist states themselves have been evolving very rapidly since the early 1990s, but are still to see stability in their state structures. The establishment of the rule of law, a professional and impartial state bureaucracy, effective regional and local self-government, plus other aspects of state transformation are long-term processes.[29] Hence, besides unstable parties there have also been unstable state bureaucracies in the region. This situation of 'dual instability' is made even more complicated in newly independent states where many institutions have to be created from scratch. It is therefore reasonable to expect that simultaneous process of state- and party-building will have a significant impact on the practice of party patronage.

Dominant accounts of patterns of patronage in Central European countries stress the importance of party system institutionalization and the degree of party power fragmentation in parliament as the main variables explaining politicization of the state. According to Grzymała-Busse, the rise of a dominant party at the early stage of party system development led to a situation where such a party politicized the state and monopolized state resources. In contrast, a dispersion of parliamentary power among several parties led to a situation of political uncertainty where parties preferred to create a strict system of control over unrestrained access to state resources. Hence, concentration of power in one party leads to widespread use of patronage, while dispersion of parliamentary power limits the level of state colonization by parties.[30] O'Dwyer's interpretation is slightly different: in his account, too much dispersion of parliamentary power among many relevant parties also creates incentives for patronage behaviour. Even though they do not significantly expand their grip on state resources, or change the system inherited from the previous period of unrestrained rule by a dominant party, small parties in government tend to maximize their individual patronage resources while expecting that responsibilities (and blame) for their behaviour will be dispersed among all ruling parties.[31]

Both models provide powerful potential explanations of the patronage practices in Slovakia. The extensive politicization of the state before the 1998 elections can be interpreted as a consequence of the dominant position of the HZDS before the 1998 elections. Similarly, because of the high fragmentation of coalition governments since 1998, and the strength of the opposition HZDS between 1998 and 2002, we can expect to see only a limited change in the existing system of patronage and the state politicization. However, while the former claim is supported by sufficient empirical evidence, the latter proposition cannot be fully confirmed. Important changes regarding the practice of patronage did take place after 1998. First, in 2001 parliament adopted a civil service act (modified several times between 2001 and 2003) that established a professional civil service and, *inter alia*, introduced a distinction between permanent civil service and political positions. It was therefore officially acknowledged that there are state administration jobs open to the practice of patronage by political parties. In contrast, the majority of state administration positions are to be filled on the basis of professionalism, impartiality and political independence. Second, between 2001 and 2004, Slovakia carried out a comprehensive reform of its public administration which introduced elected regional governments and devolved significant powers from the state to the elected regional and local government. Even though 'hard' evidence is not available, there are good reasons to assume that the scope of patronage has decreased since then. However, the decline has not been universal. While the importance of patronage in the horizontal state administration (national-level state administration) has declined, it is still widespread in the vertical state administration (that is, at the regional and district levels). Moreover, contrary to the pre-2001 practices, patronage positions are now in practice recognized by law.

Various accounts of Slovak politics in the 1990s mention the practices of the 1994–98 administration, led by the HZDS, as an exemplary case of party patronage linking state building and party building. Before 1994, the HZDS was a loosely organized entity composed of various ideological streams and interests, united only by a popular and charismatic leader. The party suffered two major defections of groups of parliamentarians in 1994, only to win the elections in late 1994 after six months in opposition. After that, the HZDS embarked upon a far-reaching organizational transformation: it stabilized its organizational structure, introduced individual membership, and announced its goal of transforming itself into a fully-fledged mass party. The party leadership was able to impose strict political discipline in the HZDS parliamentary group – not a single HZDS deputy left the party in the 1994–98 parliamentary cycle. During an infamous first regular parliamentary session after the 1994 elections, the HZDS (supported by its two junior coalition partners) launched an unprecedented purge of the horizontal state administration. In the course of a single night-long session all representatives of the opposition parties were removed from the national property fund, the supreme auditing office, and various supervisory bodies overseeing publicly owned mass media and other public institutions. Only HZDS and its allies nominated their representatives to these institutions.

Moreover, the HZDS-led government recalled about two-thirds of Slovakia's ambassadors and replaced a great many civil servants in top ministerial positions and all leading state officials at the regional and district level of state administration. Special committees composed of the representatives of the governing parties were created in all administrative districts. These committees served as political platforms where important patronage decisions at the local level were taken. The ruling political parties reportedly decided about appointments to all important positions within state institutions at the local level. According to the parliamentary opposition these changes represented the most extensive purges in the state apparatus since the regime change in 1989.[32]

The most radical form of party patronage, however, was enabled by the government's programme of administrative reform of the state. In 1996 the parliament increased the number of territorial districts from 38 to 79, and a new tier consisting of eight administrative regional units was added as well. Since the new territorial division did not bring about decentralization (new administrative units were part of the state administration subordinated to the central government), the measure was widely perceived as a tool for the HZDS and its allies to increase control over the state. Thanks to this administrative reform, the number of employees in the state administration sharply increased. The new positions were filled primarily by members of the three governing parties – or, alternatively, membership of one of them was in practice a precondition for getting the job.[33] Indirect evidence had also been provided by the HZDS itself: between 1995 and 1998, the claimed party membership increased from 28,000 to 70,000.[34]

Even though the HZDS received a plurality of votes in the 1998 elections, all its parliamentary opponents united and created a broad left–right coalition government. Parties of the new government soon embarked upon replacing HZDS-nominated civil servants with their own members. Again, the precise extent of these changes remains undocumented, although examples abound. The new minister of culture, for example, recalled all general directors of the ministry as well as directors of all state and public institutions active in the sphere of his ministry.[35] The new cabinet also recalled all top officials heading the regional and district-level state administration appointed by the HZDS-led coalition, and replaced them with individuals close to the respective parties of the government.

The frequent and massive purges in the national ministries stopped only after the 2001 civil service law was enacted. A special agency – the Civil Service Authority – was created to oversee the implementation of the act, with responsibilities for organizing competition for all permanent positions within the state administration. The authority was abolished in early 2006, however, because it was said to be ineffective and expensive; nevertheless, the principles of the civil service act were untouched. Originally, the number of political positions within the state administration (that is, positions where appointments could be made without competition) was to be kept at a minimum. Only the eight heads of the regional level of state administration were to be appointed by the government. All other positions in both the vertical and the horizontal state administration were to be filled by permanent civil servants without explicit party backing. In 2002 and 2003, however, the representatives of the new four-party coalition government agreed to increase the number of political positions. Moreover, it was not the line ministers but the cabinet as a whole who was to control appointments to the top positions in the specialized regional and district level state administration. In 2002, the new government also replaced the nominees of the two parties from the 1998–2002 government who were not represented in the new cabinet. Following a comprehensive reform launched in 2004, top positions in the specialized regional and district level state administration were again redistributed among nominees of the four governing parties.

According to the estimates of the ministry of interior, the new state administration reform should reduce the number of civil servants in the local state administration from 17,000 to about 10,000.[36] Nevertheless, doubts remain about the extent to which the vertical state administration has been truly depoliticized. There have been allegations that party patronage plays a decisive role even in appointments to the posts that are defined as non-political by the civil service act. For example, the Slovak daily *Pravda* reported in July 2004 that, even though all 46 directors of the labour and social affairs agencies operating at the district level of state administration were chosen in an open competition, most of them are members, nominees, or supporters of one of the parties represented in the government. No similar link was found between any of these top civil servants and parties of the parliamentary opposition.[37]

Two factors seem to explain why the use of party patronage has declined in the horizontal state administration but has remained significant and widespread in the vertical one. First, the parliamentary opposition heavily criticized the HZDS-led purges at the top level of national administration in late 1994. Had they wanted to maintain political credibility in the eyes of their voters after winning elections in the 1998, they could not have engaged in such extensive purges. The government, for example, recalled several top

HZDS officials-turned-ambassadors appointed in the last days of the Mečiar cabinet in 1998, but there were no changes comparable to those made in November 1994. Similarly, during 1994–98 the opposition strongly objected to the fact that it had no significant representation in important state institutions and in the bodies governing public broadcast media. After 1998, the parties of the parliamentary opposition were given a chance to appoint their nominees to these bodies. Hence, at the horizontal level of state administration, the patronage opportunities either decreased or have been shared more proportionally among all parliamentary parties.

In contrast, patronage in the vertical state administration remains widespread. These positions have been distributed almost exclusively among nominees of the parties in government. The capacity to appoint party members and activists to the top positions of the state administration at regional and district level remains an important asset of governing parties. One reason for this is that party nominees in the regional state administration serve as important contacts between the regional party organizations and the party leaders in charge of the ministries. These nominees, even though employed by the state, carry out important functions on behalf of the party that nominated them. Typically, they would arrange meetings of the top party representatives with local economic elites, organize educational activities for the party members in the region, and perform similar party-related tasks. As most Slovak political parties are organizationally underdeveloped and understaffed (especially at the local level), patronage opportunities increase the selective incentives that motivate otherwise inactive party members and activists. Patronage opportunities in the vertical state administration are therefore more valuable in this respect, since they help to maintain and activate party activities at the local level.

Conclusion

The state has played an indispensable role in the life of Slovak political parties since the beginning of the post-communist transformation. There have been three aspects of party–state relations that have made the state a crucial actor in creating and maintaining political parties. First, most parties that have been represented in the post-1989 parliaments did not originate in society but were established within the state institutions. Ambitious members of parliament and government often used their institutional positions to relaunch their political careers in internally created new political parties. Even though only electorally successful parties are eligible for direct state subsidies, leaders of new parties created in parliament between elections manage to gain access to important start-up resources available to members of parliaments and government.

Second, direct state subsidies were available to political parties since the very beginning of party development. Unchallenged by significant opponents, political parties have systematically increased the amount of direct state subsidies available to them. These increases have been paralleled by only symbolic changes to the largely ineffective control mechanism of party finances.

Third, party patronage remains an important asset in the hands of parties in government. Political positions within the regional state administration remain particularly important as selective incentives, often used by parties to invigorate their otherwise understaffed and inactive sub-national party units. Compared with the 1990s, however, the number of patronage positions within the horizontal state administration has decreased, and in some institutions party nominations have been distributed more proportionally among all parliamentary parties. Changes of the early 2000s included a major overhaul of the public administration in 2001–4 and the civil service act reforms of 2001–3, and these indicate that a substantial de-politicization of the state is possible even in a situation of growing fragmentation of the parliament, a finding that contradicts the predictions of an influential explanatory model.[38] However, more research is needed to confirm whether patronage by Slovak parties has been indeed confined to the political positions officially singled out by the new legislation, or whether parties exert hidden influence over appointments that should be filled by independent and professional civil servants.

It is interesting to note that access to substantial state resources does not guarantee party survival in the rather volatile context of Slovak party politics. Even though parties represented in the Slovak parliament have consistently increased the amount of money they receive from the state budget, and have exploited opportunities offered by indirect state resources, stabilization of the party system remains unattained. New parties have succeeded in securing parliamentary representation, but established parties have failed to do so. Therefore, despite the significant role that the state plays in the party development process Slovakia, parties' access to state resources has not led to the emergence of a party cartel preventing new political forces from entering the political stage.

NOTES

1. See Richard S. Katz and Peter Mair, 'Changing Models of Party Organization and Party Democracy: The Emergence of the Cartel Party', *Party Politics*, Vol.1, No.1 (1995), pp.5–28.
2. See, for example, Richard Gunther and Larry Diamond, 'Types and Functions of Parties', in Larry Diamond and Richard Gunther (eds.), *Political Parties and Democracy* (Baltimore, MD and London: Johns Hopkins University Press, 2001).
3. The Communist Party of Slovakia was a territorial branch of the Communist Party of Czechoslovakia (KSČ). The KSČ was federalized in 1991, with the Party of Democratic

Left as its Slovak component and the Communist Party of Bohemia and Moravia (KSČM) constituting its Czech equivalent; in 1992 the federation of the two parties was dissolved.

4. The VPN and OF used the communist-era constitutional provisions and, on the basis of an agreement with the communist regime representatives, nominated ('co-opted') their own people into the federal and state parliaments even before the free elections were held. These 'co-optations' were made possible because many members of these legislatures were forced to give up their parliamentary seats.
5. Darina Malová and Kevin Deegan Krause, 'Parliamentary Party Groups in Slovakia', in Knut Heidar and Ruud Koole (eds.), *Parliamentary Party Groups in European Democracies: Political Parties Behind Closed Doors* (London: Routledge, 2000).
6. The ZRS was a member of the 1994–98 coalition government.
7. The PSNS was a breakaway faction from the Slovak National Party (a junior coalition member in 1994–98); the SF split from the Slovak Democratic and Christian Union (the senior coalition member since 2002) in 2003.
8. The SOP became a member of the government in 1998; the KSS was elected to the parliament for the first time in 2002.
9. For the argument see Paul G. Lewis, 'Party Funding in Post-Communist East–Central Europe', in Peter Burnell and Allan Ware (eds.), *Funding Democratization* (Manchester: Manchester University Press, 1998), p.150.
10. Author's interview with Braňo Ondruš, deputy chairman of the Party of Democratic Left, 2001.
11. Geoffrey Pridham, 'Transnational Party Links and Transition to Democracy: Eastern Europe in Comparative Perspective', in Paul G. Lewis (ed.), *Party Structure and Organization in East–Central Europe* (Cheltenham: Edward Elgar, 1996), p.201.
12. See Erik Láštic, 'Parties and Government in Slovakia: A Fatal Attraction?', in Oľga Gyarfášová and Grigorij Mesežnikov (eds.), *Party Government in Slovakia: Experience and Perspectives* (Bratislava: Institute for Public Affairs, 2004), pp.101–12.
13. See Shaun Bowler, Elisabeth Carter and David M. Farrell, 'Changing Party Access to Elections', in Bruce E. Cain, Russell J. Dalton and Susan E. Scarrow (eds.), *Democracy Transformed? Expanding Political Opportunities in Advanced Industrial Democracies* (Oxford: Oxford University Press, 2003), pp.81–101.
14. For a detailed discussion of the financial consequences of the change see Láštic, 'Parties and Government in Slovakia'.
15. According to a HZDS deputy the party voted against the proposal primarily because it was proposed by the government: see Zuzana Petková, 'Na stranícke účty dajú ľudia miliardu', *Pravda* (Bratislava), 5 Feb. 2005.
16. The creation of a new parliamentary party group in the period between elections requires approval by parliament; the new party group must consist of at least eight parliamentarians.
17. KDH was a founding member of the Slovak Democratic Coalition; however, owing to a new electoral law that effectively banned coalition of parties from taking part in the elections, the SDK was transformed into a new party and contested elections on behalf of the founding parties. The KDH parliamentary faction was restored in 2000 after its members left the SDK parliamentary party group.
18. See Petr Kopecký, 'Political Parties and the State in Post-Communist Europe: The Nature of Symbiosis', in this collection.
19. See Milan Čič and others, *Komentár k Ústave Slovenskej Republiky* (Martin: Vydavateľstvo Matice slovenskej, 1997).
20. See *Informácia o predložení výročných finančných správ politických strán a politických hnutí za rok 1998: Materiál č. 256* (Bratislava: Národná Rada SR, June 1999).
21. See Zuzana Wienk, 'Financovanie politických strán', in Emília Sičáková-Beblavá (ed.), *Korupcia a protikorupčná politika na Slovensku* (Bratislava: Transparency International Slovensko, 2005), pp.173–87.
22. See 'Strany si pridelili opäť viac peňazí', in *SME*, 5 Feb. 2005.
23. See Jon Pierre, Lars Svasand and Andreas Widfeldt, 'State Subsidies to Political Parties: Confronting Rethoric with Reality', *West European Politics*, Vol.23, No.3 (2000), pp.1–24.

24. See Wienk, 'Financovanie politických strán', p.184.
25. See Emília Sičáková-Beblavá and Daniela Zemanovičová, *Politické strany a financie: tajomstvo alebo dôvera?* (Bratislava: Transparency International Slovensko, 2002), esp. pp.23–8.
26. See Wolfgang C. Müller, 'Patronage by National Government', in Jean Blondel and Maurizio Cotta (eds.), *The Nature of Party Government: A Comparative European Perspective* (Basingstoke: Palgrave, 2000), pp.141–60.
27. See Connor O'Dwyer, 'Runaway State Building: How Political Parties Shape States in Post-communist Eastern Europe', *World Politics*, Vol.56, July 2004, p.521.
28. Láštic, 'Parties and Government in Slovakia', p.108.
29. See Anna Grzymała-Busse and Pauline Jones Luong, 'Reconceptualizing the State: Lessons from Post-Communism', *Politics and Society*, Vol.30, No.4 (2002), pp.529–54.
30. See Anna Grzymała-Busse, 'Political Competition and the Politicization of the State in East Central Europe', *Comparative Political Studies*, Vol.36, No.10 (2003), pp.1123–47, and O'Dwyer, 'Runaway State Building'.
31. O'Dwyer, 'Runaway State Building', pp.531–4.
32. See for example 'SDL': Slovensko ohrozujú akčné pätky', *SME*, 17 Jan. 1995; 'Šimko prečítal v NR SR zoznam akčných pätiek vládnej koalície', *SME*, 13 May 1995.
33. Viktor Nižňanský, 'Verejná správa', in Martin Bútora (ed.), *Slovensko 1996: Súhrnná správa o stave spoločnosti a trendoch na rok 1997* (Bratislava: Inštitút pre verejné otázky, 1997), pp.59–70.
34. Mária Ondruchová, *Organizácia politických strán a hnutí na Slovensku* (Bratislava: Inštitút pre verejné otázky, 2000), p.52.
35. See 'Kňažko uskutočnil personálne zmeny a tvrdí, že budú verejné konkurzy, HZDS hovorí o čistkách', *SME*, 6 Nov. 1998.
36. See 'Okresné úrady sú zrušené, nahradia ich iné', *SME*, 15 Dec. 2003.
37. 'Koaličné strany si rozdelili úrady práce', *Pravda* (Bratislava), 30 July 2004.
38. O'Dwyer, 'Runaway State Building'.

From Private Organizations to Democratic Infrastructure: Political Parties and the State in Estonia

ALLAN SIKK

The changing relationship between political parties and the state in modern democracies has been a major topic in party studies at least since the seminal article on cartel parties by Richard Katz and Peter Mair.[1] Their propositions have triggered considerable reaction in terms of both criticism[2] and their application to party politics in the post-communist democracies.[3] While the cartelization hypothesis focuses primarily on the role of public party financing in shaping the relationship between political parties and the state, recent accounts have widened the scope of research to analyse further dimensions in this relationship as well as the status of parties more conceptually.[4]

This article analyses the developments in the status of political parties in Estonia since the country regained independence and held its first parliamentary elections in 1992. While competitive politics and principally free and fair elections were introduced much earlier (arguably already in 1989), the first political parties act was passed only in 1994. Although earlier developments could be illuminating, the present article focuses more narrowly on the status of political parties since the time they gained a specific status in legal terms.

In general, political parties have undergone a clear development from being basically private NGOs with relatively little state regulation to being 'public utilities'[5] that are seen as an essential part of political life and regulated heavily. The trend has been consistent and several remarkable changes have occurred in slightly more than a decade. The increasing interconnectedness of political parties and the state has, somewhat surprisingly, not been inhibited by the liberal nature of Estonian politics and economics. This could indeed indicate that political parties are increasingly seen as 'public utilities'. Even the staunchest liberals believe that the free economic market needs a legal infrastructure for its functioning; similarly, political parties are seen as a necessary 'democratic infrastructure' for the smooth functioning of a liberal and representative democracy.

We begin with a short overview of Estonia's electoral and party system. This is followed by a discussion of the role of political parties in a post-communist country that has a small population and has undergone a period of dramatic changes. As regards the latter, Estonia has faced more changes than some other post-communist countries. For example, in contrast to those that were independent during the communist era, Estonia has faced the enormous task of building up many state institutions from scratch.[6] I will argue that these factors lead us to expect a particular relationship between the political parties and the state.

The second half of the article considers empirically the three dimensions of the state–party relationship put forward by van Biezen and Kopecký: the dependence of parties on the state (in terms of public financing), the management of parties by the state (in terms of regulations regarding political parties), and parties' control of the state (in terms of patronage over administrative appointments).[7] The analysis is developed around two main topics: the development of direct public subsidies to political parties and the relationship between political parties and public offices. Regarding the latter, the study uses data on the career paths of MPs and ministers in Estonia since 1992 to analyse the movement of people from political to bureaucratic positions and vice versa during a period of 13 years. It is shown that members of the administrative elite have entered the political elite at a higher rate than vice versa. The political recruitment of bureaucrats and the appointment of political figures into administrative positions may be somewhat related to the 'personification' of small country politics and administration[8] rather than being simply an indication of patronage. The essay concludes with an analysis of the debates on the political neutrality of the most senior civil servants – county governors and secretaries-general of ministries. The developments regarding these positions have been divergent: while the political neutrality of secretaries-general was rather settled by 2005, the county governors had principally changed from being non-partisan civil servants to clearly political appointees.

Political Parties and the State: Legal Status and Legacies

Since becoming independent in 1991, Estonia has used a system of proportional representation with a five per cent national threshold to elect Riigikogu (the national parliament). This system has led to a rather fragmented party system. Still, the number of parties entering parliament has decreased somewhat: the effective number of parliamentary parties declined from 5.9 in 1992 to 4.7 in 2003. The party systems of post-communist countries have usually been considered unstable and showing at best only slight signs of stabilization and consolidation. The traditional measures of party system stability, such as electoral volatility and programmatic competition, likewise would depict the Estonian party system as only partially consolidated.

However, the 'menu' of nationally viable parties changed surprisingly little from 1992 to 2003. The vote shares of parties have swung dramatically at times, but often only to change direction again in the following elections. The programmatic profile of some parties has changed, yet the ranks of key politicians remained largely constant throughout the decade. Only the parliamentary election of 2003 brought with it a genuinely new party, Res Publica, whose sudden rise seemed to undermine the previous relative persistence of the party system.[9] All other major parties or their direct predecessors had been present in politics since 1992. These include the moderately leftist Centre Party under the charismatic leadership of Edgar Savisaar; the market liberal Reform Party, which has participated in all coalitions since 1999; the national-conservative Pro Patria Union; the rural People's Union (with elements of the once powerful but now defunct Coalition Party); and the Social Democrats, formerly called the Moderates.[10] While the parties are ideologically distinct and differ in their social bases of support, ideology has not been a decisive factor in coalition-making. The Moderates have participated in right-wing coalitions under Mart Laar (Pro Patria Union), and remarkable differences in economic programmes have not impeded the Centre Party and Reform Party from sharing governmental responsibilities. In fact, there are very few inconceivable coalition combinations in Estonia today.

The Estonian perception of the role of parties and their relationship to the state does not simply reflect the status of parties in modern democracies, but has particularities that can be traced to the recent transition from communism and its legacies. These will be discussed below. In addition, Estonia poses an interesting question about the status of political parties in a small country. The question of whether parties should be primarily private or public organizations was extensively discussed in the parliamentary debates preceding the passing of the political parties act in 1994. The eventual version of the law saw them mostly as private organizations – the law was basically an addendum to the non-profit associations act, with a few added regulations. In matters not covered by the political parties act, parties were subject to the same legal provisions as NGOs (that is, as private organizations).[11]

Since then, the political parties act has been amended on several occasions and considerably increased in length and scope. Political parties have come to face many more restrictions and requirements, including those related to financial income and its declaration (discussed below). Also, the number of members required for the registration of a party has been quite high since 1996, set at 1,000 (more than 0.1 per cent of adult citizens). Originally that implied presenting membership lists upon registration, but since March 2002 the lists have become public and are constantly updated. If the number of members falls below 1,000, the party faces liquidation. Hence, Estonian parties have become much more publicly regulated institutions than they used to be. After successive amendments, the political parties act had become so lengthy and confusing that drafting a completely new law was debated before another round of revisions in 2003. That new law would certainly have seen a weakening of the status of parties as NGOs of a special kind and a strengthening of their status as public institutions.

The most important privilege granted to Estonian parties is their virtually exclusive right to the political representation – and even political organization – of citizens at the national level. Both the initial political parties act and the parliamentary debates preceding it were guided by the idea that if an organization wants to be engaged in politics, or have any political aims at all, it has to be registered as a party. The status of political parties was strengthened by the ban on electoral coalitions introduced in 1998 that applied both to coalitions composed of two or more parties and to any ad hoc coalitions. Since the 1999 parliamentary elections, only officially registered parties may run in national elections alongside individual candidates, who are effectively subject to more restrictive electoral rules. A proposed further ban on party and ad hoc electoral coalitions at the local level has been a subject of a lengthy controversy. The parliament adopted the respective changes to the local elections act in March 2002, but at the time of writing these have twice been overturned by the Supreme Court.[12]

The privileges for parties can partly be explained by a pragmatic wish to exclude non-partisan actors from the electoral competition, but some more objective reasons have been significant as well. The main reasoning behind the ban on coalitions has been the strengthening of political accountability. Clearly, electoral coalitions are temporary organizations, and accountability can dissolve among their constituent parts. On the other hand, Estonia has also seen once powerful parties simply dissolve after a spell in power. The most remarkable case was that of the Coalition Party, which became the most powerful actor in the 1995 parliament and fielded two prime ministers, only to almost fade from the scene in 1999 and disband two years later. This step was hailed as an honourable one by some of the party's members – that the party did not stick to power after completing its mission (whatever that was). But the fate of the Coalition Party was also somewhat notorious because its term in power was tainted by numerous corruption scandals. These included bringing down Prime Minister Tiit Vähi, who has since become one of the wealthiest entrepreneurs in Estonia. While the present strict membership requirements for parties should in principle enhance the prospects of accountability, even the publication of membership lists has not made them thoroughly trustworthy.[13]

A more implicit and ideational reason for strengthening the role of political parties can be related to communist legacies. During Soviet times, non-communist political organizations were acting underground. In a multiparty democracy, a non-party political actor can be seen as a phenomenon of a previous era, as there are no longer any restrictions on the establishment of genuine political parties instead of looser organizations. On the other hand, the Soviet-era communist party was pervasive in government affairs. Many members of the post-independence political and administrative elite spent their formative years under such a system and are possibly still tied to the mentality. While having learned the basic democratic principles and being in favour of a multi-party system, they can perceive the playground of governing parties in very broad terms. The multiplicity of parties can be seen as a safeguard against a permanent penetration of single parties into state structures, but parties currently in government can be seen by many as temporarily all-powerful in the public realm.

Even though some parties and individuals are less tainted by communist socialization, their incentives are formed with reference to the expected behaviour of older elites. The governing parties after the 1992 elections were idealistic and young, or had a fiercely anti-communist background, and possibly had a different conception of political parties. Yet, they always faced a risk of being voted out of office and replaced by elites of a different persuasion – as indeed happened in 1995. Therefore, they had to ensure maximum impact before others acquired any. To some extent that led to a vicious circle – administrative elites were often replaced on the pretext of getting rid of the politicized persons in the civil service – whether or not the old appointments actually were partisan or the new ones were not. The line between correcting the old wrongdoings and new misconduct has often been fine and the two may sometimes coincide.

The dynamics of the democratic transition have also strengthened the possibility of parties' penetration of the state, especially in the 1990s. On the one hand, many decisions had to be made that shaped the future of the country, possibly for decades. Several senior officials had to be appointed virtually for the first time, especially as the building of state structures often started from scratch,[14] and a campaign of decommunization swept through the ministries. Most other post-communist countries did not share one of the conditions: the Central European countries did not start with a clean sheet of institutions, and in contrast to Estonia most of the former communist parties have retained positions in their country's party politics. Here, most of the parties in the 2005 parliament have been present there since the early 1990s and some of them were responsible for creating the state institutions. In effect, the parties can be considered to be an endogenous factor in state-building. Thus, the institutional setup of the country and its staffing policies may well reflect the interests of political parties that created them.

Furthermore, the parties in power in the early 1990s were probably aware of the prospect of electoral backlash that only strengthened their willingness to leave a strong impact on the state quickly and appoint people from their own circles to influential administrative positions. The latter was of course preferably done covertly to enhance the chances of outliving the government. However, even in cases when appointees' party political background was evident, once in office these individuals acquired unparalleled and highly needed experience and developed strong networks, making them difficult to replace by successive governments. Most of the old cadre had fallen prey to the decommunization efforts or were just considered incompetent for serving in the administration of a democratic country. Thus, there was a lack of well-trained administrative counter-elite. Many senior civil servants lacked the appropriate training as well, but they had had a chance to acquire necessary skills while in office.

These phenomena have only been strengthened by the small population of Estonia.[15] It has been argued that the public administration of small countries differs qualitatively from that of larger countries as personal relationships connect more people and there is a lack of a reserve cadre of specialists; this results in a tendency of 'personification' of the civil service.[16] In turn, mixing politics with the civil service can become a more widespread and even more accepted practice for pragmatic reasons because able people are often in short supply.

An example illuminating the above discussion is posed by Indrek Tarand. Once a governmental adviser and a special envoy to north-eastern Estonia (where ethnic tensions were high in the early 1990s), he subsequently became the secretary-general of the ministry of foreign affairs in 1994. He stayed there until 2002, and was largely behind the building up of Estonia's foreign service. Tarand was mostly well liked in the ministry and, despite problems with his public image (including drunk driving in 2002), he managed to hold on thanks to his good relationship with the ministry's staff and his experience in Estonian foreign policy matters until 2002.

In general, while Estonian bureaucratic structures can be considered to have become relatively settled by 2005, recent developments could bring important changes. Estonia's accession to the EU has changed the relative importance of institutions and has even created new organizational structures. For instance, financial control and agricultural support agencies have gained importance. Thus, one of the largest new institutions in the country is the Estonian Agricultural Registers and Information Board; the staff of the ministry of agriculture has increased considerably.[17] At the same time, some institutions such as the Bank of Estonia and others in areas where more power will be delegated to Brussels (or Frankfurt, for that matter) might lose importance in the bureaucratic hierarchy. Thus, one might foresee continued state-building that may provide interesting cases for the study of the relationship between political parties and state structures.[18]

Public Financing of Political Parties

As noted above, the legal status of political parties in Estonia has changed from private organizations to public institutions. The same tendency can be seen in the party-financing regime: there has been a notable shift towards increased state financing of parties complemented by restrictions on private contributions to party coffers. Also, public financing has been rather biased in favour of established parliamentary parties. This has helped them to become institutionalized and made it harder for external or new contenders to rival them.

Estonia has a relatively advanced system of public party funding. The principle of state budget subventions to political parties was introduced in the original political parties act of 1994. It became effective in 1996, because it was decided that using the party composition of parliament before the 1995 elections would be too confusing: most MPs elected in 1992 were running in electoral coalitions, sometimes not affiliated to any parties, and many had changed camps during the parliamentary term.[19]

However, it is important to note that the will to introduce state financing was there some years before it was actually put into effect.

Initially, public financing was introduced following foreign examples (such as Germany), with the aim of limiting the undue influence of other sources of financing, including both corrupt corporate donations and foreign donations. The latter were seen as problematic because of the inflows from both the East and the West. Donations from the East would have been self-evidently controversial in 1993 as there was a reasonable fear of Russian penetration into Estonian party politics.[20] Western money was not well liked by the parties that lacked strong contacts with foreign parties or political foundations: German, Swedish, British and European parties were rather strongly supporting parties of the centre-right.

Estonia witnessed a significant increase in the total state of subventions to political parties after 1996: the total level of subsidies has increased more than tenfold (see Table 1). The sharpest increase came in 2004 when public financing of political parties increased threefold, with the introduction of significant restrictions on private financing (see below).

Calculating the share of public financing of total party income is difficult because reporting on routine income has until recently been inadequate. The share of public subsidies in campaign finance reports (that are submitted more satisfactorily) is very low: some parliamentary parties have not listed the state budget as a source of income there at all. Therefore, Figure 1 charts the rise in public subsidies against the increase in reported campaign spending. Both have had markedly higher growth rates than national GDP (which increased only 1.65 times between 1996 and 2004, according to the Statistical Office of Estonia, reporting in 2005). During the first electoral cycle after the introduction of public subsidies, campaign expenditures grew at approximately the same rate as the subsidies. Even though the campaign expenditures in 1999 were higher compared with 'year zero' than public donations, some campaign activities started already in 1998 when public subsidies were higher than before (the elections always take place in early March). Yet, by 2003, growth in

TABLE 1
PUBLIC SUBSIDIES TO POLITICAL PARTIES, ESTONIA, 1996–2004

	1996	1997	1998	1999	2000	2001	2002	2003	2004	2005
Million euro	*0.32*	0.64	0.84	*0.54*	1.02	1.28	*1.28*	**1.28**	3.83	*3.83*
€ per registered voter*	*0.40*	0.81	1.07	*0.63*	1.19	1.49	*1.49*	**1.49**	4.46	*4.46*

Notes: In bold – the years of parliamentary elections, in italics – the years of local elections.
    * In 1995, 1999, 2003.

Sources: Sven Mikser, 'Eesti kogemus erakondade rahastamisel', *Riigikogu Toimetised* (2001), No.4, pp.22–6; State Budget Law 2003, 2004 and 2005.

FIGURE 1
REPORTED CAMPAIGN EXPENDITURES AND PUBLIC FUNDING OF POLITICAL
PARTIES, ESTONIA, 1995–2004 (1995, 1996 = 100)

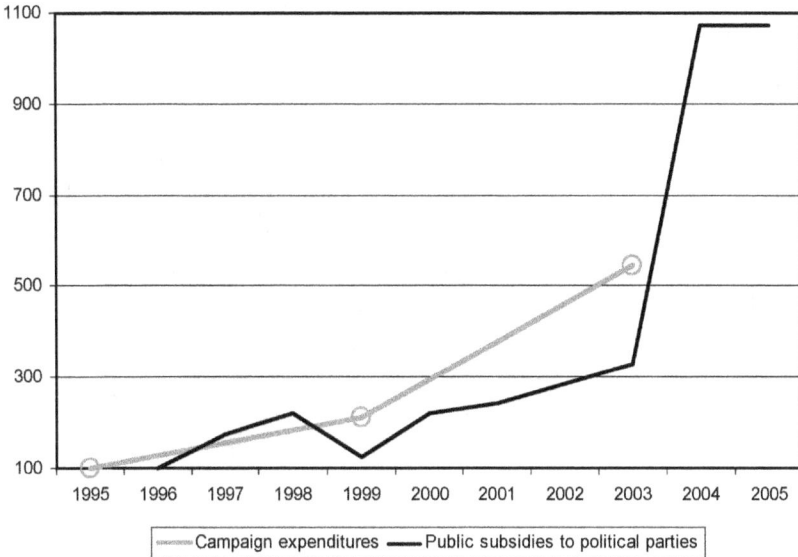

Note: Parliamentary elections took place in March 1995, 1999 and 2003, indicated by dots.
Source: Allan Sikk, 'Party Financing Regimes and Emergence of New Parties in Latvia and
Estonia', paper presented at the ECPR Joint Session of Workshops, Uppsala, 13–18
April 2004, updated.

campaign expenditures had clearly surpassed the increase in public subsidies.
That is partly a consequence of a new big spender, Res Publica, that was at
the time excluded from receiving subsidies from the state budget (since it
was not yet represented in parliament). The trend has probably reversed since
2003 as public funding of political parties has surged. It is unlikely that
future levels of campaign expenditure will keep pace with public subsidies as
they have already been high by international standards.

More information on the breakdown of parties' sources of income has been
available since 2002, when routine reporting became more regular. Figure 2
shows a sudden increase in party incomes related to parliamentary elections
(2003, first quarter). The year 2004 saw a slight increase in total party
income compared with the other period without national elections, 2002. This
increase is primarily due to the sharp increase in public subsidies for political
parties. Donations from other sources actually declined for most parliamentary
parties compared with 2002. For some quarters in 2004, several parties reported
only a few hundred euros of income from sources other than the state budget.

FIGURE 2
TOTAL REPORTED INCOME AND % OF PUBLIC FINANCING, 2002–4

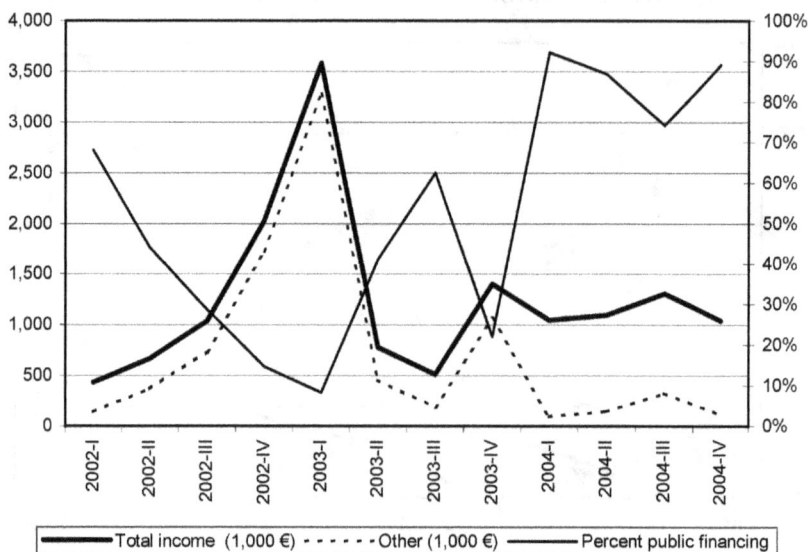

Note: Only parliamentary parties as of 2005.
Source: Author's calculations based on party financial declarations.

The shift towards higher levels of public financing in 2004 was accompanied by a major restriction regarding financing from other sources: all corporate donations were banned. The influence of this change was rapidly seen in the last quarter of 2003 – corporate donations to all political parties increased considerably before the amendment came into effect (see Figure 2).

While membership fees are rather insignificant as a source of income for most political parties – one parliamentary party has no membership fee at all – individual donations by MPs and MEPs have increased considerably. That is routine practice in all parliamentary parties bar the Reform Party.[21] Even though these contributions do not constitute a major element in party income, they strengthen the relationship between political parties and their office holders, and this in turn strengthens party cohesion. Generous subventions by parties' top politicians who receive substantial salaries from the state can also be considered a type of indirect subsidy that further strengthens the link between the parties and the state.

Public party financing in Estonia is based on the number of seats, which is rather different from parties' vote shares in national elections as the electoral formula used is a disproportional modification of the d'Hondt method.

Distribution of public financing based on votes rather than seats has been discussed at times, but the only amendment put forward in this direction was revoked before it took effect. Only parties reaching the five per cent national threshold have been eligible for public financing. An exception was introduced in 2003 for parties receiving at least one per cent of the national vote: they currently receive some funding from the state, but that is very small compared with the subventions to parliamentary parties, in both absolute terms and per vote. In 2005, the two largest parties in parliament received slightly over eight euros for each vote won in the 2003 election; the smallest parliamentary party received over six euros per vote. The two parties not represented in parliament but eligible for public subsidies received only 0.7 and 1.8 euros per vote. The difference in absolute numbers is even more drastic. The formula for distributing subsidies strengthens the larger parties that have also been more instrumental in governments, further strengthening the linkage between the state and political parties.

A striking case of fusion between political parties and the state concerns the submission of campaign finance declarations. The issue concerning which government institution should be charged with receiving parties' campaign declarations was debated both before the passing of the original political parties act and during the substantial amendment of the act in 2003. Until 2004, the campaign declarations were submitted to the national electoral commission, although the latter did not have enough administrative resources to check them effectively. From 2004, the function was transferred to the parliamentary select committee on the application of the anti-corruption act. This has been criticized because it leads to a situation where the parties effectively check their own declarations. Submitting the declarations to the state auditor has also been discussed, but the idea was rejected as this might divert attention away from the state auditor's main tasks. Ultimately parliamentary transcripts show that the decision about which institution should be responsible for party financial declarations was taken with relative haste. The change is indicative of the still blurred boundaries between political parties and the state. Indeed, the Estonian political parties receive 3.8 million euros a year – that is probably the largest support allocated from the state budget without any guidelines on how to use the money and no effective inspection on whether the parties fulfil the regulations set out in the political parties act. Furthermore, it gives a favoured position to the parties represented in the parliament compared with extra-parliamentary parties, independent candidates and local electoral coalitions.

Political Parties and Public Officials

A further aspect of fusion of political parties with state institutions is political patronage – the appointment of party members to administrative positions or appointments that are simply politically motivated. Such politicization can take place at both national and local levels. Political parties may also possess appointment powers beyond the public administration, extending to directors of public companies and different semi-public institutions, including directors of public broadcasting companies and quangos. However, certain public institutions can be fundamentally beyond the reach of direct party political influence. A good example is public universities in Estonia, where rectors are elected by electoral colleges composed of university professors and student representatives.

In this section I concentrate mainly on the circulation of individuals among political and administrative positions at the central government level, but in doing so I do not argue that all or even most patronage takes place at this level. Since patronage is presumably controversial, if not outright unpopular, the most striking cases of patronage take place more covertly. By covertly, I mean two things. First, such patronage takes place where it is less visible – the central government is a rather poor place for conducting controversial partisan appointments. Rather, it can take place in local governments, and be related to less significant appointments. For example, before the 2005 local elections, the incumbent mayor of Tartu was accused of appointing school heads who only a few months later agreed to run on her party's list. Second, the party affiliation of appointees may often be very well hidden. Certainly, some of these individuals have never run in an election for 'their' party, let alone have they been MPs or cabinet ministers. A typical example of that are senior career bureaucrats who are loyal to one or another party but not card-carrying members of it;[22] another example might be businessmen related to certain political parties who get appointed either to senior civil service positions or to directorships of publicly owned companies.

I have chosen to concentrate only on the tip of the iceberg – the career paths of members of the political elite – for two reasons. First, the data on the more covert instances are not available or are anecdotal. Second, as will be shown, looking at the issue from the perspective of the political elite's career paths reveals an interesting phenomenon: while (former) members of the political elite in Estonia have often been appointed to administrative positions, it has been more common for political parties to recruit new elite members from the ranks of civil servants. While in most cases such practices cannot be regarded as patronage (however, sometimes they can: see below), this should be seen as another kind of strong linkage between political parties and the state administration. It is a link that corroborates well the finding that in small countries the mixing of politics and civil service can be surprisingly widespread not because of patronage but because of the pragmatic need to find competent and experienced people willing to run for political office.[23]

Circulation of Political and Administrative Elites

The figures presented in Table 2 are derived from a newly compiled database containing information on the public careers of all MPs and cabinet ministers from 1992 to 2005, a total of 361 individuals. The list has been checked against the telephone directories covering public officials (*Riigitelefon*: The State Telephone). These volumes contain information on parliament, ministries, county governments, courts, local governments and various other governmental bodies (inspectorates, boards, foundations, universities and public companies). The books cover a few top levels for all institutions; in the case of ministries this usually includes secretaries-general, their deputies, and heads of department. For some ministries, even some lower levels were covered – but that was not the case with the ministries of foreign affairs and defence. Below, the category of political elite (P) is composed of cabinet ministers, MPs, mayors and local council chairs.[24] The category of administrative elite (A) basically includes all other people listed in the telephone directories, thus covering all positions in these institutions (except for those included in the category of political elite). In principle, almost all of these are supposed to be non-political administrative positions. However, in a limited number of cases it has been difficult to distinguish between political and non-political advisers at ministries; in these cases the author's discretion has been used. Also excluded from the category are university rectors and vice-rectors, who are also listed in *Riigitelefon* but appointed internally.

TABLE 2
CAREER PATTERNS OF POLITICAL AND ADMINISTRATIVE ELITE

Career pattern	Number (%*) of persons	% cabinet ministers therein
P	295 (–)	23
P → A	13 (20)	33
A → P	37 (57)	43
P → A → P	6 (9)	67
A → P → A	7 (11)	83
P → A → P → A	1 (2)	100
A → P → A → P	1 (2)	100
Total	360 (–)	48

Note: This table excludes positions in public universities and political advisers.
  * Among persons (65) who have been both in administrative (A) and political positions (P).

Source: Calculations based on author's database. For overview of the database, see text.

From 1992 to 2005, out of 360 people from the political elite (who had been MPs or ministers) 65 (18 per cent) had at other times served in administrative positions. Out of 328 MPs included in the database, 16 per cent had also served in public office at times, while the same figure for ministers was much higher: 34 per cent. The latter number seems especially high, and it would be even higher (40 per cent) if we included all ministerial advisers – some possibly non-political – and various academic positions: several members of political elite have served as rectors before or after holding political positions. It is telling that clearly more than a third of Estonia's cabinet ministers have also served in at least nominally non-political higher civil service positions. Yet, as some of the examples presented below will reveal, the circulation between political and administrative elites may at times not relate to patronage but rather to the recruitment strategies in small countries – when good people are in short supply, the bureaucracy and the parties cannot be too selective.

In the previous analysis the calculations were made regardless of whether the political career preceded or followed the administrative one. However, when tracking the patterns of succession, six different paths can be seen: first, there are politicians who have later become public officials $(P \rightarrow A)$; second, public officials can become politicians at a later stage $(A \rightarrow P)$; third, administrative positions may have been held in-between political positions $(P \rightarrow A \rightarrow P)$; or, fourth, vice versa $(A \rightarrow P \rightarrow A)$; the list is completed by instances of three changes in status $(P \rightarrow A \rightarrow P \rightarrow A$ and $A \rightarrow P \rightarrow A \rightarrow P)$. Note that I disregard here periods when the persons in question have held neither political nor administrative positions or when they changed their political or administrative positions. All other members of the political elite who have not held administrative positions form a residual category (P).

Table 2 gives an overview of such career patterns. It is notable that it has been much more common to enter politics after holding administrative positions than vice versa: the number of persons following the career pattern $A \rightarrow P$ more than twice outnumbers the opposite. When looking at particular persons in this category, cabinet ministers have been more numerous than in the opposite category of $P \rightarrow A$. Also, more than half of the people in the $A \rightarrow P$ group have been affiliated with two parties formed after the parliament elected in 1992: the Reform Party (established in 1994) and Res Publica (2002). That is not surprising, since senior civil servants are an appealing pool for finding experienced and well-known candidates for newly formed parties. The category of $P \rightarrow A$, on the other hand, mostly consist of people belonging to the 1992 parliament or corresponding cabinets. Nevertheless, the comparatively small number of people in this group compared with $A \rightarrow P$ is an indication that the intermingling of administrative and political elites has been much more connected to recruiting activities of political parties among civil servants than former politicians making their way into administration.[25]

Nearly a quarter of those who have held both political and administrative positions have changed their status more than once. Approximately half of these cases can be explained by technocratic cabinet nominations; the same applies to several people in the A → P category.[26] Other cases include senior people moving back and forth between administrative and political positions. Examples of this include Andres Lipstok, who after serving as county governor became minister of finance in 1994, and later a senior parliamentary figure for the Reform Party, but was appointed president of the Bank of Estonia in 2005. Another example is Trivimi Velliste, prominent in the independence movement from the late 1980s, who became an MP in 1992 and a cabinet minister in 1993; he later served for four years as a head of department in the ministry of foreign affairs, before re-joining parliament in 1999.

Two persons included in the database have managed two spells in the political and two in the administrative elite over the course of 13 years. One is Jüri Luik, who became the foreign minister in Europe in 1994 representing the Pro Patria party. Following the electoral defeat of the party in 1995, he served as an ambassador to the Benelux countries and NATO, but following the party's electoral success in 1999 he became minister of defence, only to return to the diplomatic ranks in 2004 as ambassador to United States. The other person in this category is Robert Lepikson, who has been a member of several parties. He entered politics after serving as a director of a publicly owned metal-exporting company and a deputy secretary-general at the ministry of defence, becoming the mayor of Tallinn and minister of the interior. Thereafter he served three years as a county governor, and then returned to parliament in 2003. The two cases reflect in fact two quite distinct variants of individuals moving between political and administrative positions. Luik is considered by many to be one of the most able ministers and diplomats in recent Estonian history. By contrast, Lepikson is often characterized as a political opportunist who has cleverly moved between administrative and political positions, and also from one party to another.

Regarding different political parties, the Reform Party stands out as the one with the most people (14) who have been members of both political and administrative elites. This is somewhat surprising given the party's business-friendly and occasionally libertarian stance. While the Reform Party has indeed recruited many of its MPs and ministers from the ranks of senior civil servants, the figure for the Coalition Party (11) may be surprisingly low, considering its relatively technocratic image. The divergence highlights an interesting difference in parties' recruitment practices. While the Coalition Party sometimes invited non-members to take cabinet posts, the standard practice of the Reform Party has been to make such appointments conditional on joining the party.

The Reform Party has also been remarkable in that several of its politicians have later been appointed to major public offices. In addition to the above-mentioned example of the central bank president, the current chief justice of the Supreme Court and the head of Estonian radio are former ministers for the Reform Party. That party has also proposed its MPs as 'candidates' for the offices of legal chancellor and state auditor when there has been a stalemate between the president – who nominates candidates for these offices – and parliament.[27]

When looking at the electoral experience of senior civil servants as of 2005 (Table 3), it is apparent that most of them have no electoral experience; thus in that respect the higher ranks of bureaucracy are supposedly non-partisan. While about one in ten has run for parliament, one in three has participated in local elections. Electoral experience is remarkably higher among county governors compared to other categories of top civil servants – more than a quarter of them have run for the parliament and almost two thirds for local councils. Around half of those contesting local elections have also been successful. At the same time, only one top civil servant in the database has previously been elected to the parliament. However, one should certainly not expect too strong links here, as competing in elections is clearly one of the most advanced ways of party political involvement. Still, the table highlights an interesting development in Estonia's civil service – the politicization of county governors.

Politicization of County Governors and Secretaries-General

The final sections of this article concentrate on one of the most central debates regarding the politicization of senior civil servant appointments: county

TABLE 3
EXPERIENCE WITH CONTESTING ELECTIONS, SENIOR CIVIL SERVANTS IN 2005

	Contested elections		
Category	Parliamentary (1992–2003)	Local (1993–2005)	Total
Secretaries general	1 (9%)	3 (27%)	11
Deputy secretaries general	2 (5%)	11 (28%)	39
County governors	4 (27%)	9 (60%)	15
Heads of executive government agency (*amet*)	3 (14%)	6 (27%)	22
Total*	11 (11%)	33 (34%)	98

* Includes some civil servants not listed in above categories.
Source: Author's database.

governors and secretaries-general in ministries. The 15 county governors and at present 11 secretaries-general are some of the highest-ranking civil servants in Estonia. Both have been the subject of extensive discussions regarding whether they should be party political appointments or politically neutral career officials. For some time the viewpoint was that they were supposed to be neutral. More recently, county governors have become subject to much more partisan appointments.

According to the government of the republic act, as amended in March 2004, the county governors are appointed by the government after being nominated by the minister of regional affairs. In addition, the prospective appointees require endorsement by the county organization of local governments, since the governors were seen as representatives of the central government at the county level and vice versa. Some of the nominees supported by the government have at times failed the latter test. However, the consent of local governments is not seen as obligatory; in other words, they are not seen to possess a direct veto power over nominations.

Open public competition for county governorship vacancies was introduced in 2004. The move followed tensions in the government over appointments that had led to a situation whereby most counties were run by acting governors (appointed for three months by the prime minister).[28] It became quite obvious that the issue was related to ensuring the balance of appointments among the coalition partners. This trend became public when in 2003 a list of candidates supported by one of the coalition partners was published in an Estonian daily newspaper.[29] Furthermore, three county governors nominated by the minister of regional affairs in October 2004 were members of the three parties that formed the government coalition at that time.[30]

The status of secretaries-general of ministries has also been subject to political controversy. That became especially acute after the 1999 elections when the newly formed coalition replaced five secretaries-general out of 12 in one month; later, several of them successfully challenged the decisions in court. So, in December 2000 an amendment was introduced to the public service act that enabled the government to replace secretaries-general on a minister's initiative if 'co-operation between the two fails' but not less than one year after the investiture of a minister. However, despite contrary fears, waves of replacement did not occur at the time: in fact, only two secretaries-general had been replaced by the end of 2005.

To some extent the problem for ministers with non-partisan, or hostile, secretaries-general was further eased by the introduction of the position of assistant minister in 2003.[31] Until then, the only political appointees in ministries were a couple of advisers; one of these has commonly not been an expert on the ministry's affairs, but a means of liaison between ministers and their party headquarters and parliamentary faction. Given the sometimes

wide scope of Estonian ministries,[32] the ministers working with less
co-operative secretaries-general have faced a situation where they had little
if any control over the work of the ministry.

The more politicized nature of county governors compared with
secretaries-general is also reflected by looking at the rate of joining politics
among the two groups. County governors have been entering politics very
actively in recent years. For example, in 2005, seven MPs and cabinet
ministers were governors as late as 2002. In other words, almost half of the
governors serving at that time subsequently entered politics. The same
applies to only one secretary-general.

A related debate has addressed the restrictions on party membership for
certain categories of public officials. In 1994, after intense debates and not
unanimously, some restrictions were introduced: the legal chancellor and
his or her advisers, higher civil servants of the state audit office, judges, pro-
secutors, police personnel, acting members of defence forces and border
guards were barred from being members of political parties. In 2003, the
restrictions were revoked (except for the defence personnel), but the
changes were delayed until 2008. The amendments faced considerable opposition in parliament because it was feared that the government might attempt
to 'partify by force' the officials in question. On the one hand, the amendments
do increase the personal freedom of public officials to organize politically, but,
on the other hand, doubts remain whether Estonian political culture is
sufficiently advanced so that the independence or impartiality of judges or
police personnel can be maintained.

Conclusion

The preceding discussion may leave an impression that close connections
between political and administrative elites are not justified from a normative
perspective. While this is probably true for many cases of party patronage,
the circulation of elites and the appointment of people with a political background may sometimes be justified and good for a country. As noted above,
in Estonia the circulation has more frequently occurred in the direction of political parties recruiting candidates from administrative circles. By doing so, the
parties and their policies clearly benefit from the expertise brought in. On the
other hand, a small country's civil service can sometimes not afford to be selective just because of the individuals' party background, as that may lead to
recruiting non-party people with poorer skills, knowledge or experience.

Whatever the normative implications, this study has demonstrated a close
and strengthening relationship between political parties and the state in
Estonia. That has been visible in different arenas. First, regarding the
parties' legal status, there has been a clear movement away from parties

being conceived of as specific NGOs to a conception of them as part of the 'democratic infrastructure'. The regulation of parties' internal life has increased – exemplified by strict membership requirements – and an exclusive role in national elections has been granted to political parties.

Second, since the introduction of public financing in 1996, Estonian parties have become markedly reliant on public subsidies. These subsidies have been biased in favour of larger parliamentary parties – those 'closest' to the state because of the more prominent role they play in governing coalitions. The recent ban on corporate donations has cut off the alternative source of funding that has dominated much of the post-independence period and substantially helped a recent successful new party to emerge.

Third, the circulation of individuals between senior administrative and political positions has been noteworthy. Interestingly, parties' recruitment of civil servants to fill political positions has been more common than has the nomination of political elite members into administrative offices. Both of these can be instances of party patronage, and there are good reasons to believe that it has been occurring. However, such close ties are not necessarily related to patronage in a traditional and entirely negative sense. A good deal of it can be attributed to the legacies of communism and the recent building up of state institutions in Estonia. Much of the Soviet-era cadre of civil servants was widely regarded as too unreliable or unskilled to serve the independent country. They were often replaced by persons with relatively little experience yet who were politically more trusted; the same applies even more to the institutions that were built up from scratch. Later, some had to leave office as their political masters changed. However, others became virtually irreplaceable owing to the unparalleled experience gained during their term in office. They were also 'helped' by the small size of the country, and the recent nature of independence, which both implied a weak or absent reserve pool of civil servants. These people often formed a basis on which a professional civil service could be established. However, the political neutrality of some categories of senior civil servants has been prone to change. Whereas in the mid-1990s secretaries-general of ministries were subject to clearly politically motivated appointments and withdrawals, they became less partisan by 2005. An opposite tendency can be seen regarding country governors, who have effectively become party political figures.

NOTES

1. Richard S. Katz and Peter Mair, 'Changing Models of Party Organization and Party Democracy: The Emergence of the Cartel Party', *Party Politics*, Vol.1, No.1 (1995), pp.5–28.
2. Herbert Kitschelt, 'Citizens, Politicians, and Party Cartellization: Political Representation and State Failure in Post-industrial Democracies', *European Journal of Political Research*,

Vol.37, No.2 (2000), pp.149–79; and Ruud Koole, 'Cadre, Catch-all or Cartel? A Comment on the Notion of the Cartel Party', *Party Politics*, Vol.2, No.4 (1996), pp.509–25.

3. Ingrid van Biezen and Petr Kopecký, 'On the Predominance of State Money: Reassessing Party Financing in the New Democracies of Southern and Eastern Europe', *Perspectives on European Politics and Society*, Vol.2, No.3 (2001), pp.401–29, Michal Klíma, 'Consolidation and Stabilization of the Party System in the Czech Republic', in Richard Hofferbert (ed.), *Parties and Democracy* (Oxford: Blackwell, 1998), pp.70–88; and Aleks Szczerbiak, 'Cartelization in Post-Communist Politics: State Party Funding in Post-1989 Poland', *Perspectives on European Politics and Society*, Vol.2, No.3 (2001), pp.431–51.

4. Ingrid van Biezen and Petr Kopecký, 'The State and the Parties: Public funding, public regulation and party patronage in contemporary democracies', paper prepared for the conference 'Political Parties and Political Development', National Democratic Institute, Washington DC, 31 Aug. 2005; Ingrid van Biezen, 'Political Parties as Public Utilities', *Party Politics*, Vol.10, No.6 (2004), pp.701–22; and Anna Grzymała-Busse, 'Political Competition and the Politicization of the State in East Central Europe', *Comparative Political Studies*, Vol.36, No.10 (2003), pp.1123–47.

5. The term has been proposed in Van Biezen, 'Political Parties as Public Utilities'.

6. Tiina Randma-Liiv, 'A Small Civil Service in Transition: The Case of Estonia', *Public Administration and Development*, Vol.21, No.1 (2001), pp.41–51.

7. Van Biezen and Kopecký 'The State and the Parties'.

8. Tiina Randma-Liiv, 'Small States and Bureaucracy: Challenges for Public Administration', *Trames*, Vol.6, No.4 (2002), pp.374–89.

9. At the time of writing, its fortunes have turned and the party is struggling near the five per cent threshold in opinion polls.

10. Although ethnic Russians comprise more than a quarter of Estonia's population, the ethnic dimension has faded in party politics since 1999. At present there are no Russian parties in the parliament and most major parties also try to mobilize ethnic Russian voters.

11. Interestingly, when presenting the draft Act to parliament, the minister of justice linked the special and semi-public status of political parties to the fact that other NGOs do not receive subventions from the state budget.

12. Elections in many smaller municipalities have been fought mostly or exclusively between electoral coalitions. Indeed, in municipalities with a few thousand voters, there would be a contradiction between the party membership requirement and ensuring genuine political competition. The amendments to the local elections act were also criticized as an attempt to 'partify' municipalities by force. The criticism was fuelled by the fact that coalitions were outlawed only six months before the 2002 local elections.

13. When the lists were publicized, many people found themselves listed without being aware of their membership. They were normally deleted from the lists. However, many probably remain ignorant even of the fact that the lists are public and will not have checked them (it is possible only over the internet). Not too much trust should be put in the membership lists. Some parties with the required number of members have failed to contest any elections. Also, there has been a party with a voter:membership ratio below one – despite fulfilling the membership criterion, the Russian Party in Estonia won less than 1,000 votes in the 2003 parliamentary elections.

14. Randma-Liiv, 'A Small Civil Service in Transition'.

15. The number of inhabitants was 1,347,510 in 2005: Statistical Office of Estonia, at <http://pub.stat.ee/px-web.2001/dialog/statfileri.asp>; accessed 18 June 2005. A considerable portion of adults are Russophone non-citizens; the number of adult citizens was only 859,714 in 2003: Vabariigi Valimiskomisjon (Estonian National Electoral Committee), at <http://www.vvk.ee>; accessed 30 Oct. 2005.

16. See Paul Sutton, 'Political Aspects', in C. Clarke and T. Payne (eds.), *Politics, Security and Development in Small States* (London: George Allen & Unwin, 1987), pp.3–25; and Randma-Liiv, 'Small states and bureaucracy'.

17. Very little assistance to farmers existed in Estonia prior to the accession to the EU, except for ad hoc support in case of drought or other adverse climate conditions.

POLITICAL PARTIES AND THE STATE IN ESTONIA

18. The ministries of agriculture and environment have received their share of attention regarding partisan-based nominations: Hindrek Riikoja, 'Rahvaliitlased on võtnud enda kätte põllumajandusvaldkonna juhtimise', *Postimees*, 31 Oct. 2005.
19. Until the political parties act of 1994, the parties were registered according to the civic unions' act, and were not differentiated from other NGOs.
20. That also led to the provision that Estonian parties could not form sub-units abroad, because of fear of the formation of divisions of Russian parties in Estonia.
21. Ülle Madise and Allan Sikk, 'Die Institution der politischen Partei in Estland', in D. Th. Tsatsos, D. Schefold and H.-P. Schneider (eds.), *Parteienrecht im europäischen Vergleich, Die Parteien in den demokratischen Ordnungen der Staaten der Europäischen Gemeinschaft*, 2nd edn (Baden-Baden: Nomos, forthcoming, 2006).
22. For such practices in Hungary see Jan Meyer-Sahling in this collection.
23. Randma-Liiv, 'Small states and bureaucracy', p.39.
24. The latter two categories only in cases when the person has also been in national political office.
25. However, the reasons for civil servants entering politics may be more complex, including the possibility of being afraid of losing their position after a change in government when they remain neutral or appear to be on the 'wrong' side of the political divide.
26. That mostly covers more recent cases, and some may join the civil service again in the future.
27. 'Reformierakond pakub Ignar Fjukki riigikontroloriks', *Eesti Päevaleht*, 28 Aug. 2002, 'Reformierakond pakub Tiit Käbinit õiguskantsleriks', *Eesti Päevaleht*, 22 Nov. 2000.
28. The regional minister threatened to resign over the issue, as the prime minister sometimes did not discuss the nominations of acting governors with him: Kalle Muuli, 'Minister Jaan Õunapuu ähvardas ametist lahkuda', *Postimees*, 5 Dec. 2003.
29. Ibid.
30. 'Õunapuu esitab kolm maavanema kandidaati', *Eesti Päevaleht*, 8 Oct. 2004.
31. As of October 2005, four assistant ministers were serving in Estonian ministries.
32. Estonia has a total of 11 ministries; the latest merger included the ministries of economics, and transport and communications.

The Influence of Party Patronage and State Finance on Electoral Outcomes: Evidence from Romania

While much has been written about the relationship of post-communist civil societies to the state, only recently has scholarship begun to examine the links between parties and the state.[1] The lack of literature in this area is surprising given, as Ganev argues, that the 'symbiosis of party and state was arguably the most important feature of communist political systems in Eastern Europe'.[2] Perhaps one of the reasons this relationship has not been more studied is the difficulty of operationalizing appropriate measures. While terms such as 'state capture' and 'clientelism' have been used to describe the party–state relationship, empirical measures for these phenomena are difficult to establish. However, this is an important literature for scholars to engage with, as it raises the question of whether the politicization of the state is a function of such issues as regime legacy, the provision of state public goods, the structure of state incentives or the distribution of party power in parliament.[3]

The issue of state capture involves the use of state resources for private gains as a form of rent seeking. The interests that can benefit from state resources include both economic (such as businesses) and political (for example, parties). Many argue that this form of rent seeking creates market distortions that engender corruption. Therefore, campaign finance and other practices are often viewed as a panacea for the capture of the state by economic interests. The question remains whether these practices simply substitute one principle for another as the state continues to serve as the agent for other interests. This is no small matter as there are numerous links between the post-communist state and parties that broadly influence party development, policy formation and voting behaviour.

In this research, I focus on two forms of the party–state relationship that have often been described as areas in which corruption and rent seeking occur. First, I examine the development of party patronage as a dimension of the party–state relationship. Given that party patronage can facilitate the creation of clientelistic networks that emphasize rent-seeking characteristics, it is important to understand how patronage is used by parties to control state resources. Patronage as a practice is distinct from corruption. While the awarding of state positions by party elites can produce corruption, party patronage is often a constitutionally recognized prerogative of the ruling party in most democratic countries. Indeed, some such as Schneider argue that party patronage creates a rotation of bureaucrats that can actually facilitate better policy-making.[4]

Often missing from these accounts of civil service practices is the international environment in which the party penetration of state structures occurs. Particularly in the case of post-communist countries that have had pending applications with the European Union (EU), the issue of civil service reform has become part of the larger discussion concerning fulfilling requirements of the *acquis communautaire*. While the theories that have been developed to account for the politicization of the state vary in their explanation, students of parties often view state capture and the use of party patronage as a *domestically driven* process. While the initial development of the civil service sector in post-communist societies was driven by domestic concerns, the reform of this sector is properly seen as an *internationally driven* process.

Moreover, party patronage becomes an ideal type in which the rent-seeking behaviour within parties and ministries is viewed as systemic. Michalak argues that the pattern of civil service reform is not necessarily uniform throughout a country.[5] In many post-communist countries, certain ministries have reformed their civil service practices so as to limit the use of party patronage while other ministries have lagged behind. What accounts for the different level of reform among ministries? One possible answer would be the amount of international and EU penetration into the state bureaucracy, which erodes previous party patronage. Another related question is whether parties are uniform in their ability to use patronage. Every post-communist country has witnessed rotations in power (in some cases with a tremendous change in party ideology) which leads to the question of how 'new ruling parties' use patronage to reward supporters and to dislodge opponents.

The second part of the research explores the issue of party and campaign finance (PCF) as an example of the party–state relationship. PCF is often viewed as a means to limit the influence of economic interests and create a more level playing-field among parties; however, the actual influence of PCF varies among European countries. The differential impact of PCF on European countries has less to do with the legacies of communism and more to do with the mode of the transition to democracy. Therefore among post-communist countries, the difference in the impact of PCF on parties and the state is much more a function of the relative success of the transition to democracy as well as the acceptance of democratic 'rules of the game' within the political culture.

While much has been written on the ability of PCF to curb corrupt political practices, corruption should be placed within the context of the party–state relationship and not as a separate analytical category. In other words, the ability to subvert legislative intent or the creation of defective PCF legislation influences parties to engage in corrupt campaign practices that transform the party and the state. Indeed, as parties develop from cadre to cartel organizations, corruption can become an institutionalized practice.[6] PCF calls into question whether the 'path-dependency approach' and the design of completely new democratic institutions destroy previous institutions and rules of the game or simply redefine the rules. Moreover, using the West European experience with PCF as a basis for analysing post-communist finance is wrought with difficulties. As van Biezen argues, PCF in so-called 'new democracies' can have a very different impact on party formation from that in more established democracies.[7]

In this research, I explore the impact that party patronage and PCF have on Romanian parties and the state by examining the various forms of patronage and influence of PCF as a form of party income. More specifically in terms of patronage, I examine the use of patronage by analysing the appointment process of civil servants, local government and media structure and how external monitoring by the EU influences civil service reform. With respect to PCF, I examine the level of party subsidies and how the state subvention contributes to total party income in order to understand how PCF shapes party development. The study concludes by examining whether these state resources translate into electoral advantage for parties and politicians. While patronage and PCF are used by parties and politicians to enhance their electoral chances, I find that in the case of Romania neither form of state support is sufficient to procure an electoral outcome. Parties that have wielded considerable patronage and have had access to significant PCF have often been unable to translate these resources into an electoral victory.

Measurements of Party Patronage

The Weberian ideal that the development of autonomy and non-partisanship is a component of an efficient bureaucracy stands in stark contrast to the use of personal and party patronage in most countries. While patronage as a practice is distinct from corruption, the use of patronage in newer democracies has a greater likelihood of leading to corrupt practices because of the lack of a professional bureaucratic culture, meritocracy, and autonomy from political institutions. While some argue that patronage and even corruption can contribute to state-building and policy-making, most of the literature finds that patronage can have a negative influence on parties and ultimately the state.[8]

A difficulty in studying 'party' patronage rather than 'personal' patronage is developing appropriate measures. In a presidential regime especially, the use of personal patronage (such as appointment of the civil service bureaucracy) is relatively easy to identify. However, in parliamentary regimes, particularly those with a coalition government, it becomes more difficult to identify the influence of parties on bureaucratic appointments. Moreover, aside from civil service appointments, a number of activities can be understood as a form of patronage. For example, Müller provides examples of a range of goods and services that are indicative of patronage, including appointments (for example, in quangos and public-sector firms) as well as policy areas (such as 'pork barrel' legislation, government contracts and public construction works).[9] Blondel argues, however, for a definition of patronage that excludes powers of appointment and instead focuses on the 'distribution of favours to individuals in exchange for political advantages accruing – or being expected to accrue – to those who give the favours'.[10]

Yet establishing that the patron–client relationship involves an actual exchange of benefits is empirically difficult. Therefore for purposes of this research, I employ the definition provided by Müller, which includes the appointment process as a fundamental basis of patronage. Since all states use patronage and appointments to some degree, the level of patronage is a result of the penetration of appointments within the bureaucracy and the state apparatus. Those states in which appointments are made throughout the bureaucracy and throughout all levels of government can be viewed as having a much higher level of patronage.

The question remains whether a higher level of patronage is correlated with a higher level of corruption. Patronage provides an exchange of public position for *possible* favour in policy making, which has obvious implications for corruption. Patronage does not necessarily entail corruption; however, patronage can create an environment that fosters exchanges at the cost of the public good. Indeed, Müller argues that patronage and corruption are related but not identical phenomena. In his survey of West European states, he finds that the states with the highest level of patronage are generally those with the lowest ranking in the Transparency International (TI) corruption perceptions index.

Most of the literature operationalizes patronage as a form of domestic exchange. The use of patronage becomes even more difficult to operationalize when the international dimension is added to the analysis. Often missing from these accounts of bureaucratic party patronage is the influence of international actors in the civil service reform process. The neglect of the international dimension is somewhat surprising given the importance that the EU has attached to bureaucratic reform as a means to achieve greater efficiency and transparency and to reduce corruption. Moreover, most studies of bureaucratic party patronage tend to examine patronage as a systemic problem without disaggregating various bureaucratic agencies. In other words, most studies tend to view party patronage as a system-wide problem rather than treating it on a case-by-case ministerial basis. In this research, I explore the domestic and the international factors of patronage in Romania by reference to civil service appointments, structure of local government and media and the influence of the EU on civil service reform.

Party Patronage and Civil Service Appointments

The Romanian Legal Framework

The first Law on the Civil Service was not passed in Romania until 1999. Romania was one of the last post-communist states to adopt such a law, and prior to its passage there was no distinction made between political and professional civil servants. Moreover, there was no system of civil service tenure to protect and insulate the bureaucracy from political control. The legislative history of this law indicates how entrenched party patronage was in Romania. The passage of this law coincided with the EU's invitation at the end of 1999 to begin the accession process. As a result of this decision, the Romanian parliament began to consider several laws that had been supported by the EU but languished in committee. While there was a general consensus between the government and the opposition favouring EU membership, there was a major difference of opinion regarding the passage of this law. The opposition, led by the Party of Social Democracy in Romania (PDSR), was concerned that this law would stymie its efforts to remove government bureaucrats after the 2000 national elections which the ruling government coalition at the time, the Democratic Convention of Romania (CDR), was certain to lose. Therefore, the CDR coalition government of Prime Minister Radu Vasile struggled to win ratification of the legislation in time for the president to promulgate it before the EU summit schedule for 12 December 1999. Ultimately, Vasile linked the passage of the law with a no-confidence vote to ensure coalition member loyalty as well as to block the opposition.[11] At the time, the opposition indicated that one of the first actions of a new PDSR-led government would be to repeal this law.

Following the 2000 national elections in which the PDSR (later renamed the Social Democratic Party or PSD) returned to power, the ruling coalition decided not to repeal the 1999 law because of a concern that this action would weaken the country's bid for EU membership, and because the ruling party understood the mechanisms necessary to subvert the intent of the law. Immediately after returning to power in 2000, President Iliescu and the government began to dismiss civil servants who had been tenured under the 1999 law. While civil servants were being dismissed under Chapter VIII of the Civil Service Law, in almost all cases the state employees who were dismissed had been appointed in 1996 by the former government coalition. The appeal process, which is part of Chapter VIII, allowed civil servants to bring suit against termination, and many of the decisions of the government were later reversed by the Court of Justice.[12]

The 1999 law not only created a classification system for civil servants but also elaborated the method for recruitment examinations and performance evaluation. However, Pralong argues that 'reforms [were] needed to deal with fundamental issues like remuneration, career structure, and accountability'.[13] While the PSD-led government initially resisted attempts at reforming the state bureaucracy, EU membership requirements forced the government to professionalize the bureaucracy further and limit the power of party patronage. In 2003, the largest anti-corruption legislative package was passed, which contained many elements designed to limit party patronage and reduce clientelism. The 2003 Law on the Civil Service included a section dealing with conflicts of interest for government ministers and civil servants.[14] The law created a new category of 'high civil servant' which professionalized several civil servant positions.

While the law was designed to depoliticize the appointment process, all civil servants had to be reappointed under the 2003 law, and there were several cases of individuals not reappointed, allegedly because of support for the opposition. Indeed, Mungiu-Pippidi argues that 'unfortunately, across the entire field of government reform there is a general impression that laws are passed to create the appearance of change rather than to truly impact the system'.[15] As a result of the government actions, civil servants organized a trade union that represents approximately 60 per cent of the 100,000 employees nationally. The trade union provides legal counsel as well as assistance in depoliticizing the hiring and firing process. However, a survey of civil servants conducted in 2004 by the Institute for Public Policy in Romania found, even after passage of the 2003 law, that almost half the respondents believed that a personal connection with political leaders was the most important factor when applying for employment in the public sector.[16]

Politicization of Prefects

While most of the attention of civil service reform has been at the national level, the use of patronage extends throughout of the various levels of government. Following the French model, the Romanian government appoints a representative (prefect) for each of the 41 counties (*judeţe*). Romania is a unitary state in which the prefect is provided with significant administrative and budgetary resources from the central government in the administration of localities.[17] The appointment of prefects is negotiated among coalition partners in the central government. During the first years of Romania's transition, prefects almost always came from the largest ruling party. It was not until the 1996 election that the appointment of prefects was divided more proportionally among coalition partners. Significantly, the opposition has never been afforded the opportunity to appoint prefects. Müller examines the style of patronage in terms of whether spoils are concentrated in government parties (majoritarian) or are shared proportionally with opposition parties. He finds that the preponderance of West European states exhibit a form of majoritarian patronage. Romania, therefore, falls within this general European pattern.

The prefect controls the local government bureaucracy in each county. Within the local government system, they have the authority to appoint, dismiss and promote individuals. Moreover, as the representative of the government, they have significant budgetary resources and are able to provide government contracts and to order inspections and audits of local businesses and individuals. They also tend to have considerable influence over local media, since Romanian newspapers and television stations tend to be heavily dependent on the government for subsidies and tax concessions. The Law of Local Public Administration was passed in 1991 and, while amended on several occasions, still retains several clauses that promote the use of patronage. Indeed, a survey of local civil servants finds that they view political interference in the hiring and the promoting of local government civil servants as natural in public administration.[18]

Throughout the 1990s, prefects used the 1991 law in order to dismiss mayors prior to a judicial inquiry. In almost all cases, the dismissed mayors were from the opposition. The Council of Europe notes that 'suspension decisions in particular do not always seem to comply with the terms of Law 69/91. Reportedly, certain mayors (at least 19 cases have been identified) were suspended without any "*judicial inquiry*" being instituted against them'.[19] This practice, in which prefects used their administrative powers to dismiss mayors and local county councillors, continued throughout the 1990s. The prefect provided the central government with a mechanism to extend party patronage to cities and rural communes. The anecdotal evidence suggests that those mayors from the ruling party were afforded support from the prefect in the form of access to material resources as well as local party support. In response, numerous opposition mayors eventually decided to switch party affiliation. In 2000, PSD won approximately 30 per cent of the mayoral and county council contests; however, by the time of local elections in 2004, the party controlled almost 70 per cent of local government administration. Clearly, there were mass defections from opposition parties to the PSD throughout the early 2000s.

In order to limit the authority of the prefect, the 2003 revised Constitution specified more clearly the powers and limitations of the prefect. Article 123(4) specifies that local government officials including mayors and county councillors are not subordinate to the prefect. In July 2004, the Law on the Corps of Prefects was established which further limited the legal powers of the prefect over other elected local government officials. Nevertheless, prefects still have substantial financial resources, including government contracts, at their disposal. Therefore, Mungiu-Pippidi argues that 'in practice, however, prefects and heads of county councils, the latter being purely honorary positions, have come to enjoy the largest influence at the county level'.[20] Because of this influence, Romanian local administration legislation forbade prefects from holding membership of a party (from 31 December 2005), so all prefects must resign either their party membership or their position. At the time of writing, the vast majority have resigned their party membership and retained their public office. However, one can question whether resigning from party membership truly insulates the prefect from party influence.

Party Patronage in the Mass Media

Patronage as a practice often blurs the distinction between public and private, state and party. One sector in which the use of patronage has an especially erosive effect on the autonomy of the state is the mass media. Indeed, what is so troubling about the Romanian mass media is that they exhibit several of the features of patronage that Müller describes, including appointments to the civil service, use of government licensing, state subsidies and grants (specifically, tax relief). Media patronage is a special case because of the importance of the media during and between election cycles. Indeed, much of the campaign finance provided by the state goes towards the purchasing of broadcasting time. Media patronage involves the appointment of individuals to the body that oversees broadcast media as well as appointments to state-run media outlets.

The state television station (TVR) is the only public station that has nation-wide coverage. Although there has been an explosion in the number of private television stations, TVR still commands a substantial market share because only approximately half of Romanians have cable. TVR has long been accused of having a pro-government bias and providing opposition parties limited airtime. Moreover, the media infrastructure is generally state-controlled. Until the recent privatization of Letea SA Bacău, the state controlled the sole newsprint mill in the country, which gave it indirect control over the operation of all private print media outlets. In addition, the print media distribution network, Rodipet, was until recently owned by the state and it determined which papers were sold at the local level.

The National Audiovisual Council (CNA) is the state agency responsible for issuing television and radio broadcasting licences and monitoring legislative compliance. The CNA is composed of 11 individuals appointed by the president, the government and the parliament. The CNA wields significant influence on the entry and financial structure of broadcast media. Leeson and Coyne argue that the CNA appointment process is subject to political corruption, 'leading to the control over the substance of media-provided programs ... government leaders appoint their friends to the council, who in turn refuse to grant broadcasting licenses to media outlets that might be critical of the ruling party'.[21]

Since its creation, the CNA has issued a large number of broadcasting licences. There are over 100 privately owned television stations in Romania; however, many observers have commented on the 'Berlusconiza-tion' of the television media as almost all stations are owned by high-ranking party leaders, especially from the PSD. The Romanian advertising market is not large enough to provide income for these stations, particularly in smaller cities. As a consequence, one of the problems facing these private stations is the amount of debt owed to the state in taxes and other state dues. Every private station is indebted to the state, and some, such as the popular ProTV, owe as much as $50 million in back taxes.[22] Empirically, it is difficult to establish whether the government uses this situation to undermine the editorial independence of stations; however, the anecdotal evidence suggests that the financial situation of private stations does influence the coverage of parties and political leaders. Reports issued by the Media Monitoring Agency, a Romanian NGO, indicate that during the summer of 2003 among the four national television stations the ruling party received over 70 per cent of the coverage.[23]

Effects of International Pressure on Party Patronage

As noted above, over the past decade, the EU has been monitoring Romania's progress on public administration and civil service reform. The EU views public administration reform not only as an element of good governance but also as a vital check on the mismanagement of PHARE assistance funds. Therefore, the level of civil service reform can be viewed as a function of the external monitoring by organizations such as the EU. As discussed above, the 1999 and the 2003 Law on Civil Service were both enacted in order to satisfy EU demands regarding closer monitoring of grant programmes. While these laws deal with all categories of civil servant throughout the Romanian bureaucracy, the implementation of the legislation varies across bureaucracies. In those ministries in which EU monitoring is highest, I would expect that internal civil service reform would be most advanced. Indeed, the ministry of foreign affairs and the ministry of finance are regarded as two of the more professional Romanian bureaucracies, thanks in part to their close working relationship with the EU.[24]

However, most Romanian ministries can still be regarded as largely personalistic and patronistic. In its latest report on the status of Romania's preparedness to join the EU, the European Commission noted that, while the country has made progress, 'public administration is characterised by cumbersome procedures, a lack of professionalism, inadequate remuneration and poor management of human resources'.[25] The Comprehensive Monitoring Report released by the EU in October 2005 indicates that one of the three areas of serious concern involves the eradication of corruption in ministries due to the risk of fraud in the use of EU funds. While some ministries have made great strides in professionalizing the recruitment and retention of personnel, other ministries have been far less successful.

What accounts for the success of civil service reform in some ministries and the lack of reform in others? Michalak argues that the incentive structure of politicians influences the degree of patronage.[26] In those ministries with few divisible benefits that create a clientelistic network, the influence of politicians and parties wanes while the influence of external monitors increases. Since many Romanian ministries possess divisible benefits, it is not surprising that patronage still exerts a strong influence in decisions on appointment and retention. Pralong argues that 'although civil servants enjoy protection from inappropriate firings, political interference remains an important factor in recruitment and promotion. The Romanian central administration is still characterized by inflated staffs owing to clientelism and nepotism'.[27]

Empirically, identifying which ministries offer few divisible benefits is difficult. An attempt to correlate party patronage with indicators such as the size of the ministry (in terms of personnel or budget) is problematic in the Romanian case. While the ministry of foreign affairs is regarded as the most professionalized and least patronistic ministry, data collected by Michalak indicate that the size of the staff and the budget of this ministry are far greater than those of the less professionalized ministry of education, research and youth.[28] As pointed out by Meyer-Sahling (in this collection), indicators such as ministerial budget and personnel size are problematic proxies for patronage. Perhaps the distinction is how much of the budget is for domestic compared with international purposes. Those ministries that wield a large *domestically oriented* budget are less likely to undergo serious civil service reform because the incentive structure for politicians is based on domestic, not international, rents. Thus, politicians have a different incentive structure in regard to ministries that are internationally oriented, which allows external monitoring the ability to assist in reforms because of the lack of divisible benefits. Of course, this indicator for patronage also is problematic, as many domestically-oriented ministries, such as education, are recipients of EU funds and thus subject to external monitoring pressure. There is still much work to be done to develop appropriate measures for patronage.

Party Campaign Finance in Romania

It is interesting that the two dimensions of the post-communist party–state relationship addressed in this study, patronage and PCF, have only recently received scholarly attention. Most studies of patronage and PCF have focused on Western Europe even though patronage is a feature of all post-communist countries, and many of these countries instituted PCF very early in the transition process. In the founding election of May 1990, the Romanian government provided direct and indirect campaign financing. Article 53 of the 1990 election law provided all parties that participated in the election with a state subsidy that was to be determined at a later date;[29] in addition, the law stipulated that donations from foreign sources would not be permitted. Article 51 provided parties with free access to radio and television media during the campaign (indirect PCF).

What was the motivation behind Romania adopting PCF? In 1990, the ruling National Salvation Front (FSN) controlled the financial resources of the former Romanian Communist Party. Therefore the FSN had substantial funding for the 1990 campaign while the state subsidy provided under the law amounted to approximately 40,000 lei (roughly US$500).[30] Therefore, the subsidy that was provided did not create a more level playing field. Moreover, the prohibition against foreign donations was not created in order to minimize corruption; instead, the prohibition was designed to prevent Ion Raţiu (the opposition presidential candidate of the National Peasants' Party Christian Democratic or PNŢCD) from using the fortune (which he amassed in Great Britain) during the campaign.[31]

In addition, as mentioned above, the electronic media did not provide equal access to parties. In the early 1990s, TVR was the only nation-wide television station, and while the FSN was prominently featured in every broadcast, the opposition 'suffered from limited access to programming, unpredictable placement and uneven access to recording studios and equipment'.[32] This phenomenon is not unusual: as Katz and Mair argue, 'although new parties may get access to the state media if they nominate a sufficiently large number of candidates, that access is sometimes minimal, or is available only at the least attractive times'.[33]

If the state subsidy was not given to provide greater opportunity for parties, why then did the FSN promote PCF? The state subsidy was provided in order to encourage the proliferation of parties. The party registration law only required a party to have 251 members,[34] and this low membership requirement coupled with state financing significantly increased the number of registered parties. More than 70 parties contested the election for the lower house, and of these, about 40 were said to be sympathetic to the FSN. These parties can be seen as a form of electoral clientelism, and they were created in order to overwhelm the public with choices. A Romanian electorate that was used to no choice now faced the daunting task of deciding among dozens of parties. Under this form of voting uncertainty, the FSN emerged as the one stable and broad-based party that could effectively run government. It is not surprising, therefore, that the FSN won over 68 per cent of the lower house seats and that FSN presidential candidate Ion Iliescu won over 85 per cent of the vote. While the FSN held an absolute majority of parliamentary seats, 17 other parties were represented.[35]

In an attempt to consolidate the party system, a number of changes were enacted for the 1992 national elections. The 1992 election law imposed a parliamentary threshold of three per cent, and the PCF was changed.[36] Article 45 of the election law states that parties 'may, by special law, receive funds from the state budget',[37] although parties that received the subsidy but failed to garner five per cent of the total vote had to return the subsidy within two months following the election. However, while the law allowed for the possibility of a direct state subsidy, no party actually received a subsidy for the 1992 national elections. The parliament never passed the enabling legislation as was required to provide financing. Therefore, the 1992 national elections occurred without any direct state subsidy.

The new election law also forbade accepting funds from foreigners, public institutions or public authorities, and the prohibition against foreign contributions included all state and private organizations.[38] Article 46 provided free media time for parliamentary parties, whereas extra-parliamentary parties and independent candidates had media access on the basis of state-negotiated contracts in which the parties and independent candidates had reduced charges. Unlike the 1990 law, there was a reporting requirement of all contributions to the ministry of economics and finance, although no ceiling was imposed for contributions from either individuals or corporations.[39]

Many in the opposition complained that the free access to the media that was guaranteed for all parties was heavily tilted towards Iliescu's newly formed party, the Democratic National Salvation Front (FDSN). The opposition claimed that Iliescu used his authority over TVR to influence the reporting of the election. Just before the elections, Iliescu had established the CNA, responsible for overseeing the media's campaign coverage. The membership of the council was largely drawn from the FDSN. Although guaranteed a specified number of minutes, the opposition advertisements ran late in the evening, guaranteeing that fewer voters saw them. While the Romanian media's actions were technically legal, they were contrary to the spirit of PCF.

After the 1992 national elections, there was no significant legislation on parties or state financing until 1996. During spring 1996, the parliament finally addressed the issue of party development and registration. With local elections scheduled for June, the parliament approved a new party registration law in April 1996 to replace the law adopted in 1989. By 1996, there were over 160 registered parties. The principal provision increased the number of required members from 251 to 10,000. A number of opposition parliamentary and extra-parliamentary parties voiced concern over the dramatic increase in the membership requirement. The country's supreme court ruled, however, that no specific number is any more 'rational and moderate' than another number and allowed the law to stand.[40]

The new law on parties dealt not only with registration requirements but also with the issue of campaign finance. The sixth chapter of the law established a much more specific and elaborate campaign and party finance system than in 1990 or 1992. Under the law (which is still in force), parties are entitled to funding from membership subscriptions (fees), donations (contributions), and revenues from proper activities and the state budget. Donations received by a party may not exceed 0.005 per cent of the country's budget revenues; in an election year, however, the amount is doubled. The sum of the dues paid over the period of one year by a single person may not exceed 50 minimum salaries, and the total yearly contribution made by an individual may not exceed 100 minimum salaries; the total contribution made by a corporation in a year may not exceed 500 minimum salaries. Unlike previous legislation, the 1996 was much more specific about reporting requirements. Under the 1996 law, the contribution does not have to be reported so long as it is less than ten minimum salaries. In addition, a party does not have to report contributions as long as the total amount of contributions (from all sources) does not exceed 20 per cent of the state subsidy in a year; however, the list of contributors who donate amounts greater than ten minimum salaries must be reported and published in the *Monitorul Oficial* by 31 March of the following year.

As under the 1992 law, parties may not receive contributions from public institutions, state enterprises, foreign states and organizations; however, the law does allow international political organizations to which the party is affiliated to make contributions. Unlike the 1992 law, the current law does provide PCF to both parliamentary and extra-parliamentary parties. The amount that is allocated to all parties may not exceed .04 per cent of state revenue. Article 39 states that parties at the beginning of the yearly legislative session that are represented by a parliamentary faction in at least one of the chambers receive a base subsidy, and the total of the base subsidies is one-third of the total state subsidy allocated to all parties. It is very significant that the law provides a base subsidy not to parliamentary *parties* but rather to parliamentary *factions*. This is because the lower house standing orders require at least ten deputies in order to form a faction, so not all parliamentary parties receive the base subsidy. This creates an incentive for the creation of party faction coalitions and also punishes those parties that lose members because, according to the standing orders, MPs may not leave and join a new faction.

Parliamentary parties also receive a subsidy in proportion to their number of seats. The amount awarded per seat is established by dividing the remaining two-thirds of the total state subsidy by the total number of MPs (for the Chamber of Deputies and the Senate). This amount, however, may not exceed five times the base subsidy. In addition, extra-parliamentary parties that obtained at least two per cent of the vote (presumably in the national election) receive equal subsidies, established by dividing the remaining amount after the per seat allocation by the number of eligible parties; the total amount allocated to extra-parliamentary parties may not exceed one base subsidy.

A government decision in September 1996 described the methodology used to determine the state subsidy for that year. On the basis of the April law, 15 parties were awarded some form of state subsidy. As shown in Table 1, not surprisingly the two largest parties, the PDSR and the PNŢCD (as part of the CDR), received the largest subsidies. In addition, two extra-parliamentary parties were awarded a state subsidy based on their share of the 1992 parliamentary vote. Given that the threshold for the 2000 parliamentary election was raised from three to five per cent, this increased the number of extra-parliamentary parties eligible for a state subsidy.

TABLE 1
SUBSIDY FOR PARTIES, 1997–2000 (IN US$)

Parties	Democratic Convention of Romania[a]	Party of Social Democracy in Romania[b]	Union of Social Democracy	Party of Romanian National Unity	Hungarian Democratic Union of Romania	Party of Greater Romania
1997	5,584,431	420,770	301,417	155,622	187,068	161,339
1998	723,823	521,126	373,307	192,739	231,685	199,820
1999	655,367	471,841	338,002	174,511	209,773	180,992
2000	741,111	533,573	382,223	197,342	237,218	204,592

Source: The calculation of these sums was based on government decision 756 published in *Monitorul Oficial al României.* These data were computed by the author on the basis of budget revenues reported by the IMF. These data refer to total state subsidies to various parties based on parliamentary group representation.

Notes: [a]Once the parliament convened after the 1996 elections, there were nine parliamentary factions including two separate parliamentary factions for the Convention. I have combined the subsidy for these parties into a single Convention total. In addition while the ethnic minority parties are listed as a separate faction, it was unclear whether they received a base, and therefore, they have been excluded from this analysis. [b]The 1996 law provides that no party may receive five times the base subsidy in any year. Therefore the PDSR was the only party that exceeded this amount (in every year) and had a lower adjusted amount. In 1997, the pre-adjusted amount was $571,579; in 1998 the amount was $461,506; in 1999 the amount was $517,522; and in 2000, the amount was $585,230.

What is striking is that the ruling coalition that received the greatest amount of state subsidy during the period 1996–2000 failed to pass the threshold for the 2000 national elections: this failure by the ruling CDR to pass the threshold in the 2000 elections indicates that this was a party coalition that was out of touch with voters throughout the country. Moreover, while the CDR did well in the capital, it failed to mobilize voters in traditional power bases including the Banat and Transylvania. Therefore, the use of PCF by the governing coalition did not translate into electoral success during the 2000 national elections.

As Table 2 shows, during the period between 2000 and 2004, the largest parties enjoyed a large financial advantage over smaller parliamentary and especially non-parliamentary parties. However, because the 1996 law does not require full reporting of party income, these figures reveal only the contribution of the state to party maintenance. In addition, these figures focus on the party at the national level whereas, increasingly, party entrepreneurs at the local level are providing party finance as a means of entry into the party leadership.

In the 2004 national elections, the Pro-Democracy Association (APD), a non-governmental organization, produced a series of reports that analysed the spending of parties. During these elections, the two leading parties

TABLE 2
SUBSIDY FOR PARTIES, 2001–2004 (IN US$)

Parties	Social Democratic Pole of Romania[a]	Democratic Party	National Liberal Party	Hungarian Democratic Union of Romania	Party of Greater Romania
2001	5,778,640	244,821	242,186	231,644	447,741
2002	779,987	276,694	270,572	258,329	509,313
2003	821,072	246,068	340,937	226,346	495,876
2004	832,484	139,212	138,606	125,878	391,272

Source: These data were computed by the author on the basis of budget revenues reported by the Ministry of Finance. These data refer to total state subsidies to various parties based on parliamentary group representation.

Note: [a]The Social Democratic Pole of Romania includes the Social Democratic Party, the Romanian Social Democratic Party and the Humanist Party of Romania.

entered into coalitions: the PSD joined up with the Humanist Party of Romania (PUR) in a coalition labelled the National Union PSD + PUR, while the PNL and the Democratic Party entered into the Justice and Truth Alliance. A report issued by the Court of Audit, the institution responsible for monitoring the spending of parties, found that the declared campaign spending of the two coalitions was more than $6 million.[41] In its report, the APD found that the coalitions actually spent almost $9 million that was not accounted for under the audit done by the Court.

While state financing can be an asset to party performance, the case of the PRM is instructive. This party received substantial party finance between the 2000 and 2004 elections (see Table 2). However, the performance of the party suffered considerably as it lost almost half of its seats. This demonstrates that parties that are personalistic – the PRM was an election vehicle for the ultra-nationalist Corneliu Vadim Tudor – can suffer a reversal of fortune no matter how much money is at the party's disposal.

The importance of the party subsidy varies with parties. For some, the subvention forms the vast bulk of the annual income that the party receives. As shown in Table 3, the amount of income generated by parties (and thus the reliance of the party on the subsidy) varies tremendously. Not surprisingly, the PSD reported the largest amount of income of any party during the period 2000–3. These figures also show that on average parties spent more than their income (deficit spending) twice during the period reported. In fact, the UDMR overspent in all reported years except for 2001. Not surprisingly, parties went into deficit in 2000 (an election year) and again in 2003 (gearing up for the 2004 election). It is unclear whether these figures supplied by the ministry of finance included campaign finance. If not, then it is possible that the addition of this income, especially in 2000, would change the ratio of spending.

TABLE 3
PARLIAMENTARY GROUP INCOME AND SPENDING, 2001–2003 (IN US$)

Parties	Social Democratic Pole of Romania[a]	Democratic Party	National Liberal Party	Hungarian Democratic Union of Romania	Party of Greater Romania
2001	1,467,390^2	535,334	–	464,693	575,816
	1,059,256	445,578		410,958	492,802
2002	2,486,780	643,476	420,432	1,195,809	612,748
	2,624,598	642,430	464,322	1,218,100	520,924
2003	4,167,356	701,076	564,364	860,684	679,311
	3,488,373	722,076	539,031	861,894	702,737

Source: These data were computed by the author on the basis of budget revenues reported by the Ministry of Finance.

Note: [a]The Social Democratic Pole of Romania includes the Social Democratic Party, the Romanian Social Democratic Party and the Humanist Party of Romania.

Over the last few years, the importance of the party subsidy as a form of party income has decreased for all parliamentary parties. In Table 4, I calculate the percentage of income that the party subsidy represents for all parliamentary groups. In every case, the proportion has decreased since 2001. In some cases, such as the PSD + PUR coalition, the importance of the subsidy has decreased by well over half. Interestingly, only the extremist PRM relies heavily on the subsidy. Because of changes in coalitions and factions, it is more difficult to calculate these figures for earlier than 2001; however, for the UDMR and the PRM the pre-2001 pattern is largely the same. In 1999, the party subsidy represented 50 per cent of the UDMR's income, whereas it represented 84 per cent for the PRM. In 2000, the reliance

TABLE 4
PARTY SUBSIDY AS A PERCENTAGE OF INCOME, 2001–2003

Parties	Social Democratic Pole of Romania[a]	Democratic Party	National Liberal Party	Hungarian Democratic Union of Romania	Party of Greater Romania
2001	53	46	–	50	78
2002	31	43	64	22	83
2003	20	35	60	26	73

Source: These data were computed by the author on the basis of subsidies and income reported by the Ministry of Finance. These data refer to total state subsidies to various parties based on parliamentary group representation.

Note: [a]The Social Democratic Pole of Romania includes the Social Democratic Party, the Romanian Social Democratic Party and the Humanist Party of Romania.

on the subsidy decreased for both parties (45 and 70 per cent respectively). While the ministry of finance reports the income and spending for non-parliamentary parties, the income of many of these parties is less than US$100. I have no data for the few non-parliamentary parties that receive a subsidy; however, it seems reasonable to expect that the party subsidy as a proportion of income for these parties would be substantially higher than for parliamentary parties.

Conclusions

Ultimately, public policy must be formulated and administered by the state bureaucracy. Since Weber's analysis of public administration, many scholars have noted that patronage and the politicization of the bureaucracy leads to inefficiency and poor policy-making. If this is correct, perhaps one empirical measure to determine patronage would be the implementation of public policy in numerous sectors. Depending on how one operationalizes a 'successful' policy, policy success in areas such as privatization (where rent-seeking behaviour is opportunistic) might be one indicator of a depoliticized state. While pre-communist and communist historical legacies may offer a clue to the penetration of party patronage, it is instructive to examine individual ministries to determine the level of *possible* clientelism.

Moreover, the relationship between parties and the state is complex owing to conflicting interests and numerous pressure points. PCF is an example of how parties attempt to capture the state for financial and political gain. On the one hand, these laws are often designed by parties to exclude the entry of new parties. However, as Katz and Mair argue, the attempt to use PCF to suppress new parties can actually backfire and provide these new parties with a rallying cry against the political establishment.[42] Gryzmała-Busse argues that those post-communist countries in which power was concentrated among a small group of parties de-emphasized the importance of state finance in lieu of other forms of funding, which undermined transparency and ultimately politicized the state.[43] She argues that the lack of transparency in financing led to rent-seeking behaviour within bureaucracies, whereby party patronage formed the basis of a clientelistic state.

The relationship between parties and the state involves empirical and normative questions about the proper role of public servants, politicians and citizens in a democracy. The use of state resources by parties is not necessarily undemocratic, and in some cases can strengthen the vibrancy of democracy. Patronage and financing require transparency in order to reduce the possibility of corruption. As the Romanian case shows, laws are not enough to provide accountability. Moreover, the same case also demonstrates that the awarding of patronage and use of PCF do not guarantee electoral success. While the

PSD greatly influenced the use of state patronage and enjoyed considerable PCF throughout the 2000s, these resources did not prevent the party from suffering electoral defeats in the 2004 national elections. Moreover, the re-emergence of the National Liberal Party (PNL) in the late 1990s demonstrates that Romanian parties can survive and indeed mount an electoral challenge without access to state resources.

NOTES

1. For a broad-ranging discussion of the relative weakness of post-communist civil societies see Aleksander Smolar, 'Civil Society After Communism: From Opposition to Atomization', *Journal of Democracy*, Vol.7 (1996), pp.24–38; Bill Lomax, 'The Strange Death of Civil Society in Post-Communist Hungary', *Journal of Communist Studies and Transition Politics*, Vol.13 (1997), pp.41–63; Grzegorz Ekiert and Jan Kubik, *Rebellious Civil Society: Popular Protest and Democratic Consolidation in Poland, 1989–1993* (Ann Arbor, MI: University of Michigan Press, 1999); and Marc Morjé Howard, *The Weakness of Civil Society in Post-Communist Europe* (Cambridge: Cambridge University Press, 2003).
2. Venelin I. Ganev, 'The Separation of Party and State as a Logistical Problem: A Glance at the Causes of State Weakness in Postcommunism', *East European Politics and Societies*, Vol.15 (2001), p.389.
3. For an interesting account of state capture due to the communist legacy see Herbert Kitschelt, Zdenka Mansfeldova, Radoslaw Markowski and Gabor Toka, *Post-Communist Party Systems: Competition, Representation, and Inter-Party Cooperation* (Cambridge: Cambridge University Press, 1999). For a functionalist account of state politicization see M. Steven Fish, 'The Determinants of Economic Reform in the Post-Communist World', *East European Politics and Societies*, Vol.4 (1998), pp.31–78; and for the structure of state incentives, László Bruszt and David Stark, *Pathways from State Socialism* (Cambridge: Cambridge University Press, 1998). For an account of state capture based on the distribution of party power in parliament see Anna Grzymala-Busse, 'Political Competition and the Politicization of the State in East Central Europe', *Comparative Political Studies*, Vol.36 (2003), pp.1123–47.
4. Ben Schneider, *Politics within the State: Elite Bureaucrats and Industrial Policy in Authoritarian Brazil* (Pittsburgh, PA: University of Pittsburgh Press, 1991).
5. Katja Michalak, 'Patterns of Civil Service Reform in Romania: A Multi-Dimensional State Analysis' (unpublished manuscript, 2005).
6. Although Katz and Mair develop the concept of the cartel party, they do not see the interpenetration of the state and the party as a necessary condition for corruption: see Richard S. Katz and Peter Mair, 'Changing Models of Party Organization and Party Democracy', *Party Politics*, Vol.1 (1995), pp.5–28.
7. Ingrid van Biezen, 'Party Financing in New Democracies: Spain and Portugal', *Party Politics*, Vol.6 (2000), p.329.
8. Huntington was one of the first scholars to argue for the benefits of party patronage: see Samuel Huntington, *Political Order in Changing Societies* (New Haven, CT: Yale University Press, 1968).
9. Wolfgang C. Müller, 'Patronage by National Governments', in Jean Blondel and Maurizio Cotta (eds.), *The Nature of Party Government: A Comparative European Perspective* (Basingstoke: Palgrave, 2000), pp.142–3.
10. Jean Blondel, 'Party Government, Patronage, and Party Decline in Western Europe', in Richard Gunther, José Ramon-Montero and Juan J. Linz (eds.), *Political Parties: Old Concepts and New Challenges* (Oxford: Oxford University Press, 2002), p.241.
11. By the time the law was to be promulgated, Vasile had been removed as prime minister and replaced by Mugur Isarărescu.

12. 'Best Practices in the European Countries: The Republic of Romania', Centre for Administrative Innovation in the Euro-Mediterranean Region (Naples, Italy, 2004), p.11.
13. Sandra Pralong, 'Romania', *Nations in Transition* (New York: Facts on File, 2003), p.489.
14. While the law clarifies situations of conflict of interest by defining public interest and personal interest, the code applies only to civil servants and not to elected and appointed officials: see Alina Mungiu-Pippidi, 'Nations in Transit 2005' (2005), p.11.
15. Alina Mungiu-Pippidi, 'Nations in Transit 2004' (2004), p.17.
16. Adrian Moraru and Elena Iorga, 'Romanian Civil Service Barometer, 2004', Institute for Public Policy (Bucharest, Romania, October 2004), p.4.
17. An interesting question rarely addressed in the literature is the influence of the system of government on the use of patronage. One could argue that, while a federal system may exhibit the same level of patronage, the election of local government and separation of powers between national and sub-national levels provides a check on the use of party patronage by other parties.
18. Moraru and Iorga, 'Romanian Civil Service Barometer, 2004', p.5.
19. Giorgio De Sabbata, 'Part II Report on Local and Regional Democracy in Romania', Monitoring Report 1995 CG (2) 5 (Bucharest, Romania, 1995).
20. Mungiu-Pippidi, 'Nations in Transit 2005', p.3.
21. Peter T. Leeson and Christopher J. Coyne, 'Manipulating the Media' (unpublished manuscript, 2005), p.18.
22. Ibid, p.14.
23. 'Press Freedom in Romania: Report on 2003', Media Monitoring Agency (Bucharest, Romania, 2004), p.5.
24. In its latest report, the EU emphasized the need for the Romanian ministry of finance to be more involved in policy formation at all levels, including local government.
25. '2004 Regular Report on Romania's Progress towards Accession', Commission of the European Communities SEC (2004) 1200, 657 (6 October 2004), p.32.
26. Michalak, 'Patterns of Civil Service Reform', p.15.
27. Pralong, 'Romania', p.489.
28. Michalak reports that 597 employees work at the ministry of foreign affairs while 350 work at the ministry of education, research and youth (both figures based on civil servants in the Bucharest office); in addition, the budget of the ministry of foreign affairs is ten times that of the ministry of education, research and youth: see Michalak, 'Patterns of Civil Service Reform', p.21.
29. *Monitorul Oficial al României*, 18 March 1990.
30. Carothers argues that few, if any, opposition parties actually received the state subsidy: see Thomas Carothers, 'Romania', in Larry Garber and Eric Bjorn (eds.), *The New Democratic Frontier* (Washington, DC: National Democratic Institute for International Affairs, 1992), p.86.
31. This prohibition was supposedly amended to allow for foreign contributions if they were documented. Carothers reports that opposition parties had to wait an inordinate amount of time for their currency transfers to be approved: ibid, p.83.
32. Ibid.
33. Katz and Mair, 'Cadre, Catch-All or Cartel? A Rejoinder', pp.529–30.
34. *Monitorul Oficial al României*, 30 Dec. 1989.
35. This number does not include ethnic minority parties, which were guaranteed a seat in the lower house. Of the ethnic-based parties, only the Hungarian Democratic Union of Romania and the German Democratic Forum received enough votes to win a seat outright.
36. Significantly, there was no change to the party registration requirement of 251 members.
37. *Monitorul Oficial al României*, 5 July 1992.
38. However, governments such as the United States were very active during the 1992 national elections. As Carothers points out, the United States through organizations such as the International Republican Institute, the National Democratic Institute for International Affairs and the United States Information Agency was very active in supporting opposition parties: see Thomas Carothers, *Assessing Democracy Assistance: The Case of Romania* (Washington, DC: Carnegie Endowment for International Peace, 1996).

39. Each party had to designate a specific fiscal agent that registered with the ministry of economics and finance.
40. *Monitorul Oficial al României*, 11 April 1996.
41. The court of audit is the government body responsible for supervising the financing of parties. Interestingly, the law specifically states that the court of audit may check only the general bank account of a party. The paragraph that outlines the forms of party financing is specifically excluded from the supervisory jurisdiction of the court. Neither the 1996 election law nor the law on parties specifies that parties must submit reports to the court of audit; rather, the court has the right to investigate party bank accounts: see *Monitorul Oficial al României*, 15 Feb. 2005, and 'Alegeri la limita democrației: Analiza procesului electoral din România, Octombrie – Decembrie 2004' (Bucharest: Pro-Democracy Association, 2005).
42. Katz and Mair, 'Changing Models', p.20.
43. Grzymala-Busse, 'Political Competition and the Politicization of the State', pp.1123–47.

Managing Democracy: Political Parties and the State in Russia

HANS OVERSLOOT and RUBEN VERHEUL

In the former Soviet Union and its satellites, the communist party and the state overlapped. Decision making in all spheres of life was in effect done within the Communist Party of the Soviet Union (CPSU), which was effectively above the law and accountable only to itself.[1] Public offices were staffed through the CPSU's *nomenklatura* system.[2]

After the demise of the CPSU in 1991, what remained of the Russian state was left party-less, and after the failed coup of August 1991 Russia was actually a dictatorship. The state itself, legitimized by the people's deputies and the President – not any party – was instrumental in reasserting state power for the people and instrumental in re-creating order in the Russian Federation (RF). The very concept of 'party' was strongly, negatively, associated with *the* party, namely the CPSU, which Yeltsin and the 'new democrats' (sometimes working together in the Democratic Russia movement[3]) had managed to curtail.[4] Following the dissolution of the Soviet-era parliament, and the adoption of a new Constitution, the first genuine multiparty elections of December 1993 finally gave parties a meaningful, albeit limited, role in the political process.

This study deals with the party–state relationships that have arisen since then. Seeking to determine the extent to which political parties in Russia have been able to assert themselves *vis-à-vis* the state, and whether they are able to make use of the state, we first look at current party–state links in Russia on three dimensions: public regulation of political parties, public funding of political parties, and patronage. As some accounts demonstrate, state capture in conditions of post-communism has followed diverse patterns, for various reasons and with varying degrees of politicization. But the general trend seems to be towards increasing control of parties over the state.[5] Coupled with the 'cartelization' observed in established democracies, this means a shift from parties acting as agents of society to parties representing and managing state institutions.[6] In our analysis, the Russian case is markedly different. We observe that it is the state that is colonizing the parties, rather than *vice versa*.

We then propose a categorization of the parties in Russia. Most attention will be given to the so-called parties of power, for these reflect the extent to which, and the mechanisms by which, the state manages party politics and the administrative elites keep politics out of the state. We conclude that recent reforms by the Putin administration point towards more, rather than less, encroachment of the state in party politics.

The Relevance of Parties

While the Russian state was under construction and the new rules of the game were being written, the parties had to content themselves with a marginal role, both at the apex of the political system and within the society at large. Office benefits they can offer are confined by and large to a seat in parliament, the State Duma. And even there, as we shall see, parties have limited control.

The presidency, as will be shown below, has so far been beyond the reach of parties. Both Boris Yeltsin and Vladimir Putin remained aloof from party politics throughout their tenure. While they both employed political parties as support vehicles, and made several attempts to create 'workable' majorities in parliament, their actual power base lay elsewhere. Given the zero-sum nature of the presidential contest, and the volatility of the Russian electorate, Yeltsin and Putin have been careful not to bet on one horse and tie their fate to any particular party. As presidents of 'all Russians', they claimed wide-ranging legitimacy and room for manoeuvre.

Appointments to and careers in the executive – government and state bureaucracy – based on party affiliation are the exception rather than the rule. In Russia, it is the president who selects and appoints the members of the government. Parliamentary approval is required only for the prime minister. The Duma can refuse to confirm the president's nomination, but at a high price: 'blocking' three consecutive nominations results in the dissolution of the Duma and new elections. The prime ministers of choice of both Boris Yeltsin and Vladimir Putin have so far been a-political figures: 'technocrats', career bureaucrats and professionals from large state enterprises.

The following table illustrates this point. Listed are the prime ministers who have served under Yeltsin and Putin. Where applicable, we have indicated their involvement in a party organization, both at the 'time of arrival' and after their tenure. As is clear, with the exception of Khristenko none of Russia's prime ministers had a party political background initially. During or after serving their term, however, some of them became prominent leaders of parties of power (see below). The technocratic image applies to the cabinet of ministers as a whole. Of the 19 ministers currently staffing Mikhail Fradkov's core cabinet, only five can be linked to a political party (see Table 1).[7]

The same goes for other government officials. Bringing together data from several printed sources, Allen Lynch notes that '35 percent of all deputy ministers appointed between 2000 and 2003 [are military or security officers], and 25 percent of the Russian political elite as a whole for the same period (compared to 11 percent for business elites), representing a sixfold increase in military and security representation in government leadership posts since

TABLE 1
PRIME MINISTERS OF THE RUSSIAN FEDERATION

Name	Period	Affiliated/involved with party before appointment	Affiliated/involved with party during/after term in office
Yegor Gaidar	1992		Demokraticheskii vybor Rossii; Soyuz pravykh sil
Viktor Chernomyrdin	1992–1998		Nash Dom–Rossiya
Sergei Kirienko	1998		Soyuz pravykh sil
Viktor Chernomyrdin	1998		
Yevgenii Primakov	1998–1999		Otechestvo–Vsya Rossiya
Sergei Stepashin	1999		
Vladimir Putin	1999–2000		
Mikhail Kas'yanov	2000–2004		Planning to launch an 'opposition party'
Viktor Khristenko	2004	Nash Dom–Rossiya	
Mikhail Fradkov	2004–present		

Source: Compiled by authors.

the late Soviet period. ... [T]wo-thirds of Putin's presidential staff have backgrounds in the security services'.[8]

Presidential nominations at the regional level follow a similar pattern. Five of the seven presidential representatives who were appointed in the seven federal districts (North-West, Central, Southern, Volga, Ural, Siberian, and Far Eastern), had a background in either the military or the security forces (KGB and FSB).[9]

The only way in which political parties fulfil a political recruitment function and control access to political office is through elections, most importantly those for the State Duma (the federal parliament). Up until recently, Duma seats were contested under a mixed system, which combines plurality voting with proportional representation (PR). This formula was introduced in 1993,[10] and maintained for the parliaments elected in December 1995,[11] December 1999,[12] and December 2003.[13] Half of the 450 Duma seats were elected in single-member districts (*odnomandatnye izbiratel'nye okruga*, SMD) according to the first-past-the-post principle; the other half within one single nation-wide district (*federal'nyi izbiratel'nyi okrug*), with the help of 'party lists' (PL), each independently of the other. For the PL part, a five per cent threshold was set. Both the SMD and the PL contests employ categorical ballots, which means that voters can express their preference for only one candidate or PL; the latter is closed – voters cannot express any preference for individual candidates.

The PL elections are the most important domain for Russia's parties, since by default they nominate candidates for these elections. The SMD, however, were not their *chasse gardée*. There, party candidates had to compete against individuals, and they have not been so successful: many SMD-deputies were elected *à titre personnel*, as 'independents' (*nezavisimye*).[14] This weakness in the regions (*sub"ekty*) is also reflected in the fact that most heads of the regions ('governors' as they are informally called) are not party politicians. To this day, the 'reach' of the parties is fairly limited; only a few of them have grassroots organizations and serious representation beyond Moscow.[15] In his research on this phenomenon, Grigorii Golosov found that 'What matters is not what the candidate can gain entirely or partly with the help of the party (i.e. party support and incumbency, respectively), but something that candidates can gain mostly independently from the party'.[16]

Political entrepreneurs tend to see parties merely as instrumental. They rarely invest in maintaining and strengthening party organizations, relying on their own informal networks instead. This does not of itself make Russia a special case. As John Aldrich puts it, politicians 'turn to their party – that is use its powers, resources, and institutional forms – when they believe doing so increases their prospects for winning desired outcomes, and they turn from it if it does not'.[17] What sets Russia apart is that this logic in practice translates into an unusually fluid and unstable party system: parties – party labels – come and go with every election.[18]

Recent changes in Russia's institutional structure may further reinforce the general weakness of parties. Following the dramatic siege of School No.1 in Beslan in the Republic of North Ossetia, which took the lives of over 300 people, President Putin in autumn 2004 announced a wholesale reform of 'state power', asserting that, in order to combat terrorism, strengthening the state was crucial. Characteristically for Putin's overall programme, this boiled down to recentralizing the state. Two measures were announced: the abolition of direct elections to the heads of the federal subjects; and the aboli-tion of the SMD portion of the Duma elections.[19] Whatever the link with terrorism, the fact that the post of 'governor' will no longer be directly elected is likely to further weaken the grip of parties on regional executives.

The consequences of the shift from mixed to entirely proportional Duma elections (scheduled for the end of 2007)[20] are less obvious, however. On the one hand, this may strengthen the parties and offer them an incentive to expand their geographical reach beyond the proverbial 'Moscow Garden Ring'. They will no longer face the competition of independents. With parties in control of the candidate nomination process, aspirants to parlia-mentary seats will have to earn party endorsement. On the other hand, scepti-cally speaking, the 'nationalization' of the Duma ballot gives the central authorities even more control over party competition, leaving less room for manoeuvre and for local initiatives aimed at autonomous party formation.

A third measure, also linked to the battle against terrorism, is less ambig-uous in its impact upon parties. Early in 2005, Putin ordered the creation of a Public Chamber (*Obshchestvennaya palata*).[21] This institution, a kind of 'third chamber' of parliament, is supposed to act as a collective ombudsman, supervising government, the Duma, the media and law enforcement agencies. It was due to convene in January 2006 and number 126 members, a third of them handpicked by the president from among 'widely recognized and respected personalities', in consultation with NGOs;[22] these 42 members in turn decide on the remaining members (one-third representing federal and one-third representing regional NGOs). Representatives of parties are expressly excluded from membership. It remains to be seen what the Public Chamber will amount to in practice, but this apparent bypassing of the Duma sends a clear signal to the parties inhabiting it: legitimation (and even criticism) can be organized without them.

State Regulation of Parties

The immaturity of Russia's party system has often been criticized. Many politicians and commentators lamented the lack of a specific law safeguarding or delimiting the role of parties: 'under-regulation' was thought to be at the root of the disorder. Legislation applying to political parties, such as the *perestroika*-era law on public associations,[23] was enacted prior to the 'legalization' of multiple parties, and lacked sophistication and the tools to regulate party activity. Yet it took years of debates to adopt the 2001 law on political parties.[24] With this law, the Putin administration claimed finally to create some order, to be understood in terms of fewer, more enduring and more transparent parties.

The law and its 2004 amendments define quite strictly what it takes to be considered a political party *de jure*, and what are the concomitant rights and obligations. Party status – and thus access to the electoral arena and state funding (see below) – is dependent on membership (parties must have a broad membership base) and territorial diffusion (parties must be represented throughout the Federation). In specific terms, parties: (1) should have regional chapters in at least half of the subjects of the RF, (2) each numbering at least 500 members (other regional chapters require at least 250 members); and (3) must have a total membership of at least 50,000 citizens.[25] These members are to have equal access to leading positions within their organizations. Party status, furthermore, is dependent on continued participation in the electoral process: a party (4) must field candidates in federal, regional or local elections at least once every five years, otherwise it loses its status. It does not matter whether parties stage electoral campaigns alone, or in collaboration with others.[26]

Parties and their regional branches must annually update the ministry of justice regarding their whereabouts, activities, candidate nominations, and the number of members (since the 2004 amendment, they are also required to present a list of their members). On the basis of this information, the ministry can verify whether a party still 'exists'. Practice has shown that the state does not hesitate to use its powers *vis-à-vis* quasi- or pseudo-parties: quite a number of parties have been de-registered since 2003.[27] These bans are unlikely to have had any significant effect on the 'power configuration', however, since they concern organizations in the margins of the party landscape; in any case, they did not provoke public debate. But it is difficult to tell whether all cases have received equal treatment. A large-scale audit operation was apparently planned for October 2005, following which it was expected that about half of the registered parties would not retain their status. In January 2006, *Rosregistratsiya* (the ministry of justice's Federal Registration Service) listed 32 parties (and 25 that were de-registered).[28]

The law gives the state considerable leverage over the parties, but it also claims to delineate the state from the parties. State agencies and public officials may not interfere at will in party affairs; parties, in turn, may not meddle in organs of state power (except legislatures), law enforcement, the armed forces and education. Public officials – while they are not excluded from party membership – may not use their posts to further the interests of their parties. In turn, public officials cannot be bound by party decisions in the performance of their duties. The president of the RF has the right to suspend their own party membership during their term of office.[29] This clause – given its non-committal wording – appears to be rather gratuitous, but in the Russian context it matters, of course, whether or not the president is a party figure.

The procedures for admitting newly founded parties and monitoring existing ones are spelled out in great detail. To begin with, all aspects of a party's existence stand or fall with its registration, at both the central and regional levels. It is mandatory that newly founded parties submit to the 'registering organs' – the ministry of justice – their charters, programme, the minutes of the regional founding conference or conferences, and their contact details, *inter alia*. On the face of it, registration is a bureaucratic hurdle that can be cleared with relative ease; moreover, registration can be denied on only a few grounds, mostly procedural. The submitted documentation must be adequate and the charter must be in line with legislation (or vague enough in order to avoid conflicts). The only substantive obstacle to registration is that programmatic 'anti-system' provisions, described above, are inadmissible. Otherwise, a party's programme is irrelevant for its legalization.[30]

Party Funding

One of the most controversial issues in the debate on the law on parties was state funding. Previously, electoral associations were entitled to modest compensation of their campaign expenses, as set forth in various electoral laws, which were usually rewritten for each specific election. The party law envisages permanent state funding for parties that (1) obtain at least three per cent of the list vote in Duma elections; or (2) get at least 12 SMD candidates elected to the Duma (in which case the 'three per cent threshold' is not applicable); or (3) collect a minimum of three per cent of the votes for their presidential nominee. The first two results – those achieved in parliamentary elections – give right to a yearly subvention; the latter – the presidential vote – is translated into a non-recurrent subsidy. In all the above cases, the number of votes received is multiplied by 0.005 times the minimum wage (*minimal'nyi razmer oplaty truda*, MROT).[31] Other sources of income, besides state funding, are membership dues, donations by sympathetic 'outsiders' (both individuals and firms) and entrepreneurial activity. There appears to be no maximum set for membership fees; the authors of the law most likely expected these to remain within reasonable limits. But restrictions and ceilings are established for donations (*pozhertvovaniya*) from without the party ranks. Donors can be Russian citizens and legal persons; funds from abroad are expressly outlawed. The total sum of yearly contributions may not exceed 10 million MROT (about US$100 million).

Data regarding the actual flow of state funds to party bank accounts since 2003 have yet to be published. In that sense, the party law's attempt at transparency has not been achieved. Yet, in order to appraise the potential state contribution to party maintenance, consider the following two examples, calculated on the basis of the list vote in the December 1999 Duma elections (the last elections held before the party law was enacted) and a MROT of 300 roubles (about $10): the Communist Party of the Russian Federation (the winner in that year's list) would be entitled to a yearly subsidy of almost $810,000; Yabloko, which finished last, would earn almost $198,000.

Such donations from the state appear to be rather modest, in absolute terms. The relative weight of state subsidies in party budgets is another matter. Some parties generate a considerable income from membership dues and, especially, donations. The limited – and unfortunately incomplete – data available suggest that the latter constitute the bulk of parties' income. The Union of Right Forces (Soyuz pravykh sil: SPS) and United Russia (Yedinaya Rossiya: UR) are particularly successful fund-raisers.[32] For other parties, however, state subventions account for the bulk of their official income. Of course, party accounting is to be taken with a pinch of salt, for the 'official' data that parties disclose are likely to be incomplete.

These figures, with the exception of those for SPS and UR, might suggest that politics in Russia is not really a capital-intensive affair. Yet, campaigning in Russia is big business, especially for office-holders. Take, for example, the 1996 presidential elections, in which Boris Yeltsin – who was highly unpopular at the time – competed against opposition leader Gennadii Zyuganov. According to Andrew Wilson, spending in this election surpassed that in the 2000 contest for the American presidency: 'Yeltsin's victory in 1996 required somewhere between $1 and $2 billion ... By comparison, even with the constant escalation of expenditure in American elections, the total official amount raised in 2000 was only $529 million ($193 million for George Bush, $133 million for Al Gore, plus others)'.[33] Lilia Shevtsova's estimate is lower, at between $700 million and $1 billion. Yet she points out that public spending in 1996 skyrocketed, because the Yeltsin administration took 'popularity measures' (paying wage and pension arrears, building metros, and so on). During Yeltsin's campaign, Russia's external debt rose by $4 billion, while its internal debt grew by $16 billion.[34]

Co-sponsorship of political parties by businessmen is the rule rather than the exception in Russia. Corporate funding is usually clouded in secrecy, but it can be safely assumed that all major parties in Russia enjoy such support and that the bulk of it goes to the 'parties of power'.[35] These have the leverage to solicit contributions and access to the spoils for delivery. But as a rule they do not monopolize donations, being interested in the upkeep of the party system as a whole, not merely the infusion of funds into their own electoral organizations.

Only on rare occasions does this lead to scandals, lawsuits or both. The Khodorkovskii case is the exception to this rule. His sponsorship of SPS, of Yabloko, and even of the KPRF in preparation for the 2003 State Duma elections was clearly intended neither to support the regime nor to help the party of power indirectly. Khodorkovskii had political ambitions of his own; it was assumed that he would eventually have gone for the highest prize, bypassing the power-brokers and the plans they might have for Putin or for Putin's succession. Khodorkovskii was confronted with criminal investigations concerning his business dealings, and in the spring of 2005 he was sentenced to nine years in prison for a series of financial crimes.

There have been instances where businessmen went a step further and attempted to launch parties of their own (for example, Konstantin Borovoi's Party of Economic Freedom). But these projects have proved to be ineffective and short-lived. A much safer investment, it seems, is infiltrating existing electorally successful parties. Vladimir Zhirinovskii's Liberal-Democratic Party (LDPR) is notorious for selling Duma seats to the highest bidder. However, it is by no means the only party that maintains close ties to business: even the Communist Party (KPRF) runs party lists on which 'red' business tycoons figure prominently.

The Functioning of Russia's Pseudo-Parties

Having outlined above the institutional and legal framework in which parties in Russia operate, we now shift our focus to the functioning of parties themselves. Given the volatile nature of the Russian party system, we think a categorization is in place. Political parties in present-day Russia for the most part fit into the following categories:

(1) The Communist Party of the Russian Federation (KPRF) fills a category of its own. It is the continuation and slimmed-down version of the single party of the past; it is heir to the CPSU (and the Communist Party of Russia), in terms of its cadres, membership, organizing principles, and much of its ideology (and probably to a part of the CPSU's finances as well).[36] Since 1993, and to the present, the KPRF has been the only real mass party, with a membership of close to 500,000 for well over a decade.

(2) Other 'genuine parties'. These are not Duvergerian mass parties but cadre parties. The social-liberal Yabloko party is the main representative of this

category. It has been active since 1993, but is not represented in the State Duma at present, as it failed to pass the five per cent threshold for the PL vote in the December 2003 elections. Its support is concentrated in the big cities, notably St. Petersburg and Moscow. Yabloko caters primarily for highly educated urban professionals and the remaining intelligentsia.

(3) A third category is the so-called 'party of power' (*partiya vlasti*).

(4) Yet another holds what we suggest calling 'party of power helper parties', among which several sub-categories can be distinguished: (4a) 'satellite' parties and (4b) 'adjunct' or 'alternative' parties of power. Satellite parties of power circle round the party of power, attract a small number of voters who do not identify themselves with the electoral branch of the party of power proper, but whose actual mode of behaviour is supportive of the party of power. Satellite parties are not opposition parties: the SPS, at least initially, was such a party. 'Adjunct' or 'alternative' parties of power do not distinguish themselves ideologically from parties of power, only the cadre and the leadership are different. The adjunct party is quite acceptable to the party of power; in fact it is set up by the power-holders (to which category the adjunct party's leadership belongs), but it is not yet operational as the electoral branch of the real party of power – instead it is kept in reserve. Its two major functions seem to be to serve as a testing-ground for political and administrative personnel, and to keep local leaders of the party of power alert and disciplined. Their replacement, it might be said, is on permanent display in the adjunct party.

(5) Also important are the 'favoured opposition parties'. Their purpose is to express opposition to the regime, to serve as 'alternatives' to the party of power, and to channel the electorate's dislike of the power-holders. Favoured opposition parties are created or co-opted or at least aided by the power-holders to help gather the votes of the disenchanted and other oppositionists in order to disarm the real, independent, opposition, and transform citizens' votes for opposition parties into regime support via the votes of their representatives in parliament. Oppositionist sentiment is transformed via these parties into actual policy support in the legislative body. These parties mimic opposition parties, and may even present themselves as anti-system parties, but they are professional double-crossers and fakers. We have given these parties their own separate category, but much is to be said for categorizing them among the 'party of power helper parties'; nevertheless they are special in that they thrive by being successful in suggesting they are not.[37]

(6) The number of subcategories can be extend further by distinguishing the species of 'harassment-parties' (in Russian: *mukhi*, flies) and 'harassment-candidates', or, if one prefers, 'parties of distraction'. These are parties

with no other function than to hamper opposition parties, for example by using a similar party label and defending a similar political programme, or by organizing the risk of mistaken identity by putting candidates on the ballot with the same name (preferably the same first name, the same patronymic and the same family name) as the candidate selected by the power-holders for harassment.[38] In effect these are 'helper parties' too, but also help by suggesting they are not what they are.

(7) A final category is what could be called 'vanity parties' or 'advertisement' or 'self-advertisement parties' (and associated vanity candidates), which seem to exist for the sole purpose of providing party support for a candidate who stands little or no chance of winning a seat, or being voted into office, but who loves the limelight and the general public's attention. An example is Vladimir Bryntsalov, who managed to get elected to the State Duma in December 1995, and was the founder of the Russian Socialist Party in 1996. There is little of a socialist discernible in this crook and multimillionaire, the kind of person who gives even 'new Russians' a bad name, and who was a hopeless candidate in, *inter alia*, the 1996 RF presidential election. Sometimes vanity and business acumen go very well together. Having access to the corridors of power (and having voting power in legislative bodies) can be economically rewarding.

Category 3 and following parties, with the exception of 'vanity parties', are set up or co-opted and heavily sponsored by the political power holders, that is, by the presidential administration or the government in a wider sense: by federal ministers, federal services heads and their apparatuses. They operate directly, or indirectly, such as by organizing support by 'favoured business leaders', who thereby hope to receive preferential treatment by the administration. Many of these parties have their beginning close to the federal political centre, Moscow, and from there branch out more or less intensively to the federal subjects' centres – the capitals of the 89 provinces, republics, autonomous regions and other units that constitute the federation. In some cases parties were set up and sponsored by the heads of the executive branches of subjects of the federation, and were to branch out from there. Noteworthy examples of these 'local' parties of power were Fatherland (*Otechestvo*) and All Russia (*Vsya Rossiya*) (see below).

Parties of Power

We suggest that the most interesting, and quintessential, element of Russia's party system – and political system as a whole – is the phenomenon of 'party of power'.[39] The party of power defines Russia's party political scene, as it also generates the concomitant 'party of power helper parties', and 'favoured parties of opposition'. Here, the party–state relationship theme – the encroachment of the state apparatus into electoral politics – comes to the fore to its full effect.

We need to clarify at the outset that in Russia there is no ruling party in the 'ordinary' sense. Certainly, there exists at any given moment close to Duma elections (which precede presidential elections) an organization set up, financed and staffed by the RF's political centre (presidential administration *cum* government) which presents and recommends its candidates for parliament. The aim of the party of power is to ensure political support in the legislative branch for the present or future head of the executive branch and their *komanda* (team). If this enterprise is successful, reference is to what is merely the temporary electoral branch of the true 'party of power' as 'the ruling party'. Russia's Choice (*Vybor Rossii:* VR), Our Home is Russia (*Nash Dom–Rossiya*: NDR), Unity (*Yedinstvo*) and United Russia (*Yedinaya Rossiya*) were never 'ruling parties'. Describing them as 'ruling parties' reverses cause and effect and inverts its members' actual dependencies and loyalties.

The party of power is not the party of power because it is the formal organization that, having succeeded in getting its candidates elected, exerts power as a coherent unit of people's representatives in the legislative or in the executive branch of government. The party of power is the actual group whose members wield power in and through the executive branch of government, and which creates an 'electoral branch' in order to hold on to power by organizing adequate support in the legislative branch of government. Formally a party, or a so-called political bloc, these organizations have so far been created *ad hoc*. The party of power's centre of gravity is always located in the executive branch of government and its actual centre is the future president of the Russian Federation. The so-called 'ruling party' does not have a life of its own; it is in fact neither 'ruling' nor much of a party at all.[40]

In Russian history since 1993, the 'party of power' has been (or has produced) not one but a succession of electoral organizations. Each Duma election has brought to the fore another political party serving as the electoral branch of the party of power. In the December 1993 elections, VR was the executive's designated winner. It may have been less President Yeltsin's favourite than acting Prime Minister Yegor Gaidar's intended support-group. Yeltsin probably did not want to commit himself too much, since his stance was above all anti-communist. VR came first at the polls, but was a less clear winner than Yeltsin's *komanda* or team had counted on.[41]

The failure of VR to secure an overwhelming majority in the Duma eventually prompted Yeltsin to dismiss Gaidar and some of his ministers. Out of power, the leaders of VR could no longer claim to be power brokers. Their response was an attempt to convert VR into a membership-based party, tightly organized, with closed and disciplined ranks. Russia's Choice renamed itself Russia's Democratic Choice (*Demokraticheskii vybor Rossii*: DVR) but this strategy did not succeed. Some representatives of the older organizations of Democratic Russia, weary of centralized control, preferred to stick to the movement mode of organization and split off. More importantly, voters also turned their backs on the party: in the December 1995 elections, DVR fell back from 76 to a mere nine seats (out of a total of 450 in the State Duma). It even failed to cross the five per cent threshold in the party-list vote.

In preparation for the December 1995 State Duma elections a new electoral vehicle for the party of power was set up: Our Home Is Russia (*Nash Dom–Rossiya*: NDR). This movement, launched in May 1995, was headed by Viktor Chernomyrdin, Gaidar's successor as prime minister, and much less of a market ideologist, more a Soviet style managing director – literally, as he had been heading Russia's natural gas giant Gazprom. As with VR in the early days, NDR was able to make use of governmental and other state facilities (so-called administrative resources) and enjoyed the help of private businessmen and state enterprise managers who were either ordered or expected to provide support, or volunteered to do so, eager to ingratiate themselves with those in the highest echelons of state power.

Like VR in 1993, NDR fell short of what was hoped for and expected of it: Chernomyrdin's party managed to win only 55 seats. NDR was more successful as an 'operator' at the regional level (and thus more successful in the second chamber[42]) – at least until the spring of 1998 – by cleverly supporting and co-opting certain candidates for governorships, sometimes incumbents, sometimes main opponents, some of whom were and some of whom were not formal members of NDR, but close enough to warrant the investment.

In March 1998, Chernomyrdin was dismissed as prime minister by President Yeltsin. The reasons given for Chernomyrdin's dismissal were that a new political-economic situation required a change at the helm of the cabinet and an overall change of government, and that Chernomyrdin, relieved of his duties as prime minister, could now devote himself to leading NDR and prepare himself for the presidency. In fact, to dismiss Chernomyrdin as prime minister was the worst way to 'help' Chernomyrdin, if Yeltsin was serious in his attempt to support him for the presidency. Deprived of his power-base – a senior post in the executive branch of government – Chernomyrdin lost the means to further his candidacy and lost his attraction as a potential winner in the presidential contest. Who would jump on the bandwagon now? Quite a number of politicians started looking for a better place to go. With the dismissal of Chernomyrdin, NDR lost its appeal as electoral branch of the party of power and eventually withered away.

After the 1995 State Duma elections, the Russian Federation's political centre, the Kremlin, continued to experience difficulties in establishing its grip over the vast and diverse country. Meanwhile, the leaders of the 89 'subjects' became more dominant players. Before December 1995, many of them owed their position to the president, which assured the Kremlin of their loyalty. Thereafter, all the regional executives had become elected, rather than appointed, leaders. This independence was reflected, *inter alia*, in the regional leaders' autonomous – and diverging – stance at home and in the Federation Council (the second chamber). Russia's regions were to become an important focal point for party construction (*partstroitel'stvo* in Russian).

By the time it had become clear that Yeltsin would not try to obtain a third term as president, Moscow's mayor, Yurii Luzhkov, started preparing his succession bid. At the end of 1998, he launched his own party, Fatherland (Otechestvo). This patriotic label was to serve in the December 1999 State Duma elections, and, more importantly, the RF presidential elections scheduled for June–July 2000. At the outset Fatherland seemed to have at least a fighting chance of becoming NDR's successor as the electoral branch of the party of power. As the unchallenged leader – the 'boss' – of Moscow, one of the most influential and prosperous of Russia's regions, Luzhkov could dispose of a power base that was close to Russia's centre, yet autonomous. On the other hand, since Moscow is both central and exceptional (rich, privileged in many ways, international but self-centred, admired, envied, but not generally loved), Luzhkov would have had to work exceptionally hard to gain acceptance in many parts of the country.

At the same time, in the absence of an electoral organization of the federal party of power, other subjects' leaders – most prominent among them were Tatarstan's president, Minitimer Shaimiev, and St. Petersburg's governor, Vladimir Yakovlev – also set out to prepare themselves for future federal elections by organizing All Russia (*Vsya Rossiya*).

Both Fatherland and All Russia set out to rally the support of Russia's other regional leaders. Eventually they teamed up in the tandem Fatherland–All Russia (*Otechestvo–Vsya Rossiya*: OVR).[43] Luzhkov never declared his candidacy, but no one doubted his ambition in this direction. Later, he made it clear that Yevgenii Primakov was the only candidate he would stand aside for and would support. Primakov scored very well in polls as the most trusted and respected federal politician during his short tenure as prime minister. As long as he headed the government, Primakov maintained his posture as a non-party politician, being first and foremost a statesman. After his dismissal as prime minister, Primakov teamed up with the OVR alliance but did not subordinate himself to it. Primakov and his 'support group' seemed to be in an ideal position, first to win a substantial number of seats in the December 1999 State Duma elections, and then to gear up for the RF presidential elections; there was substantial party political support for the 'stately figure' of Primakov.

However, OVR's claim to represent the party of power did not remain unchallenged. Yeltsin and his entourage apparently felt uncomfortable about the efforts at party building by Luzhkov and his colleagues. In September 1999, with only a few months to go until the Duma ballot, a new bloc was launched. This bloc, Unity (Yedinstvo), was intended to neutralize OVR, beating it by employing the same weapons. Unity attempted to organize regional executive leaders – those who had not joined OVR – and also to convert those who had pledged allegiance to Luzhkov. But unlike OVR, the new bloc had a leader who was associated with the central government, the then relatively unknown minister for emergencies, Sergei Shoigu.

The foundations for Unity were laid in the Federation Council. In September 1999, a group of 39 senators signed a joint declaration in which they expressed their concern with the 'political hysteria', 'demagoguery' and 'dirty games' that surrounded the Duma election campaign. The senators offered to counterbalance this by using their 'power, experience and authority' to ensure that the next parliament would be filled with 'honest and responsible deputies'.[44] Unity's programme, in fact, was hardly more than a declaration of support for the incumbent government, led by Vladimir Putin.[45] The prime minister remained aloof from party politics, but he did declare that he personally preferred Unity above all other parties. The new SPS, in which a number of famous (or infamous) market-liberals co-operated (Boris Nemtsov, Anatolii Chubais, Yegor Gaidar, Irina Khakamada), circled around Unity and Putin in order to collect votes so as to 'help Putin keep a market-liberal course'. It was a true satellite party, serving the needs of the expected president-elect. The social-liberal Yabloko party declined invitations to join SPS.

The December 1999 State Duma elections were an enormous success for Unity: it won 106 seats. The KPRF maintained its position as the largest faction, with 113 seats – an impressive number, but the communists were virtually isolated in the Duma. SPS collected 29 seats and Yabloko 20 in total, and half the single member districts went to independents, quite a number of whom would later opt for Unity. Even before the elections results were officially declared, Shaimiev, one of the leaders of OVR, which had secured only 67 seats, made it known that, as far as he was concerned, it was not at all clear that OVR and Unity should form a joint faction in the State Duma. He was already disengaging from Luzhkov and Primakov, and making overtures to Unity (and to Putin), in an obvious move to side with the winner. Primakov immediately understood that he was heading for an uphill fight.

Luzhkov and Yakovlev reconsidered their position. In the new Duma, Unity and OVR joined forces, creating a comfortable majority for the party of power in the legislative branch of government. This was noticeable, too, in the ease with which government proposals met their first and subsequent readings in parliament, as well as in the drop in number of bills originating in parliament itself: by far the majority of bills now originated in the executive branch. During this whole period, Putin's popularity ratings remained enormously high: close to 70 per cent.

The resulting merged organization, United Russia (*Yedinaya Rossiya*: UR), was the designated winner of the December 2003 State Duma ballot. It took half of the seats in the elections, and grew to no less than two-thirds of the Duma seats in the ensuing weeks and months, as the bandwagon effect continued after the elections. Independents sided with UR, and a number of those who had held party-list seats also changed their allegiance. For the first time, the party of power could truly claim success. The KPRF's strength was halved; Zhirinovskii's LDPR resurged (he had been cautious not to attack Putin); SPS passed the five per cent threshold, whereas Yabloko did not and disappeared from the Duma.

The March 2004 presidential election result was a foregone conclusion: the incumbent was not even seriously contested, and parties other than the party of power played a marginal role – indeed, a less than marginal role if such a thing is possible: the other electoral parties' leaders (and former presidential candidates), were practically invisible. Irina Khakamada campaigned, but not as the SPS's candidate and without its formal support; the LDPR and the KPRF had preferred to send in some third-rate politicians to take a beating, to save the faces of Zhirinovskii and Zyuganov. Putin did not campaign; he acted presidentially, not lowering himself to 'politics of a lesser kind'.

Personal Politics: Linking Parties and State

President Putin at present explicitly aims to strengthen the role of political parties as institutions linking 'state' and 'society'. Whether this will translate into a stronger role for parties in the area of political recruitment remains to be seen. Given Putin's track record (and that of his predecessor, Yeltsin), we do not expect a radical departure from the past. Using parties' mobilization and legitimation capacity is one thing; indebting oneself to one or several specific organizations and entrusting them with strategic administrative positions is quite another. Personal loyalties, rather than institutionalized relationships, sometimes seem to be the key to Russian politics. In this respect, the abolition of Soviet rule has not meant a departure from past practice. The former CPSU General Secretary Leonid Brezhnev led a *Seilschaft* (that is, he was the chief patron) of colleagues, friends and people he found otherwise useful, whom he had met in different functions, in different places, and took along with him up the career ladder – and they, in turn, supported him during his climb. As general secretary he was close to and surrounded by, among others, people he had met in Dnepropetrovsk,

his place of origin, and Moldova in the early 1950s. Yeltsin, as president of
the RF, was aided by many people whom he already had come to know in
Sverdlovsk, where he had been a party secretary (and by many other former
CPSU functionaries), and by some whom he had met later. This group
included notably Aleksandr Korzhakov, his bodyguard who held the rank
of major when Yeltsin was the main party functionary of Moscow, and
who made a career along with Yeltsin when Yeltsin became president,
finally reaching the rank of three-star general – and was then 'let go'.[46]

Actual and aspiring political heavyweights must also know when to 'let
go', and no longer be bothered by old sympathies and loyalties. Putin
brought many people to the fore, and helped to promote them – or himself
directly promoted them – to the highest state and party functions. These
were often individuals whom he had previously known in Leningrad, his
city of origin, where he had been deputy mayor under Anatolii Sobchak,
before being called to serve in Yeltsin's presidential administration; they
also included former colleagues from the KGB (and its successor, the FSB);
more specifically, he promoted KGB functionaries with a Leningrad
(St. Petersburg) background.

However, loyalty is rarely its own reward: it often expects to be rewarded.
Making all kinds of material and non-material desirables available is a way of
inducing and maintaining loyalty. Loyalty is a 'personal' and 'non-material
thing', but its concomitant expressions are less often non-material. In a political system that is highly personalistic, such as that of Russia, material rewards
given irrespective of formal bureaucratic rules and distributed even in flagrant
breach of the law are to be expected. Rewards may well take the form of
bureaucratic (administrative) rank; and indeed, under Putin probably even
more so than under Yeltsin, patronage has taken on an administrative, bureaucratic guise.

Incumbents, then, when unhampered by the 'higher echelon', have a
major advantage in the electoral process. The party of power has a major
advantage here, and for this reason a strenuous policy aimed at limiting
party spending is not to be expected. It is hard to win political office, and
especially hard to acquire elected executive office, as an outsider. Politics
in Russia to a very large extent is 'insider dealing'. Russia is not a multi-
party democracy, although it has (the tough criteria of the law on political
parties notwithstanding) a plethora of political parties; the number of parties
with representation in the State Duma has been reduced, and the single
faction of UR absolutely dominates the party-political scene. Some of the criteria contained in the law on political parties may in future also reduce the
number of registered parties.[47]

It is not merely the number of parties that determines whether or not
the concept of 'multi-party democracy' or 'multi-party system' applies. In a

'true' multi-party system political parties select and train their candidates for elected public office. In a multi-party-system it is, as a rule, parties that bring forward candidates for state leadership, and for the offices of prime minister or president, or both. And as a rule parties have a longer life-span than the people who lead them and are selected by the party for public office. Parties are, in short, real institutions. Whereas in multi-party systems access to the highest echelons of state power is provided via political parties, in Russia access to the highest echelons of state power is achieved by being co-opted by those who hold superior rank in the state apparatus, possibly, but not necessarily, after a period of 'outplacement' in a party-position – be it *de facto* or symbolic – perhaps coupled with membership of the legislative branch of government via the party of power. Many of the top candidates presented by subsequent parties of power in State Duma elections never occupied their seats in the legislature. And notwithstanding the tighter criteria of the law on political parties, the rules for the next Duma elections still allow parties to fill half of their candidate lists with non-members.[48] It is the government, or rather the administration – the 'true' party of power, with its domain first of all in the executive branch – that 'defines' the 'ruling party', and not the other way round.

At the provincial level, that of the subjects of the RF (provinces, republics, city of Moscow and so forth), in many instances the same applies, but not always. In some cases one party, or rather one political *cum* business grouping, always centred upon the executive head, has been (or still is) more dominant in its province than the president of the RF has ever been in the country as a whole. Simply put, one individual, with his family and political and business clientele, is 'boss' there.[49] In some instances there is no real 'parallel' between the federal and the provincial level, because what happens at the provincial level is first of all an extension of federal politics, in which case the subjects are the 'working ground' and the 'extension' of federal politics. It is to be expected that, as a result of Putin's policy of subordinating provincial executives to the head of the federal executive – that is to himself, as president of the RF – the number of provinces in this category will grow.

In Russia the electoral branches of the party of power have been created and discarded as has been deemed fit, with an eye to the enduring interests of the 'real party of power', or with an eye to the changing composition – the change of personnel – of the 'real party of power'.

Conclusion

Political parties are by no means fully autonomous actors, let alone key players, in Russia's political system. As we have seen, their potential for capturing the state is fairly limited. The power-holders, on the other hand, have plenty of possibilities for curtailing, manipulating and creating parties. The existing party and political system has served the party of power so far. It is not a multi-party system, but there is definitely a system discernible, with rather specific characteristics that will become lasting traits if they are not tampered with too much.

So why try to change it, as seems to be the purpose of the law on political parties and the move away from the plurality vote? And why change it at a time where the party of power has finally proved capable of dominating the ballot? The SMD have provided many recruits for the UR faction since the 2003 elections. Perhaps the party of power hopes and intends to enlist this support prior to the elections, making sure that its electoral branch will dominate the Duma. If so, the new proportional electoral system seeks to express a further phase in the quest for control of 'opportunistic' politicians by the party of power, and expresses the desire to provide a surer guide or a more secure lead to the electorate to help it choose to support the backers in the Duma of the future leader of the state. It is much harder to image that the desire may also have been to provide a surer route to a genuine and steadfast opposition as well.

If the intended effect of the law on political parties has indeed been to make entry into the political sphere as a political party and the upkeep of a small political party more difficult or even impossible, is this to the benefit of the party of power? The party of power has so far made full use of disposable electoral parties, so why would it choose to create a more durable state-party? The answer may well be that the law does not seriously limit its options. It is still fairly easy for the party of power to organize a party that meets the criteria regarding number of provincial branches, numbers of members and so on, and to arrange its financing. It may become more difficult for 'real outsiders' to enter the field. If the 'old' electoral organization of the party of power is judged to have lost its appeal, or changes of personnel in the party of power seem to require fresh expression in a new electoral party, the old one can still be easily discarded, and a new one – or several new ones – activated with relative ease, as it still has all the administrative resources at its disposal.

Possibly more disquieting, for those who have the prospect of 'real democracy' at heart, is that a 'lining up' of the executive branch of power is taking place: all heads of the executive of the federation's subjects will in future be appointed by the president of Russia, and in fact quite a number since 2005 have already been appointed by him. They will no longer be directly elected and so they will behave more like members of the presidential administration, their career prospects depending upon subordination, and so they will be much less inclined to set up or help sponsor electoral

organizations of local parties of power if these organizations are considered –
by administrative superiors – to be insufficiently helpful to the greater cause
of the 'overall' party of power. In Russia the state (the administration) produces the most important party political leaders.

The state, however, has so far been less of a unity than the singular
noun 'state' suggests. The state has been, and to a large extent still is, a territorial and functional plurality. The state, therefore, has tended to reproduce
plurality, and a certain level of competition, in the political sphere. The continuing subordination of the constituent elements of the RF, plus the dominance of a limited number of power ministries and services in the
administration – dominance that 'flows over', as it were, into the political
sphere – may well have a greater effect on state–party relations than either
the introduction of a law on political parties or the abolition of single-
member districts. If there is logic to our reasoning, the prospects for the
development of a true multi-party system, with less politics of patronage,
seem altogether bleak.

NOTES

1. Ronald J. Hill and Peter Frank, *The Soviet Communist Party*, 3rd edn (Boston, MA:
   Unwin-Hyman, 1987); Leonard Schapiro, *The Communist Party of the Soviet Union*, 2nd
   rev. edn (New York: Random House, 1971).
2. M.S. Voslenskii, *Nomenklatura: Gospodstvuyushchii klass Sovetskogo Soyuza* (Moscow:
   Sovetskaya Rossiya/Oktyabr', 1991).
3. Yitzhak M. Brudny, 'The Dynamics of "Democratic Russia", 1990–1993', *Post-Soviet
   Affairs*, Vol.9, No.2 (1993), pp.141–70.
4. See, for example, Stephen White, Richard Rose and Ian McAllister, *How Russia Votes*
   (Chatham, NJ: Chatham House, 1997). There is, however, some research that indicates that
   anti-party attitudes among the Russian voters are gradually decreasing: Jon H. Pammett
   and Joan DeBardeleben, 'Citizen Orientations to Political Parties in Russia', *Party Politics*,
   Vol.6, No.3 (2000), pp.373–84; Ted Brader and Joshua A. Tucker, 'The Emergence of
   Mass Partisanship in Russia, 1993–1996', *American Journal of Political Science*, Vol.45,
   No.1 (2001), pp.69–83.
5. Anna Grzymała-Busse, 'Political Competition and the Politicization of the State in East
   Central Europe', *Comparative Political Studies*, Vol.36, No.10 (2003), pp.1123–47; Conor
   O'Dwyer, 'Runaway State Building: How Political Parties Shape States in Postcommunist
   Eastern Europe', *World Politics*, Vol.56, No.4 (2004), pp.520–23.
6. Richard S. Katz and Peter Mair, 'Changing Models of Party Organization and Party
   Democracy: The Emergence of the Cartel Party', *Party Politics*, Vol.1, No.1 (1995), pp.5–28.
7. The ministers referred to are: Aleksandr Zhukov (deputy prime minister, Vpered Rossiya!,
   Otechestvo–Vsya Rossiya, Yedinaya Rossiya); Aleksei Gordeev (agriculture, Agrarnaya
   partiya Rossii, Yedinaya Rossiya), Viktor Khrystenko (industry and energy, Nash
   Dom–Rossiya); Sergei Shoigu (emergencies, Nash Dom–Rossiya, Yedinaya Rossiya), and
   Vladimir Yakovlev (regional development, Otechestvo–Vsya Rossiya).
8. Allen C. Lynch, *How Russia Is Not Ruled: Reflections on Russian Political Development*
   (Cambridge: Cambridge University Press, 2005), p.161.
9. Peter Reddaway and Robert W. Orttung (eds.), *The Dynamics of Russian Politics.
   Putin's Reform of Federal–Regional Relations* (Lanham, MD: Rowman & Littlefield,
   2003), p.87.

10. *Sobranie aktov Prezidenta i Pravitel'stva Rossiiskoi Federatsii*, 41/1993, item 3907.
11. *Sobranie zakonodatel'stva Rossiiskoi Federatsii*, 26/1995, item 2398.
12. *Sobranie zakonodatel'stva Rossiiskoi Federatsii*, 26/1999, item 3178.
13. *Sobranie zakonodatel'stva Rossiiskoi Federatsii*, 51/2002, item 4982.
14. Robert G. Moser, 'Independents and Party Formation: Elite Partisanship as an Intervening Variable in Russian Politics', *Comparative Politics*, Vol.31, No.2 (1999), pp.147–65. In the 1993 Duma elections, 141 unaffiliated candidates won in the SMD; in 1995, this number dropped to 77; in 1999, it rose to 106; in 2003, 67 independent deputies were elected.
15. Kathryn Stoner-Weiss, 'The Limited Reach of Russia's Party System: Underinstitutionalization in Dual Transitions', *Politics and Society*, Vol.29, No.3 (2001), pp.385–414.
16. Grigorii V. Golosov, 'Party Support or Personal Resources? Factors of Success in the Plurality Portion of the 1999 National Legislative Elections in Russia', *Communist and Post-Communist Studies*, Vol.35, No.1 (2002), pp.23–38 (p.35).
17. John H. Aldrich, *Why Parties? The Origin and Transformation of Party Politics in America* (Chicago, IL: University of Chicago Press, 1995), p.24.
18. Richard Rose in this context uses the metaphor of the market: Russian political entrepreneurship is predominantly about 'supply', rather than demand: Richard Rose, 'A Supply-Side View of Russia's Elections', *East European Constitutional Review*, Vol.9, No.1/2 (2001), pp.53–7.
19. Anatolii Kostyukov, 'Restavratsiya: Prezident obnarodoval plan gosudarstvennogo pereustroistva', *Nezavisimaya gazeta*, 14 Sept. 2004, p.1.
20. *Sobranie zakonodatel'stva Rossiiskoi Federatsii*, 21/2005, item 1919.
21. *Sobranie zakonodatel'stva Rossiiskoi Federatsii*, 15/2005, item 1277.
22. Some names circulating for leading positions in the public chamber suggest an emphasis on 'celebrity' rather than democratic credentials: oligarchs Mikhail Potanin and Mikhail Fridman and the former chess world champion Anatolii Karpov: see Sergei Varshavik, 'Antitsenzor', *Nezavisimaya gazeta*, 17 Nov. 2005, p.2.
23. *Vedomosti S"ezda narodnykh deputatov SSSR i Verkhovnogo soveta RSFSR*, 42/1990, item 839; see also S.A. Avak'yan, *Politicheskii plyuralizm i obshchestvennye ob'edineniya v Rossiiskoi Federatsii: konstitutsionno-pravovye osnovy* (Moscow: Rossiiskii yuridicheskii izdatel'skii dom, 1996).
24. *Sobranie zakonodatel'stva Rossiiskoi Federatsii*, 29/2001, item 2950. For a detailed analysis of the Law, see Ruben Verheul, 'Planned Politics: The Russian Law on Political Parties', in William B. Simons and Ferdinand Feldbrugge (eds.), *Human Rights in Russia and Eastern Europe: Essays in Honor of Ger P. van den Berg* (The Hague: Martinus Nijhoff, 2002), pp.223–39; and V.V. Lapaeva (ed.), *Kommentarii k Federal'nomu zakonu O politicheskikh partiyakh* (Moscow: Institut zakonodatel'stva i sravnitel'nogo pravovedeniya pri Pravitel'stve Rossiiskoi Federatsii, 2002).
25. This amounts to 0.046 per cent of the 2003 electorate; citizens may be members of only one party. The criteria mentioned here are set forth by a 2004 amendment of the law: *Sobranie zakonodatel'stva Rossiiskoi Federatsii*, 52/2004, item 5272. The requirements in the original version were less strict: regional chapters were to number 100 members (50 for other chapters), and minimum membership was set at 10,000.
26. It must nominate candidates in one of the following elections: State Duma (as a 'list' in the proportional elections or in at least five per cent of single-member districts); presidency; highest executive office in at least ten per cent of the federal subjects; legislatures of at least 20 per cent of the federal subjects; or organs of self-government in more than half of the federal subjects.
27. The website <http://www.cityline.ru:8081/politika> lists 21 rather obscure parties that were 'outlawed' for failing to meet the criteria of the law on political parties. Most of these bans are related to insufficient regional chapters.
28. Yelena Rudneva, '100.000 chlenov–potolok dlya partii', *Vedomosti*, 21 Sept. 2005; website of the Federal Registration Service, <http://www.rosregistr.ru/>.
29. The Central Electoral Commission, considering its draft version of the party law, originally intended to impose 'impartiality' upon the president by default. Yet the chairman, Aleksandr

Veshnyakov, and other CEC members have on various occasions stated that they do not in principle oppose a partisan presidency: see, for example, Denis Babichenko, 'Prezident ostanetsya bespartiinym', *Segodnya*, 5 Jan. 2001; Ol'ga Tropkina, 'Veshnyakov podyskivaet nachal'nika dlya Putina', *Nezavisimaya gazeta*, 23 Aug. 2001, p.3.

30. See Ye. Sidorenko, 'Pravovoe polozhenie politicheskikh partii', *Rossiiskaya yustitsiya*, 2001, No.10, pp.53–5. The author, a deputy minister of justice, points out that, while the law considerably extends the control over party activities, at the same time it leaves the registering organs few possibilities to verify whether aspiring associations actually qualify for party status. Sidorenko's plea for the possibility of demanding additional documentation has been heard, in that the 2004 amendments to the party law require party chapters to present membership lists to the ministry.

31. Politicians who are opposed in principle to receiving taxpayers' means can opt out and refuse state subsidies.

32. The ministry of justice has published financial reports of some parties for 2003 at <http://party.scli.ru/finansy.htm>. The figures available are, for dues and donations respectively: KPRF – ca. $77,430 and $118,300; SPS – $44,130 and $6,360,000, UR – $405,000 and $33,262,000; Agrarian Party – $10,800 and $1,000,400.

33. Andrew Wilson, *Virtual Politics: Faking Democracy in the Post-Soviet World* (New Haven, CT and London: Yale University Press, 2005), p.85.

34. Lilia Shevtsova, *Yeltsin's Russia: Myths and Reality* (Washington, DC: Carnegie, 1999), p.191; see also Joseph R. Blasi, Maya Kroumova and Douglas Kruse, *Kremlin Capitalism: Privatizing the Russian Economy* (Ithaca, NY and London: Cornell University Press, 1997); David E. Hoffman, *The Oligarchs: Wealth and Power in the New Russia* (Oxford: Public Affairs, 2002).

35. See, for example, Vladimir Gel'man, 'Blurry Boundaries, Biased Contests: Public Offices, Private Money, and Russia's Party Politics', paper presented at the workshop 'The Effect of Party and Campaign Finance on Post-Communist Party Development', Riga, 20–23 Oct. 2005.

36. Joan Barth Urban and Valerii D. Solovei, *Russia's Communists at the Crossroads* (Boulder, CO: Westview, 1997); Luke March, *The Communist Party in Post-Soviet Russia* (Manchester: Manchester University Press, 2002).

37. In the 1995 Duma elections, about half the party list votes were cast for parties that did not manage (and in many cases did not intend) to cross the five per cent threshold; thus, one might say, a significant share of the 'protest vote' was effectively neutralized.

38. Valentin Poluektov, *Polevye i manipulyativnye tekhnologii: nastol'naya kniga menedzhera izbiratel'nykh kampanii* (Moscow: Russkaya panorama, 2003).

39. Hans Oversloot and Ruben Verheul, 'The Party of Power in Russian Politics', *Acta Politica*, Vol.35, No.2 (2000), pp.123–45.

40. This is in obvious contrast with parties we are familiar with in many western countries, where a party can be truly a party, and can be truly governing or not. If the SPD in Germany does not supply the chancellor and the ministers, it is not the governing party, but it may become the governing party. If the Conservative Party in England has the majority in the House of Commons, the Labour Party is not thereby less of a party: it is still a party, although much less powerful. A Republican president in the USA, plus perhaps a Republican majority in both the House of Representatives and the Senate, does not thereby eradicate the Democratic Party; the Democratic Party does not lose its past and future because of the temporary domination of the Republicans.

41. Timothy J. Colton, 'Russia's Choice: The Perils of Revolutionary Democracy', in Timothy J. Colton and Jerry F. Hough (eds.), *Growing Pains: Russian Democracy and the Election of 1993* (Washington, DC: Brookings, 1998), pp.115–39.

42. After a change of the Federal law, President Putin began in 2005 to appoint the heads of the executive branches in the RF's subjects. The heads of the executive branch of the subjects (called governors, presidents, mayor [of Moscow], head [of Karelia] or some other term, but often referred to as 'governors' as their generic name) no longer hold a seat *ex officio* in the Federation Council (upper house): for the original law see *Sobranie zakonodatel'stva*

Rossiiskoi Federatsii, 42/1999, item 5005; and for Putin's amendments, *Sobranie zakonodatel'stva Rossiiskoi Federatsii*, 50/2004, item 4950.

43. B. Makarenko, 'Otechestvo–Vsya Rossiya', in Michael McFaul, Nikolai Petrov and Andrei Riabov (eds.), *Rossiya v izbiratel'nom tsikle 1999–2000 godov* (Moscow: Moskovskii tsentr Karnegi, 2000), pp.155–66.

44. Ivan Otdel'nov, 'Ocherednoi gubernatorskii blok fakticheski sozdan', *Nezavisimaya gazeta*, 23 Sept. 1999, p.1.

45. Yekatarina Grigor'eva, 'Ideologiya "Yedinstva"–v otsutstvie ideologii', *Nezavisimaya gazeta*, 29 Sept. 1999, p.3; Timothy J. Colton and Michael McFaul, 'Reinventing Russia's Party of Power: "Unity" and the 1999 Duma Election', *Post-Soviet Affairs*, Vol.16, No.3 (2000), pp.201–24.

46. Aleksandr Korzhakov, *Boris Yeltsin: Ot rassveta do zakata* (Moscow: Interbuk, 1997).

47. Compare the websites of the Russian ministry of justice on political parties, <http://party.scli.ru>, and of the Federal Registration Service, <http://www.rosregistr.ru/>.

48. *Sobranie zakonodatel'stva Rossiiskoi Federatsii*, 21/2005, item 1919.

49. For example, Roman Abramovich is the one dominating figure in Chukotka, where virtually nothing, it appears, is beyond his political and economic reach; there is no semblance of multi-party politics in Chukotka – in fact, nothing akin to politics *tout court*. Yurii Luzhkov, to mention one other example, has dominated the political scene in the city of Moscow almost since the moment in June 1992 when Gavriil Popov stepped down as the first elected mayor of the city before the expiry of his term and Luzhkov, his unelected deputy mayor, took charge. After that Luzhkov has been directly elected mayor repeatedly, with impressive, overwhelming majorities. Luzhkov is not the 'product' of his party-political organization: Luzhkov had produced his party-political organization, re-creating and re-aligning it as he saw fit, also with an eye to his ambitions on the federal scene. Less appealing examples of local political and political 'big men' are to be found in Tatarstan, Kalmykia, and Bashkortostan.

Index

For Product Safety Concerns and Information please contact our EU
representative GPSR@taylorandfrancis.com
Taylor & Francis Verlag GmbH, Kaufingerstraße 24, 80331 München, Germany